FOG ON THE TYNE

Bernard O'Mahoney is the bestselling author of *Essex Boys*, *Bonded by Blood*, *Wannabe in My Gang?* and numerous other acclaimed true-crime titles. He lives in Birmingham.

FOG ON THE TYNE

THE STORY OF BRITAIN'S BLOODIEST GANG WAR

BERNARD O'MAHONEY

MAINSTREAM
PUBLISHING

EDINBURGH AND LONDON

First published in Great Britain in 2011 by
MAINSTREAM PUBLISHING COMPANY
(EDINBURGH) LTD
7 Albany Street
Edinburgh EH1 3UG

ISBN 9781845967642

A catalogue record for this book is available
from the British Library

Printed in Great Britain by
Clays Ltd St Ives plc

1 3 5 7 9 10 8 6 4 2

ACKNOWLEDGEMENTS

SINCE I BEGAN writing this book, I have married my girlfriend, Roshea, a Geordie lass with supermodel looks, the voice of an angel and a heart of gold. On 15 January 2010, my mother's birthday, Roshea gave birth to our beautiful son, Paddy. My first name is Patrick, my father's name was Patrick and Roshea's grandfather was Patrick, and so naming our son did not demand much thought.

Five days later, I spent the night at New Cross Hospital, in Wolverhampton. For 14 long, painful hours, I watched helplessly as my lifelong heroine fought the hardest fight of her life. At 8.31 a.m. on 20 January 2010, I held my dear mother's hand and cuddled her as she gracefully conceded defeat and breathed her last.

This book, as you can imagine, has been written while experiencing every possible human emotion. So many good people have helped me through the numerous highs and lows. You know who you are, so please forgive me for not mentioning you by name, but I am sure that you will understand. I can only dedicate this book to two very special people. The first is my son Paddy O'Mahoney, who has given me hope and belief in a bright future. The other is my mother, Anna O'Mahoney, who has given me a mind awash with beautiful memories and a heart overflowing with love. Thank you both for yesterday, today and tomorrow.

CONTENTS

Introduction

CONROY

ON 11 AUGUST 2006, I received a late-night call on my mobile phone from a withheld number. 'You murdered Tucker, Tate, Rolfe and Danny Marlow, the taxi driver,' a man with a strong Geordie accent ranted.

'Really?' I replied. 'You'd better go to the police and tell them that the wrong men are in jail then, hadn't you?'

'No,' the Geordie sneered. 'I want £10,000 in cash from you, or I'm going to go to the newspapers with tapes that prove you killed them all.' I told the man, who was clearly intoxicated, that I would pay him the £10,000 he was demanding but that he would have to pop around to my house to pick up the cash. 'Do you think I'm fucking stupid?' he replied. 'I will give you a time and a place to drop it off.'

'Perhaps I can put it in a bag and leave it in my front garden for you?' I joked. 'Do yourself a favour, you maggot, and fuck off!'

I replaced the receiver and thought that would be the end of the matter. It had been 11 years since my former associates Pat Tate, Tony Tucker and Craig Rolfe had been executed as they sat in their Range Rover. In the early '90s, we had started out as a nightclub security company, which, fuelled by drugs, soon transformed itself into a ruthless gang that immersed itself in murder, extortion and drug importation and distribution. Following my associates' executions in 1995, which made national headline news, the media began calling us the Essex Boys firm, and overnight a mythical monster had been born. Our gang's rapid rise, and kamikaze fall, became the subject of numerous books, television documentaries and feature films. Blatant lies and exaggerated stories have been manufactured by hangers-on, wannabes and never-will-bes since our demise; most are told by people we never even met. As with the Kray gang before us, every chancer and loser in the UK seemed to want to be associated with the Essex Boys firm and its imaginary exploits.

I did know the late Danny Marlow. He was a family man, a taxi driver from Leicestershire. He owed an associate of the Essex Boys firm a relatively small sum of money, which I had gone to collect from him just a few hours before he was murdered. The debt had nothing to do with crime. The guy he owed it to had a chain of video rental shops that had gone bust. I never bothered asking the details of how Danny's debt came into being. The guy he owed was a friend of a friend, and so I agreed to help him retrieve his money. I was interviewed by the police about Danny's death, but I honestly played no part in it. Two men were later convicted and sentenced to life imprisonment for the killing. Two men were also convicted of the triple murders in the Essex Boys case, and they too are serving life imprisonment.

Taking into consideration those facts, I failed to see how a drunken Geordie was going to convince the police that they had locked up the wrong men, although all four do claim that they are innocent. I knew, of course, that my late-night caller had no intention of contacting the police. I had been receiving regular phone calls for more than a decade from strangers or strange people who were either in awe of my deceased associates or who were abusive and issued death threats because I had quite rightly described their heroes as arseholes. It can be a tad annoying and frustrating, and occasionally depressing, but never have I felt threatened. If somebody did intend to cause me serious harm, I am in no doubt that they would not give me the courtesy of a warning. The drunken Geordie was not the first person to accuse me of being a murderer, but it was most certainly the first time that somebody had demanded money from me.

I put the call down to the evils of drink, drugs or gangster rap and thought that I would hear no more once the sad wretch had sobered up. The following morning, I was awoken by the insistent ringing of my mobile phone. Still half asleep, I picked up the handset, but before I had a chance to speak the caller said, 'Because of your fucking cheek, O'Mahoney, we now want 20 grand or we go to the police and the newspapers.'

'Who the fuck is "we"?' I replied.

INTRODUCTION

The man, whom I recognised as the Geordie who had called the night before, screamed, 'I am one of the Conroys! CONROYS! CONROYS! Have you got that?' I had no idea who the Conroys were or what business they thought they had with me, and so I asked the man to explain just what his problem was. 'We have proof that you murdered Tucker, Tate, Rolfe and Marlow. We want 20 . . . no, fuck it, 50 grand off you, or you are going to jail. The people in prison didn't kill them, O'Mahoney. You did.'

Rather than debate my innocence or guilt with an obviously mentally challenged monkey, I switched my phone off and tried to get back to sleep. These nuisance calls continued for three weeks, and on each occasion the Geordie became more and more abusive. During the first week, he threatened to cut my eyes out, and the following week he promised an unsavoury death unless I met his increasing demands for more and more cash.

A 26-year-old 'man' named Michael Strawbridge, from Pelton, in County Durham, was eventually traced and arrested by the police. He confessed that he was responsible for the calls, which he had made 'for a laugh', and was subsequently fined the princely sum of £80. When Strawbridge had claimed that he was 'one of the Conroys', I had researched the name on the Internet in the hope that I could find out who they were and how I could contact them. I must admit that the information that I did find available about the Conroy family made for very uncomfortable reading. In their 'manor', which is the north-east of England, they are as well known as Alan Shearer, Newcastle Brown Ale, doner kebabs and Newcastle United.

After Strawbridge had been arrested and admitted that he had never even met the Conroys, my interest in the family naturally waned. That was until one evening when I was watching Donal MacIntyre's television series *MacIntyre's Underworld*. The programme examines the day-to-day lives of notorious criminals. Paddy Conroy, a snarling, spitting Geordie with serious anger-management issues and an eyepatch, growled at the camera and began ranting about destroying his rivals, the Sayers family, who he claimed were registered police informants. In 1995, Conroy had been sentenced to 11 years' imprisonment for his part in the kidnapping and torture of a fellow criminal who was alleged to have desecrated the grave of Conroy's father. The unfortunate fellow had had his teeth removed with a pair of unsterilised pliers. Although Conroy denied the work was his own, he did admit to dropping the patient off where the emergency dental work was performed. However, Conroy rather undermined his case by physically attacking the prosecution barrister in court and was subsequently found guilty. Towards the end of the show, Conroy went off on a terrifying four-minute rant against his perceived enemies, which culminated in him shouting, 'Put that in ya fookin' documentary!'

At the time, I was working on a book entitled *Faces* with a rising star in photojournalism named Brian Anderson. *Faces* is a collection of classic black and white photographs of the most infamous villains in the UK. I knew immediately that Paddy Conroy, the man who was threatening to explode out of my television screen, would just have to be included in it. A week later, I had managed to contact Conroy, he had agreed to pose for photographs for the book and I had visited him at his home in the West End of Newcastle. Talking at length with Conroy, I learned that he has lived a life saturated with extreme violence and hardship but has somehow managed to lace it heavily with his own brand of morality and infectious humour. I am not saying Conroy is a saint. On the contrary, he would be the first to admit that he has been responsible for many of the crimes committed in Newcastle over the last three decades, although, in fairness to him, Conroy and his infamous family have been wrongly accused of so much more. A whole host of unsavoury allegations, including murder, has been laid at their door.

Like the Conroy family, their rivals the Sayers clan have a mafia-type reputation in the north-east. Blackmail, robbery, drug dealing and allegations of murder are synonymous with their name. I had also contacted the Sayers family to request that they pose for photographs for inclusion in the book. At the time, John Henry Sayers was in prison and Michael Sayers was 'out of town' and therefore unavailable, but Stephen Sayers agreed to meet me. I found Stephen to be polite, intelligent and surprisingly honest. He conceded that he and his family had been involved in criminality in the past but said that it was not something that he or they were proud of. 'I don't mind helping you with your book,' Stephen said. 'You can take a few photographs of me while I talk to people here, but I don't wish to pose for them. The last thing I want to be seen as is a gangster.'

INTRODUCTION

A few weeks after that meeting, Stephen was arrested for perverting the course of justice in a murder trial that had involved his brother John Henry. He had stood trial at Leeds Crown Court in September 2002 accused of the gangland execution of a small-time crook named Freddie Knights. While giving evidence, John Henry had stunned everybody by announcing that he was totally innocent and that the Conroys were not only responsible for ordering Knights' murder but had also been the driving force behind the murder of Tyneside legend Viv Graham. John Henry was later cleared of any involvement in Knights' murder. It's hard to gauge just what the Conroys actually know, if anything, about either murder, because for many years they have been embroiled in a bitter war with members of the Sayers family. It has waged for so long now that I doubt either side can honestly say how it started.

When I heard that Stephen Sayers had been arrested for perverting the course of justice in the Knights case, it did make me wonder if Stephen had deliberately tried to mislead me when we had met or if he was, at that time, genuinely trying to walk away from his past. Like the Conroys, the Sayers family has a long, bloody history that they have excused over the years by quoting their own code of morality. It is therefore hard to try to decipher who is and who is not telling the truth about the crimes each family accuses the other of committing. All I can do is repeat the stories that I have been told and let you, the reader, decide what the Conroys and the Sayers families may or may not be guilty of.

Chapter One

ONCE UPON A TYNE

PADDY CONROY WAS born in the West End of Newcastle upon Tyne on 23 April 1960. Lee Majors, who played a former astronaut with bionic limbs in the popular television series *The Six Million Dollar Man*, shares his birthday. So, too, did the world's most famous playwright, William Shakespeare. In some ways, the three men are linked. Like Shakespeare, Conroy's time on earth has been spent immersed in one bloody drama after another, and like the Six Million Dollar Man, many of Conroy's adversaries have ended up being rebuilt or having false limbs fitted.

Conroy's parents had eight children: Lenny, the eldest, Billy, Maureen, Denny (Denise), Paddy, Michael, Neil and Dawn, the youngest. In the summer of 1963, Conroy's mother and father were involved in a bitter argument at Newcastle Central Station. Leonard Conroy was trying to board a train bound for London, and his long-suffering wife was begging him not to go. In desperation, Mrs Conroy grabbed Leonard's jacket, pulled it off his back and ran out of the station. Without his jacket, which contained his money, train ticket and wallet, Leonard was unable to make his planned trip. Paddy Conroy, aged just three at the time, stood with his father on the platform and watched as the powerful locomotive huffed and puffed before gathering speed and disappearing from view, cloaked in its own steam and billowing smoke. The atmosphere between Mr and Mrs Conroy during their journey home was extremely uncomfortable. Leonard did not say one word to his triumphant wife; he just sat on the bus glancing at her occasionally and shaking his head.

Several years later, it was revealed that Leonard had planned to travel to London to meet up with a gang of fifteen men who had gone on to commit one of the most infamous crimes in British history. They had halted a Glasgow to London mail train and stolen £2.6 million in used banknotes. Friends claim that when the enormity of the gang's heist was broadcast on the radio Leonard Conroy couldn't bring himself to be in the same room as his wife, because he was so upset. Stifling tears and screams, he would stare vacantly at the newspaper headlines about the robbery and mumble, 'No, no, no.' Five days later, Mrs Conroy had the last laugh. The police discovered the train robbers' hideout, which turned out to be an Aladdin's cave of damning evidence. Just eight months after the crime had been committed, thirteen members of the Great Train Robbery gang, as they became known, were jailed for a total of three hundred years. Leonard Conroy lost count of the number of times he heard his wife say, 'I told you so. Are you still upset that I stopped you going?' Mothers always do know best.

When Paddy Conroy was five years old, he was sent to a school in Cruddas Park. This area, in the West End of Newcastle, was named after George Cruddas, a director of the local Vickers-Armstrong armament factories. Cruddas Park attracted the weak and the poor simply because it was the cheapest area of Newcastle to live in, and this shaped the district's abnormal social make-up. The suicide rate and the incidence of respiratory TB were both three times the average for the rest of the city, while cases of venereal disease were twelve times the average. The area became a gravitation point for many of Newcastle's problem families. In fact, five times as many families deemed criminal or antisocial ended up living around Cruddas Park than were found in any other suburb.

One of the biggest eyesores in this very deprived area was the Noble Street flats. Thomas Daniel Smith, the man responsible for building what was nothing more than a high-rise slum and much of the rest of the neighbourhood that Conroy was reared in, was the Labour leader of Newcastle City Council at the time. Smith believed strongly in the need to clear the almost derelict housing people lived in and so put a great deal of effort into his regeneration plans. At Smith's suggestion, the city was nicknamed 'The Brasilia of the North'. Smith clearly had a fertile imagination: war-torn Beirut maybe, Brasilia never.

Unfortunately, Smith's unquenchable thirst for money became linked to his equally powerful political ambitions. A maintenance firm owned by him won more than 50 per cent of all the available council-housing contracts in the area. Smith soon expanded his business, setting up a PR company to support redevelopment in other cities throughout the country. This company was hired by John Poulson, an architect who paid Smith £156,000 for his work, which involved paying local councillors to secure contracts for Poulson's pre-packaged redevelopment schemes. Poulson earned more than £1,000,000 through Smith, but the pair were eventually arrested on corruption charges and imprisoned.

It seems that everybody connected to the West End of Newcastle at that time had some form of criminal enterprise on the go, even those who were supposedly beyond reproach. In those days, the West End community was made up of undoubtedly proud, hard people who created wealth for the nation while living in abject poverty. That wealth was generated in the large industrial factories, such as Vickers-Armstrong, that lined the banks of the River Tyne, producing ships, trains, tanks and armaments. Men would work long, gruelling shifts for little more than a pittance and never complain. As long as they had enough money to put a roof over their families' heads, food in their families' mouths and a few brown ales in their own, they were content.

Those who lived in the West End at that time did not look upon villains as bad people. Committing crime in order to make ends meet was not considered wrong unless you were involved in unforgivable immoral acts against the old, infirm or very young. Leonard Conroy was an old-school villain who robbed post offices, stately homes and mansions throughout the UK. He knew all the notorious London villains, such as 'Mad' Frankie Fraser, the Kray brothers and Freddie Foreman, because of the numerous times he had been in jail. Leonard's choice of profession meant that the police were regular visitors to his home. His children would watch in horror as officers tipped personal possessions onto the floor while searching for evidence of their father's latest misdemeanour.

The only time the police gave the family any peace was when Leonard Conroy was residing as a guest at one of Her Majesty's prisons. Because of all the upset and trauma this caused at the family home, Paddy Conroy chose not to spend too much time there. He preferred the stability and relative peace and quiet that his grandmother Sally's home offered. Sally was a large, kind and wise woman who enjoyed a drink. She would often visit the numerous pubs along Scotswood Road, where she would sing for the locals.

Scotswood Road was the inspiration for the Geordie anthem 'Blaydon Races'. It was known locally as 'The Road of One Hundred Pubs', but in reality there were never more than forty-six trading at any one time. The atmosphere outside those pubs was as fiery as the blast furnaces that roared endlessly at the nearby armaments factories. It is said that, along the four miles that make up Scotswood Road, every Saturday night there would be a brawl on every street corner, and on bank holidays the brawling would last into the early hours of the morning. The police who patrolled the area were hand-picked for their brawn rather than for their brains. For instance, it is said that a certain PC Elija 'Ben' Goulden once made an arrest in Corporation Street but took the prisoner to Pitt Street to charge him, because he could not spell or pronounce 'corporation'.

In time, Paddy tired of flitting from his family's home to his grandmother Sally's, and so he moved in with her on a full-time basis. Even today, a child moving from one home into another is nothing unusual in the West End. School friends will visit a fellow pupil's house to play and not go home for a month, if ever. It's just the way communities are in the north-east: everybody knows everybody, and they all look out for one another.

Both of Paddy's grandfathers had been sergeant majors in the Army. During the war, his mother's father, Billy Bell, had been stationed at Featherston Prisoner of War camp, in Haltwhistle, Northumberland. He would often tell stories of how both Italian and German POWs would be marched from the train station through the village to the camp. During the day, the prisoners would work in the fields picking vegetables or fruit. Billy Bell claimed that they had little or no desire to escape. In fact, the prisoners were considered to be such a low risk that they were allowed to go to a dance that was held in the village hall every Saturday night. I suppose that a simple life in Northumberland was far more desirable than running away to face the horrors of war.

Paddy's mother's family are law-abiding, decent people who have never so much as sworn in their lives. They have never owned anything of material value, and they have never asked anybody for anything.

Considering the community they were brought up in, they are unique to say the least. Leonard Conroy's family was the total opposite. Born and bred in Belmullet, County Mayo, on the west coast of Ireland, they were extremely hard people who wouldn't take shit off anybody. Leonard's mother, Sally, fell pregnant with him in the early 1930s, when the county of Mayo was experiencing a baby boom. This was due in part to the massive loss of life Ireland had suffered in the late 1800s during the potato famine. The Irish were dependent on their potato crop, which had failed three years out of four, and this resulted in an estimated one million people dying of starvation or disease.

County Mayo, a non-industrial area, was particularly hard hit. The unusually high birth rate that followed the famine presented its own problems: there wasn't enough work to employ or house all the additional people that it produced. In an attempt to resolve the issue, the Irish government built workhouses, or poorhouses, as they became known. The able-bodied were forced to work in return for a place to sleep and enough food and water to stay alive; the men broke stones, and the women knitted or washed linen in the laundry. These inhumane establishments were overcrowded, cold and damp places where violence and sexual abuse were rife.

The only true hope many of the people living in poorhouses had for a brighter future was to try to emigrate to America or England so that they could present themselves as cheap labour to be exploited in slightly better conditions. Leonard Conroy's father had the misfortune to spend his formative years in a workhouse in Belmullet. When he learned that his wife was expecting, he decided to save his unborn child from a similar wretched existence and so acquired the means to travel to England. He and his wife eventually washed up in the West End of Newcastle, where Leonard Conroy was subsequently born. One day, Leonard's father was walking down Scotswood Road when a bull escaped from an abattoir. Fearing innocent people would be trampled to death by the rampaging beast, Leonard's father ran, gripped the bull in a headlock, wrestled it to the ground and broke its neck. From that day onwards, everybody referred to him as 'Kill the Bull'.

A few years after that incident, in a similar manner, Kill the Bull accidentally snapped an off-duty policeman's back during a melee that he was trying to break up, again on Scotswood Road. Unfortunately, the officer died later that night in hospital. Kill the Bull was convicted of manslaughter and subsequently spent several years in prison. When he was eventually released, he was advised to move out of Newcastle because of the ill feeling some of the deceased man's colleagues held towards him. Kill the Bull refused to accept his guilt, because he had always maintained that the death was nothing more than a tragic accident. It is unclear if there were any further incidents linked to the policeman's death, but Kill the Bull never did leave Newcastle.

Paddy didn't bother going to school very often. In fact, the only time he ever did attend was to steal coal from the boiler room cellar. The 1970s was a decade blighted by strikes and industrial action by the then powerful unions. Homes were regularly plunged into darkness during power cuts caused by the miners striking, and the streets were often piled high with rotting rubbish because the binmen were working only a two-day week. Coal, the fuel that heated homes and cooked food, was scarce, and so Paddy and one of his sisters would steal it from school or off the railway lines, where it was used as ballast. The coal that was stolen from school would come in lumps, while the coal from the railway had been ground down or crushed into a fine dust by the weight of the trains – but they were still able to use it. Paddy's grandmother Sally would mix the coal dust with flour and make coke cakes, which she would then burn on the fire. It saved Sally a bit of money, and it gave Paddy and his sister an excuse to stay off school.

If you are born in Newcastle, you support Newcastle United Football Club. It's like a hereditary disease that you have been destined to contract or a religion that has been drummed into you from an early age. Everybody supported 'the Toon' in the Conroy household, but Leonard never went to watch the games at 'the Cathedral', or St James' Park, as it is more commonly known. The family were surprised, therefore, when one Saturday morning Leonard announced that he was going to watch the Toon, but they were even more surprised that nobody else was to be invited.

On that particular Saturday morning, 9 March 1974, the city of Newcastle was buzzing with excitement: victory over West Bromwich Albion in the FA Cup fifth round meant that Newcastle United had reached the quarter-finals of the prestigious competition for the first time in 13 years. Their victory was sweetened by the fact that their opponents in the next round were going to be second-division side Nottingham Forest.

Thirteen thousand of the Forest faithful travelled to St James' Park to roar on their side against an apparently superior Newcastle team. The atmosphere created by both sets of fans that day has been described as electric. After just 90 seconds of play, Forest stunned the home crowd by scoring. Urged on by 'the Toon Army', Newcastle did equalise, but just before the half-time whistle Forest regained the lead. The manager's half-time team talk must have been inspiring for the Newcastle players, as they came out for the second half full of fighting spirit. Unfortunately for them, the Forest defence stood firm and resisted wave after wave of attacks. This frustrated the Newcastle players, and after a number of niggling fouls and heavy challenges a Forest player was brought down in the area. The referee awarded a penalty kick. The Newcastle fans in the Leazes End of the ground were hysterical with rage and surged towards the pitch. Many of the younger fans in that end were crushed and, in fear of their lives, sought refuge on the pitch. To add insult to injury, Pat Howard, one of the Newcastle players, remonstrated with the referee about the penalty decision and was promptly sent off for dissent. The temperature on the terraces had been raised another few notches.

When Forest scored from the penalty kick, some of their supporters ran onto the pitch to celebrate in front of the Gallowgate End. It was one insult too many for approximately five hundred Geordies, and a golden opportunity for Leonard Conroy to set his plan in motion. 'Come on lads! Howay! Howay!' bellowed Leonard as he bulldozed through a line of police officers and onto the pitch. Helmets and bodies flew through the air as he was followed by legions of crazed Geordies who were baying for the Forest fans' blood. As Leonard led the cavalry charge, ITV commentator Brian Moore said, 'Here they come. This is what they have been waiting to do.' The players stood and watched in disbelief as hundreds of Newcastle fans tried to reach the Forest supporters. The referee looked terrified and signalled for all the players to leave the pitch. It was later alleged that, before they could do so, two Forest players, Dave Serella and Martin O'Neill, were assaulted.

Fortunately for the Forest supporters, but not for Leonard Conroy, the club and the police had prepared for crowd disturbances. There were 70 officers on duty in the ground and 70 more outside with dogs. As a result of their forward thinking, the police were able to act quickly and arrest Leonard, which resulted in order being restored after just eight minutes. When the pitch had been cleared of marauding Geordies, the referee asked both sets of club officials if they wished to continue the game. Forest, who were winning 3–1 and playing against ten men, fancied their chances and elected to play on. The Newcastle officials, clearly embarrassed by the crowd disturbances, were in no position to argue.

With 25 minutes remaining, Newcastle United attacked the Forest defence with a vengeance. The steely resolve the Forest players had shown earlier in the game was now gone. Several players appeared unnerved and eyed the hysterical Newcastle fans with fear rather than watching the ball. Poise had been replaced with panic. Urged on by thousands of black-and-white-clad Geordies, Newcastle United piled on the pressure. With twenty-two minutes remaining, Newcastle were awarded a penalty kick, which they scored, and just three minutes later they drew level with a Forest side that was by now in complete disarray. In the last minute of the game, Newcastle legend Malcolm 'Supermac' Macdonald headed the ball across the goalmouth and captain Bobby Moncur scored the winner.

When the final whistle was blown, Forest manager Allan Brown was under no illusions as to who had won the game – and it wasn't Newcastle United FC. 'The crowd and the referee undoubtedly won the game for Newcastle,' he said when interviewed after the match. Newcastle United chairman Lord Westwood did not hold back in his condemnation of the home fans either. 'I was disgusted with the behaviour of a section of the fans,' he told reporters.

Following the disturbance that Leonard Conroy had sparked, 23 fans required hospital treatment, two had suffered fractured skulls and 103 others received first aid. A number of police officers suffered minor injuries, and in all 39 people were charged with violent conduct and another 40 were ejected from the ground. Twenty-four hours later, Nottingham Forest appealed against the result, and after a meeting with the FA Cup Committee a replay at a neutral venue was ordered. The replay took place at Goodison Park, home of Everton FC. It ended in a

0–0 draw. The second replay, again played at Goodison Park, saw Newcastle United win 1–0. In the semi-final, Newcastle defeated Burnley, but their dreams of FA Cup glory, which had at one point seemed possible thanks to the actions of Leonard Conroy, were dashed when they met Liverpool in the final at Wembley and lost 3–0.

Publicly, Lord Westwood may have said that he was disgusted by the fans' behaviour, but Leonard later claimed that it was Lord Westwood himself who had asked him to attend and stop the match if Newcastle were losing. When Leonard appeared in court, he was condemned by the judge as being 'the architect' of an incident that had 'shamed the city' and was imprisoned for nine months. He later told friends that he didn't care about the sentence he had received, because Lord Westwood had paid him handsomely in cash on the condition that he never talk about their agreement or darken the turnstiles of St James' Park ever again. Both men have sadly passed away since, but there is little doubt that Leonard was telling the truth; he certainly was not the sort of man who would lie to win favour.

Lord Westwood was no stranger to controversy or dodgy dealings; in 1951, he had been involved in a ticket-touting scandal after he promised FA Cup tickets to an MP. These tickets were included in a raffle before the police stepped in to stop them becoming available. Three years after the controversy surrounding the FA Cup clash with Nottingham Forest, Newcastle United were back in the news when six first-team players threatened to quit the club after their contract talks broke down. Allegations of misconduct in the boardroom were dismissed by Lord Westwood, who claimed that he and Richard Dinnis, the recently sacked manager, were being 'knifed in the back'. In an effort to keep the dispute in-house, Lord Westwood ordered a blanket ban on Newcastle United employees, and in particular the players, discussing their grievances with the media. In 1981, Newcastle United Football Club was facing financial ruin, and so each director was urged to invest a further £16,000. Lord Westwood had financial problems of his own following the stock market crash of DCM, Europe's leading toy company, of which he was also chairman, and so he declined to assist. He resigned from the board and died ten years later, in November 1991.

Shortly after Leonard Conroy's imprisonment for the pitch invasion, his son Paddy was sent to an approved school after being caught shoplifting. It was hardly an offence worthy of such punishment; he had stolen a bottle of alcohol from a shop and was apprehended by an eagle-eyed policeman who had been observing him from across the street. Paddy did have previous convictions, so no doubt the magistrates, in their infinite wisdom, felt his crimes were heinous enough that he be denied his liberty and sent to a place where he could be taught by 'respectable adults' how one should behave.

It's unclear who had 'approved' the school, but whoever it was certainly didn't have standards, because it was, in the words of one former pupil, 'hell on fucking earth'. The 'school's' official title was Netherton Training Approved School for Boys. It was, in fact, no more than four small farm cottages in the middle of what looked like moorland, somewhere near Morpeth, in Northumberland. The only lessons the school taught its pupils were the horrors of sexual abuse and the pain of extreme violence.

The first day Paddy was there, he was introduced to a man the other children referred to as 'the Major'. Apparently, he had been charged with turning the young miscreants' lives around. Within an hour of Paddy's arrival, the Major had ushered him into a medical room, where an elderly matron ordered him to stand in front of her. Without saying another word, she pulled down his trousers and underpants while the Major looked on, smiling, sweating and slobbering. Paddy instinctively pulled away from the depraved old hag and got dressed. 'Get back here, boy,' the matron bellowed, but he was having none of it and ran back to his dormitory.

Later that night, in the television room, the teacher's pet – or bully, to give him his more realistic title – walked over to where Paddy was sitting, pointed to a comb lying on the floor and asked whose it was. 'It's not mine,' Paddy replied.

'Well, pick it up,' the bully snarled.

Paddy told him again that it wasn't his comb and that he therefore had no intention of picking it up. Moments later, the bully's sidekick swaggered into the room and asked who had stolen his comb. The bully looked at Paddy and then looked at the comb on the floor beside him before nodding to his sidekick, who immediately leapt on top of Paddy. He did his best to fight back, but against two older, stronger boys Paddy's efforts were futile. He went to bed that night nursing a black eye. Paddy's father had slipped him a £5 note at court and advised him that if he did get sent away he could escape and use the cash to make his way home. Even though it was Paddy's first day at the approved school, he knew that the money would be needed before too long and so, rather than give in to temptation and spend it, he had hidden it in his sock for safe keeping. Less than an hour after Paddy went to bed, the heavy, morbid atmosphere in the school had convinced him that he should escape and head home to Newcastle. He got dressed in the darkness and tiptoed out of the dormitory.

Moments later, Paddy was running across the fields to freedom, but he had been spotted by the school bully, who informed the teachers, and was soon apprehended. Threats, slaps and promises of further punishment accompanied him back to his bed. When the onslaught had ended, rather than sleep, Paddy lay awake in the darkness, planning his next move. He couldn't see what was happening in his dormitory, but the cries of pain and anguish from within the darkness made it abundantly clear that some of his fellow inmates were being either raped or beaten, or both. Paddy could live with the threat of violence, but the very thought of being raped inspired him to run away at great speed the following morning.

Paddy didn't know it at the time, but running away from that institution was one of the wisest decisions he would ever make. The abuse, both sexual and physical, turned out to be far more sinister than he had experienced during his own short stay. In 2007, scores of former pupils at care homes throughout the north-east, including Netherton, sued for damages. It was proven that they had suffered rape and sexual, physical and emotional abuse. So much for sending young children who have stolen a single bottle of beer to such an establishment for 'rehabilitation'.

After making his way to the nearest town, Paddy used the £5 note that his father had given him to get home. Seeing the famous Tyne Bridge from the window of a bus later that afternoon would undoubtedly have been one of the happiest moments in Paddy's life. After fleeing from the approved school, he did his best to change his ways and avoid contact with the police. But, however good his intentions may have been, he still needed money to pay for his day-to-day needs and so, inevitably, returned to committing petty crime.

During the execution of one particular criminal enterprise, Paddy happened upon a pretty girl named Maureen, who later turned out to be the love of his life. Their first meeting was hardly romantic: Maureen was mugged, by Paddy, as she was making her way to the shops. Paddy had been told by a friend that Maureen was paid to do the shopping for her landlady, and so he decided that he would relieve her of the cash. In many ways, it was the perfect crime. Maureen did not argue when Paddy demanded that she hand over her cash to him, nor did she report him to the authorities when she had complied with his request.

After being robbed two or three times in as many weeks, Maureen didn't even bother waiting for Paddy to ask for the money when they next met. Paddy just stood outside the shop, and Maureen walked over to him and handed over her cash. Then, one day, Paddy decided to carry Maureen off home along with her money. They have been together ever since.

The authorities regularly searched Paddy's grandmother's home and scoured the local streets in pursuit of him. He was confident that he would never be caught, but his father sat him down one day and explained that it would be only a matter of time before they got lucky and he would be returned to the approved school. Leonard was no stranger to being on the run and advised his son that if he wished to stay free he would be better off moving to London to live with a good friend of his named Jack Mulholland. Paddy knew Jack, as he had been a regular visitor to the Conroy household over the years. Paddy liked him, and so he agreed that he would move to London.

Jack was a member of Leonard's criminal 'firm', and together they used to burgle country houses, hijack lorries and rob post offices. Leonard knew that Jack would accommodate Paddy, as the Conroy home had regularly been used as a safe haven for his criminal associates. Sometimes it would be because they had just got out of prison and had nowhere else to stay, but more often than not it was because they were hiding from the police. Amongst the many guests over the years were Danny Burns, Norman Short, Leonard's brother William, Kenneth 'Panda' Anderson, Billy Gascoigne, Charlie Francis and Sugar Bentley. These men were all notorious villains in the north-east during the 1960s and '70s.

Jack Mulholland was a single man who lived in the Southall area of west London. Despite his single status, Jack was hardly unattached. In fact, he was attached to a different female nearly every evening of the week. To fund his extensive wining, dining and romancing habit, Jack worked full-time as a security guard controlling the gate of a large industrial estate. Paddy grew extremely fond of Jack, who would mesmerise him with fascinating stories about his life and the criminal enterprises that he and Paddy's father had embarked upon. During one such conversation, Paddy learned that Jack held the rather dishonourable honour of being the most flogged man ever to be incarcerated at HMP Durham. Considering the establishment was built in 1810 and has housed some of Britain's most notorious prisoners, Jack's punishment record was quite remarkable.

Whenever Jack was taken from court to prison, he would spit into the face of the first prison officer who spoke to him. Then – *bang* – he would throw a punch and a fight would begin. Jack knew that he would never be able to defeat all the prison officers, but he told friends that he wanted them to know he didn't fear them. After being restrained, Jack would then be manhandled to the punishment block, stripped and repeatedly lashed with the birch. There were no general rules for administering this barbaric form of punishment, and so each individual prison officer devised his own personal preferences. Some would flog Jack across the buttocks, others across his back or shoulders. Some would administer a beating that combined all three areas. The beatings left Jack with terrible scarring and a deep-seated hatred of anybody in authority.

On the Uxbridge Road in Hayes, west London, which is where Jack worked, stood the EMI Music record factory. Any records that were marked or had covers that were in any way damaged were thrown into large skips adjacent to the factory wall. An LP back in those days retailed at around £5, and so Paddy decided that he would set up his own record stall on Brick Lane Market in the East End and sell them at a heavily discounted rate. After getting the all-clear from Jack, Paddy climbed a wall on the industrial estate and stole about ten boxes of records. The following day, Paddy 'acquired' a wheeled trolley with racks on, loaded it up with his stolen goods and caught the Tube to Aldgate East, which is just a short walk from the famous Brick Lane Market. Paddy didn't bother with the expense of hiring a stall; he just stood on a street corner, and in no time at all he had sold all his stock. He was hardly going to become a millionaire from selling damaged records, but his income wasn't bad and the overheads were no more than a return Tube ticket.

Paddy was soon expanding his business by sending boxes of the stolen records back home to Newcastle for his friends and associates to sell. Everything appeared to be going well for Paddy: he was happy living with Jack, he had built up a regular customer base on the market and he was earning more than enough to pay his own way. Then, just nine months after Paddy moved to London, tragedy struck: Jack was diagnosed with terminal cancer. He contacted Paddy's father from his deathbed and offered him his job as a security guard at the industrial estate. 'It's a cracking job,' Jack said. 'The wages aren't great, but the fiddles more than make up your money.'

At the time, the country was being held to ransom by the unions, the dockers, the car workers and the miners, and anybody else who was fortunate enough to be in employment was either on strike, working reduced hours or working to rule. Money was hard to come by, and so Leonard accepted Jack's kind offer and moved to London, taking his wife and family with him. The West End of London bore no resemblance to the West End of Newcastle, where the Conroy family had lived; in fact, it turned out to be a bit of a culture shock for them all. They had never set eyes on an Asian person in their lives, and in Southall, where they had settled, white people appeared to be in the minority. The Conroys had no problem with their neighbours being from another part of the world; they just found it difficult to converse because of their strong Geordie accents. Even the native cockneys used to ask them to slow down when they spoke so that they could try to understand what it was they were saying.

After Jack died, Paddy returned to Newcastle and moved in with Maureen, who was living in a flat with her sister Pat. When Maureen and her brothers and sisters were all very young, they had been adopted or put into care homes. Initially, Maureen had gone to live in Leeds with a foster family, but she had returned to Newcastle to reside with her sister, whose partner was a well-known villain named David Glover. He had a son, also named David, who was eight years younger than Paddy. When Paddy first moved in with Maureen and the Glovers, he got on well with David junior, but he soon realised that he was an extremely volatile and devious character.

On the day that they first met, Paddy heard a car engine roaring from behind a pair of locked garage doors. Suddenly, there was a huge crash, and a car, reversing at speed, burst through the doors and out onto the car park where Paddy was standing. Shrouded in a cloud of exhaust fumes, smoke and dust, Paddy was unable to see who was in the driving seat of the vehicle, but as the smoke began to clear he could see a small boy grinning maniacally behind the steering wheel. The boy was so short that he had put a milk crate on the driving seat to be able to see out through the windscreen. Bending down to wedge an iron bar onto the accelerator, the boy had nearly run Paddy over as the car jumped forward and then raced out of sight. David Glover was only around nine at that time, and he was already terrorising the area where he lived.

Whenever David Glover senior was sent to jail, David junior would burgle local houses to put food on the table for his family. At the tender age of 13, he was caught trying to break into HMP Durham via the high-security walls so that he could give his father contraband. The local community was absolutely terrified of David. If he couldn't get his way, or if he lost a fight, it wouldn't end there. Those who were naive enough to cross him or to take him on were usually found lying unconscious in their own bloody mess.

A kind, caring woman named Cathy, for whom Maureen regularly babysat and did odd jobs, suggested that Maureen and Paddy live with her. Maureen was often at her home from early evening until the early hours of the morning caring for the children while Cathy worked, and so it made sense to Paddy for both of them to move in there. Cathy's home was only a stone's throw from the Glovers', and so Maureen accepted her offer, as she would still be near her sister.

One evening while Maureen was babysitting, Paddy had gone out and accepted a lift from a friend in a stolen car that was subsequently stopped by the police. They were taken to the local station to be questioned. The desk sergeant soon realised, after making checks, that Paddy was on the run from the approved school, and so he refused to grant him bail. When Paddy appeared in court the following morning, he was remanded in custody to HMP Low Newton, a purpose-built remand centre that lies just four miles south of Durham. It was built in 1965 to hold 65 males and 11 female prisoners, but when Paddy arrived it housed a total of 215 inmates. To say the place was overcrowded would be a gross understatement.

Paddy's time in Low Newton during the late '70s was pretty uneventful. Because of the overcrowding, there wasn't enough work to go around, and so inmates spent the majority of their time locked in their cells. After three months of mind-numbing incarceration, Paddy appeared in court for sentencing. It was agreed by all concerned that Paddy was now too old to be returned to the approved school, and so the magistrate fined him for allowing himself to be carried in a stolen vehicle and ordered his immediate release. Shortly after that, the rest of the Conroy family returned from London to live in Newcastle. Paddy's recent stay in prison and the presence of his mother had a sobering effect upon him, and so, for the first time in his life, he decided to seek legitimate employment.

Chapter Two

AND PIGS MIGHT FLY

THE FIRST LEGITIMATE job that Paddy ever had was making sausage skins at the local abattoir. The rancid stench of animal guts and carcases clung to the clothing and skin of everybody who worked there. The workforce could scrub themselves for a week with bleach, but there would always remain a slight minty smell that identified them to others as abattoir employees. Paddy stomached the job for only two weeks, because he was offered and accepted a job as a doorman at a venue called The 69 Club.

Two legendary fighters named Paddy Leonard and Billy Robinson provided the security at the venue, and both were friends of Paddy's father. A man named 'Lucky' Joe Lyle actually owned the place, but he spent the majority of his time in the comfort of his home on the Isle of Man. The clientele tended to be made up of rough-and-ready characters, but, apart from the odd punch-up that one might witness in any establishment that sells alcohol, there was very little for the bouncers to sort out. That was because the people who frequented the club respected Paddy and Billy, and so if customers did encounter somebody they disliked they would usually ignore them and sort out their differences elsewhere.

A decade before Paddy Conroy was employed at The 69 Club, the Kray brothers had visited the venue while on a business trip to Newcastle. A Geordie named Vince Landa had made a fortune from fruit machines during the 1960s, when the gambling industry was still in its infancy, and the Krays were hiring and installing Landa's machines in the pubs and clubs that they protected throughout

31

London – for a non-negotiable fee, of course. As their business boomed, the Krays decided to cut out the middleman and purchase rather than hire the machines, and so they travelled from London to discuss a deal with Landa.

In an attempt to be the perfect host, Landa took the Krays to the Club A-Go-Go in Whitley Bay before arriving at The 69 Club later the same evening. When Joe Lyle realised who Landa was attempting to bring into his club, he told the Krays that they were not welcome and threatened to call the police. Not used to being excluded from any establishment, Reggie Kray is said to have glared at Lyle and warned him that his insolence would not be forgotten. Quickly reflecting upon his actions, Lyle is said to have given a notorious Geordie villain named Kenneth 'Panda' Anderson £1,000 in cash to give to the Krays by way of an apology.

Panda, who knew the Krays and many other cockney villains following periods he had spent with them in prison, offered Reggie the cash, and he accepted it. Very 'Lucky' Lyle's lack of tact was put down to an unfortunate misunderstanding. The stories that have circulated for years about the Krays being threatened and chased out of Newcastle are nonsense; they left of their own accord after completing their business there. Why Joe Lyle objected to the Krays going into The 69 Club is a mystery, because the only people who drank in there were villains.

Being employed as a doorman suited Paddy Conroy; he was free to do what he wanted during the day, and while he was working at night his partner Maureen was generally earning money too, by babysitting. In order to make ends meet, Paddy took on a couple of casual day jobs. For a while, he worked as a builder and, later, as a glazier at the Clayton Glass factory on West Road.

A few years earlier, Paddy's father had assaulted a policeman, whom I shall call Pinky, after a difference of opinion, and this disgruntled officer had decided to make it his life's work to cause problems for the Conroy family. Pinky and his colleague, whom I shall call Perky, used to relentlessly patrol the street where the Conroys lived. These two particular officers were generally known for throwing their weight around and slapping any teenagers they found committing misdemeanours. They didn't ever slap Paddy, despite the fact that he used to verbally abuse them whenever he saw them out on patrol. Paddy's safety was ensured by the fact that Pinky and Perky both feared his father.

When Paddy arrived at the glass factory for work one morning, he was called into the manager's office and advised that 'a problem' had arisen regarding his employment. 'The police have been in to see me,' the bleak-faced manager said. 'And they say that I am unwise to employ a man whose family is involved in serious crime.' Paddy asked if he was going to be sacked, but, to his credit, the manager replied that he would do no such thing. 'I won't be dictated to by the police about whom I employ, but if you are involved in any wrongdoing it must cease forthwith,' he said sternly.

Despite the manager's initial good intentions, things were never quite the same for Paddy at work after that. The police returned on two or three occasions and asked the manager how some of his customers would feel if they knew he was employing 'a Conroy', and so Paddy saved his boss the embarrassment of having to sack him by handing in his notice. Paddy wasn't that bothered about losing his job, but he was troubled by the attitude of the police, because he was not involved in any criminality at that time. Paddy was at the glass factory during the day and working the doors at night, and so he had more than enough money to make ends meet. Paddy believed that it was just a case of certain police officers victimising his family because of his father's criminality and the company that he chose to keep.

The Conroys were far from unique in the West End of Newcastle. Just a stone's throw from their front door lived the Sayers family. For generations, they had worked the markets in Newcastle. In fact, they were the first licensed 'barrow boys' in the city. To this day, a member of the Sayers family runs a fruit and vegetable stall that has been in Northumberland Street, the main shopping thoroughfare, since 1884. Like the Conroys, father and sons alike were villains, but neither family had much to do with the other. With the passing of time, that situation has changed. Members of the Sayers family have been accused of involvement in armed robbery, blackmail and murder, and the Conroys, Paddy in particular, have become their arch-enemies. It is widely believed in the north-east that the eldest son, John Henry Sayers, is 'the Godfather of Newcastle', a title he has done very little to disown.

The Sayers clan promoted themselves as a Kray- or mafia-type family, charitable and willing to assist the needy but equally willing to punish those they deemed to have transgressed the criminal code.

In one incident, Stephen and John Henry heard that someone had robbed St Nicholas's Cathedral of a valuable jewelled staff. It was 100 years old and of historical importance to the city of Newcastle. Stephen and John Henry were in a pub one day when a lad apparently came in trying to sell the staff. Quite what a beer-swilling Geordie would do with such an item has never been explained. Stephen and John Henry took it from the thief and returned it, undamaged, to the church. Within days, the Sayers family were in the evening newspaper having praise heaped on them.

As the Conroy and Sayers children grew older, they began to socialise with one another, but egos got in the way, and so they elected to tolerate one another's presence rather than mix. One of the local lads whom the Conroy family did embrace was Michael Bullock, who lived in the not so Noble Street flats. His mother, 'Connie the Copper', as Paddy used to call her, was a straight-laced lady who was adamant that her son should not have anything to do with the Conroy family. If Connie ever saw Paddy up to no good, which was often, she would immediately pick up the phone and ring the police. Michael, or 'the Bull', as he was known, was about the same age as Neil, the youngest of the Conroy brothers. Despite Connie's continuous protests, the Bull and Neil became close friends. Taking Neil to his own home caused the Bull too many headaches, and so he used to spend a lot of time at the Conroys'. Eventually, the Bull moved in.

Leonard was always lecturing the Bull and Neil about the need to be honest with those you depend on in life. 'I don't care who else you lie to,' Leonard would say, 'but you must never lie to me or anybody else close to you.' One evening, Neil and the Bull met a couple of girls in town and stayed out all night. As soon as they walked through the door the following morning, Leonard ushered the Bull into the sitting room. 'Where were you last night?' he asked.

Embarrassed, the Bull meekly replied, 'We had a few drinks in town. The landlord let us stay late, and we got so drunk we booked into a hotel afterwards rather than come home.'

Fixing his eyes firmly on the Bull, Leonard said, 'What have I told you about lying to those close to you?'

The Bull apologised and told Leonard the truth. That is how Leonard raised all his children. They had no secrets between them, and if somebody crossed one Conroy then they crossed them all. In time, the Bull became an honorary member of the family.

In order to earn money, Neil and the Bull used to burgle factories and shops or steal cars and use them to carry out ram raids at the MetroCentre shopping complex in nearby Gateshead. They would then supply Paddy with the stolen goods, which he would sell through his network of friends and acquaintances in Newcastle. Paddy also worked the Sunday markets, which were an ideal outlet for the type of stock his unorthodox suppliers provided. From ski suits to children's buggies – you name it – Conroy's discounted wholesalers stocked it, and if he didn't he could place an order and the Bull and Neil would guarantee an overnight delivery.

Unsurprisingly, the police eventually raided Paddy's home, in the Noble Street flats, searching for stolen property. After ransacking the place, the only thing that the officers did find was a big, heavy widescreen television. Paddy had bought it from the Bull and Neil after they had stolen it during a burglary at an electrical shop. Huffing and puffing, two detectives struggled to carry the bulky TV out of the lounge. 'Put it down. You're both useless,' Paddy said. 'I carried it up here on my own, and so I will carry it down for you.' After the panting and wheezing officers had stood aside, Paddy picked up the television, walked out of his lounge, through the front door and dropped it straight over the balcony and onto the street far below. *Boom!* There was a huge explosion as the television disintegrated into a thousand pieces.

Paddy stood there laughing as the detectives did a funny kind of dance on the spot. One ran towards Paddy and then back into the flat. The other detective held his head in his hands and swayed back and forth, as if bowing. 'Get Conroy in the fucking car,' one shouted. 'Get him in the fucking car while I sort out this mess. And don't let the bastard touch anything else,' he added, almost as an afterthought. Paddy knew that these two Keystone Kops would have trouble explaining to their bosses how he had come to be in possession of what was an exhibit of evidential value seized from his home. Paddy spent the next 30 minutes sitting in the police car, looking out of the window and laughing at them as they scurried about, picking up all the pieces of the smashed television and putting them into evidence bags.

When the matter came before the courts, Paddy pleaded not guilty. The prosecution summoned the owner of the television to identify his property, which was now in approximately 20 different evidence bags. Bemused, the man looked at each bag, looked at the magistrates and shook his head. 'Sorry,' he said, 'I don't recognise any of this.' Moments later, Paddy was walking out of the court having been told that there was no case to answer.

After a few months of working at The 69 Club, Paddy was relocated to work at a bar in the centre of Newcastle called The Lowthers. Paddy used to work there until it closed, at 10.30 p.m., and then he would cross the Tyne Bridge into Gateshead to work at a nightclub called Wheelers. That was where all the local heavy drinkers used to congregate once the pubs had kicked them out. It is an indisputable fact that alcohol and humans do not mix, and so Wheelers was quite a lively club, to say the least. The regulars who managed to remain upright until closing time tended to fight one another, and those who had failed in their efforts to consume twenty pints of brown ale before the bar closed were left where they fell to help soak up the vomit and beer from the sopping-wet, sticky carpet.

One evening, Paddy broke up a fight near the bar in Wheelers between Michael Sayers and another man, who had somehow offended him. As Michael was from the West End and Paddy knew of him, he told Michael to step aside and grabbed his opponent by the arm. Another doorman, named Derek, gripped the man's free arm and together with Paddy began frogmarching him out towards the exit. Before they had left the bar area, somebody ran up behind them and rammed a beer glass into the neck of the man they were in the process of ejecting. Blood gushed from a gaping wound, and Paddy thought the man was in danger of bleeding to death. He told the bar staff to fetch beer towels, and these were then used to apply pressure to the wound until an ambulance arrived. As the trembling man was carried from the premises on a stretcher, he was advised to keep his mouth shut if questioned by the police. Nodding furiously, the victim was loaded into an ambulance and taken to hospital, where he received more than 30 stitches before being discharged the following day.

As a result of that incident, Paddy barred Michael Sayers from the club. The following week, Michael's mother, Yvonne, arrived at Wheelers and began shouting and screaming at Paddy for having the audacity to exclude her son. Even when Paddy tried to explain what had happened to an innocent man, Yvonne was not prepared to listen. Despite his mother's protests, Michael Sayers remained barred from Wheelers, and that, as far as Paddy was concerned, was the end of the matter. Not long after this incident, Michael's eldest brother, John Henry, started work at the club as a doorman. John Henry was an ex-paratrooper who kept himself in extremely good shape: he never drank and he never smoked.

One evening, a gang of men from Gateshead burst through the door of Wheelers and came running up the stairs. Paddy had no idea of their intentions, but he was pretty sure that they were not making a social call. After launching himself at the mob, Paddy began knocking them back down the stairs, punching each face as it came into view. When the snarling, spitting mound of writhing bodies reached the reception area, Paddy found himself buried beneath two or three of his opponents and so looked up to see if any of the other door staff were coming to his aid. Suddenly, John Henry appeared and stood above Paddy and the Gateshead men. 'Thank fuck for that,' Paddy said. 'Help at last.' But his relief was both short-lived and misguided. All John Henry did to assist Paddy was shout, 'Howay, lads, if you want to fight, make it one against one.' Fortunately for Paddy, John Henry's 'intervention' broke up the fight and the men made their escape via the front door. 'Disappointing' is how Paddy described John Henry's unwillingness to fight that night.

Because Paddy and Maureen were both working hard and not spending money socialising, Paddy had managed to save approximately £5,000, which he decided to invest in a business rather than waste on brown ale. The Tyneside economy had originally been founded on the coal industry. As demand for the fuel increased, deeper pits were excavated, which led to a huge rise in production, a railway network being introduced and large cargo ships being built by Vickers-Armstrong at their factory on the banks of the Tyne. The Newcastle shipyards became so successful that they began to take orders for the construction of naval and commercial vessels from all over the world. An ever-increasing migrant workforce, needed to meet the labour demands, resulted in a rapid expansion in house building, which in turn brought new shops, pubs, churches and, eventually, a thriving community. In keeping with this, Vickers-Armstrong built a pub, called the Hydraulic Crane, for its 50,000 employees. After the war, however, the workforce was dramatically reduced, the pub closed and it and the surrounding area fell into disrepair.

Paddy and his eldest brother, Lenny, had made enquiries about the availability of the pub, and much to their surprise they were able to purchase it for a meagre £6,000. It was their belief that the Hydraulic Crane could be renovated and revamped to sell food as well as drink, which would once more attract the Vickers-Armstrong workforce at lunchtimes, and locals in the evenings.

Lenny's enthusiasm for the venture waned when a friend of his who worked for the local council suggested that he would never get planning permission. Paddy, on the other hand, has never backed down from a challenge and decided to go it alone. He sold everything he owned and other items that he didn't quite own, including his partner Maureen's jewellery, to raise the £3,000 he needed in order to buy out his brother's share. The last thing Paddy wanted was for Lenny to sell his stake in the pub to somebody he couldn't or didn't wish to work with.

Having secured total ownership of the Hydraulic Crane, Paddy brought in a new partner, who was aptly named Stuart Beveridge. Paddy planned to use the money that Stuart had invested in the project to pay for the renovation work, but before that could begin Stuart and Paddy had to apply for the planning permission that everybody had doubted they could ever obtain. Initially, their application was turned down, but, while reading and researching every possible clause and law relating to the planning procedure, they discovered that the then prime minister, Margaret Thatcher, had earmarked certain deprived areas in many major cities for special concessions. Thatcher had named these areas 'Enterprise Zones' and stated that anybody seeking planning permission for business premises within these zones could not be refused.

Rolling out a map to compare the position of the Hydraulic Crane with the boundaries of Newcastle's Enterprise Zone, Paddy and Stuart were pleasantly surprised to find that the pub fell just inside. They immediately sat down and penned a letter to Margaret Thatcher, complaining bitterly that Newcastle City Council was ignoring the government's directive by refusing them planning permission. It is not known if Thatcher personally intervened, but within weeks Stuart and Paddy had been granted permission to renovate the pub. As soon as it became common knowledge that the Hydraulic Crane was going to reopen and Paddy was a partner, one particular police officer did everything in his power to make life difficult for him.

Knowing Paddy ran a market stall was upsetting enough for some members of Northumbria Police, but the very thought of him running a public house was clearly tipping others over the edge. When the warnings came that the pub would never get a licence to sell alcohol while Paddy was involved in the running of it, he refused to be deterred and the renovation work continued. When it was nearing completion, Paddy was approached by a man who claimed to represent a third party who wished to purchase the pub. Thinking it was some sort of underhand tactic or ploy to glean information about his future plans, Paddy threw caution to the wind and said that the asking price was £45,000. Expecting the man at least to raise a wry smile, Paddy was surprised when he simply said, 'I will be in touch,' before turning and walking away. Later that evening, the man returned and said that the third party he represented was willing to pay the full asking price. A few weeks later, the sale went through; Paddy paid his partner back his investment and walked away with more than £35,000 profit.

Paddy must have felt like the richest man in Newcastle. It was certainly a lot of money to have back in those days. However, he decided that he wasn't going to get carried away. He had one or two debts to settle, and the remainder of the cash was going to be invested in his family's future. Paddy's first mandatory purchase was to replace the jewellery that he had sold belonging to his partner, Maureen. Now that he had a bit of capital, he promised her that he was done with being a villain, that he was going to try to make a legitimate living and, in the hope of sounding sincere, that he wasn't even going to buy any more heist (stolen property). It was an ambitious statement for Paddy to make, and for a while he actually believed it himself.

Paddy purchased a derelict three-storey town house for £15,000, which he then converted into eleven bedsits. Paddy named the property 'The Happy House', which he had engraved in large letters above the front door. The rooms were furnished with the assistance of the burglary business of his brother Neil and the Bull. The end result seemed to justify the fact that he had broken his promise to Maureen about buying stolen property.

On 19 July 1988, Paddy went for a drink in Newcastle city centre with three friends named Tommy Findlay, Tony Thomas and Barry Redfern. Paddy wanted to speak to a bouncer by the name of Viv Graham, who worked in town, about an incident at a restaurant called Santino's that had resulted in Viv barring some of Paddy's other friends. Viv was later to become a fighting legend in the north-east, but Paddy never considered him to be the lean, mean, unbeatable fighting machine that some have described him as. Viv had begun his career as a bouncer at the Travellers Rest pub in the village of Burnopfield. The owner had two other pubs in the area, and, after witnessing just how competent Viv was at preventing and breaking up trouble, he employed him to clear his other premises of undesirables. From the village of Burnopfield, Viv's reputation as a hard man soon spread, and he accepted work at venues such as the Whitemare Pool Hotel and Finnegan's nightclub, in Gateshead.

It was while working at Finnegan's that Viv really made a name for himself. He had fought a man named Paul Ashton while Paddy's boss on the doors, Billy Robinson, looked on. According to those present that night, Viv gave a very good account of himself during 20 gruelling minutes of fighting at the end of which Billy Robinson recruited him to work for his security company.

Within a relatively short period of time, Viv Graham had become the name that landlords uttered whenever a pub or club in or around the city of Newcastle was experiencing trouble that needed sorting out. Some even began to refer to him as the fourth emergency service. There are, of course, others who claim Viv was just a bully who picked on those he knew he could beat. Paddy's opinion of Viv fell between both camps. He was undoubtedly an able-bodied fighter, but there was also undeniable evidence of his bullying. In Newcastle, at least one brain-damaged young man bears testament to that.

When Paddy went to Santino's restaurant to speak to Viv about why he had barred his friends, he knew that there was a good chance the debate would end in violence, but Paddy had decided that if Viv wanted to resolve the grievance that way then so be it. As Paddy approached the restaurant where Viv was working, one of the bouncers recognised him and locked the door. A dustbin flashed past Paddy's head as he tried to attract the bouncer's attention, and the window he was peering through exploded into a thousand pieces. One of the lads Paddy was with had clearly grown impatient. A burglar alarm and diners in the restaurant immediately began to wail and scream. The bouncers ran out of the main dining area and into the safety of the kitchen, while Paddy and the others ran, laughing hysterically, to their car.

As they sped away, a policeman noticed that their BMW Cabriolet was travelling the wrong way up a one-way street and decided to pull them over. At first, they thought the policeman was going to question them about the dustbin being thrown through the restaurant window, but it soon became apparent that he wasn't aware of the incident. 'Where have you been, lads? Have you been drinking?' he asked. The driver of the vehicle, Tommy Findlay, stared straight ahead and didn't bother to reply. He had been drinking all day and knew he would fail a breathalyser test, so he just slammed the car into gear and sped off, leaving the officer shrouded in a cloud of tyre smoke. The policeman ran back to his own vehicle, activated the siren and blue flashing lights, and gave chase.

Within a few minutes, the speeding car had left the city centre and was careering through the streets of Paddy's neighbourhood, where the occupants believed that they would be safe. Paddy rang Maureen on his mobile phone and told her to make sure the back gate was open for the driver. Paddy knew that if Findlay was able to get into his house via the rear entrance there was no way the police would give chase, because he had a couple of huge Rottweilers roaming around in the garden. Paddy was living at 113 Northbourne Street at the time and should have known things wouldn't go according to plan, because over the years the property had been a magnet for bad luck for his family. Paddy's 19-year-old cousin Jimmy Conroy had lived in the house before him, and he had ended up being convicted of murder.

One evening, Jimmy had gone down the town to meet his friends for a drink. When the pubs had closed, they had begun walking to a taxi rank. Jimmy, who was drunk but not incapable, had picked up a crash helmet that had been left on the seat of a motorcycle parked at the side of the road. It was a stupid, pointless act, but Jimmy was behaving as many young men do when in drink: fooling about with friends, oblivious to the upset and concern that their loutish antics may cause to others.

When a taxi arrived, Jimmy got into it, still clutching the crash helmet, and asked the driver to take him home. His friends lived in other areas of Newcastle, and so they caught separate taxis.

As the driver turned into Northbourne Street, Jimmy could see that a fight involving a group of men was in progress. Rather foolishly, when Jimmy climbed out of the taxi, he tried to break the fight up, but several bystanders remonstrated with him, saying he should mind his own business. Because Jimmy was so well liked, it didn't take long for people to come out of their houses to back him up. As Jimmy tried to pull the lads apart, he was punched in the face, and in no time at all a skirmish between half a dozen lads had turned into a full-scale battle involving between 20 and 30 people. The lad who had punched Jimmy was trying to get him into a headlock, and so, instinctively, Jimmy lashed out while still holding the crash helmet. Another of the combatants had fallen nearby, and two men were kicking his head repeatedly. Jimmy was adamant that this was the person who later died from head injuries, but the police maintained it was the guy Jimmy had struck with the crash helmet. When the two men who had repeatedly been kicking their opponent were questioned, both denied kicking anybody and both made statements alleging that it was Jimmy who had killed the victim, using a crash helmet. Unsurprisingly, Jimmy was convicted of murder and served a total of 17 years for a crime that he still maintains he did not commit.

When Tommy Findlay screeched to an abrupt halt at the rear of Paddy's Northbourne Street home, Barry Redfern threw a survival-style knife he had on him out into the street and dashed for the gate. The pursuing police car arrived moments later, and an officer gave chase. Unfortunately for Findlay, Maureen hadn't had time to open the garden gate, and the policeman pounced on him as he tried to climb over it. Drawing his baton, the officer began to club Findlay, and he soon fell to the floor. As reinforcements arrived, they too drew their batons and began striking Findlay, who was screaming with fear. Paddy thought it was totally unnecessary for them to hit a man who wasn't offering resistance, and so he ran to his aid. As soon as the police left Findlay alone and focused their attention and batons on Paddy, Findlay got to his feet and ran away.

In the battle that ensued, Paddy was badly beaten and several police officers were injured. Paddy doesn't remember too much about the fight, because he was knocked unconscious by a baton that was wrapped around the back of his head by an overzealous policeman. When a neighbour named Mickey Burke saw two police officers sitting on top of Paddy, and their colleagues striking him with batons, he ran over to assist him. Picking up a long piece of wood, Mickey struck one of the officers over the head. The wood smashed into two pieces, and the officer fell to the pavement beside Paddy. Both men were unconscious.

When Paddy awoke in the cells some hours later, he was informed that his injuries had been sustained when he had put his own head through a window at the front of the police station and that a knife had been found in his pocket. The intense beating Paddy's head had been subjected to had obviously affected his memory, because he couldn't recall head-butting a window or carrying a knife. A doctor who examined Paddy said that he had bruising around his head and eyes, a half-inch abrasion on his forehead and a swollen lip. He had suffered 'severe contusions', some of which 'may well have been caused by truncheons'. It is, of course, possible, given the nature of Paddy's injuries, that the police were mistaken and that he had in fact been thrown head first into the window and the knife had been planted on him. The only 'weapon' Paddy could recall possessing that night was his mobile phone. Surely the police, honest and true, wouldn't fit somebody up, would they?

The following morning, Paddy was charged with wounding a police officer named John Middleton with intent to resist lawful arrest, assaulting another in the execution of his duty, criminal damage and possessing a knife. In the charge room, the desk sergeant informed Paddy's solicitor, Peter Hedworth, that the injuries caused to PC Middleton had been inflicted by a lump of wood and not the knife that Paddy was alleged to have had in his possession. Paddy knew that such a comment was of evidential value, as he had not been accused of wielding a piece of wood, and so he asked his solicitor to ask the officer if he would confirm his last statement. Mr Hedworth did as he was asked, but the officer totally ignored him. Paddy thought that the police were being rather discourteous to his solicitor, but unbeknown to him at that time they were investigating Hedworth in connection with a million-pound mortgage and property fraud.

When Hedworth was eventually arrested and charged with these offences, he pleaded not guilty and stood trial at Doncaster Crown Court. During the proceedings, which lasted three months, a jury heard how he had ripped off clients and building societies so that he could pay for a farm in the Lake District. Despite his plea of innocence, Hedworth was found guilty, sentenced to serve six years' imprisonment and struck off the roll of solicitors.

Had Paddy been guilty as charged and known that his legal representative was partial to breaking the law himself, he might well have asked him to assist him somehow above and beyond the call of duty. However, Paddy believed he was genuinely innocent and that justice would prevail. To add to his dismay and outrage, he was denied bail and remanded in custody to await trial.

The West End of Newcastle was incensed by the treatment Paddy had been subjected to and what they believed to be the trumped-up charges that he faced. The identity of the person who had hit the policeman with the lump of wood was the worst-kept secret in Newcastle. Everybody in the street where Paddy lived knew that he was being wrongfully accused of wounding the policeman. They believed this strongly, simply because the shouting and screaming that night had brought all his neighbours out into the street and they had witnessed the incident as it unfolded. Seventeen people attended the police station to make statements on Paddy's behalf. One said that the police van that he was put into was 'rocking from side to side as they kicked and beat him, despite the fact that he was already unconscious'.

The night after Paddy's arrest, an angry mob numbering more than 70 people attacked a police station in the West End. Windows were smashed, and a barrage of bricks, bottles and thunderflashes was thrown. In the street outside the station, a line of parked police vehicles had windscreens smashed and bodywork damaged. 'Skinny' Gary Thompson, who lived near Paddy, was arrested and charged with no fewer than 16 counts of criminal damage. Several other locals also faced similar charges. However, the arrests failed to have the desired effect on the community: instead of deterring protests, they inflamed the situation. Cars were stolen and set alight across the entrances to strategic streets in the neighbourhood. If the police attempted to remove the vehicles, or if the fire brigade attempted to extinguish the fires, they were attacked by mobs patrolling the area. Police cars were rammed by stolen vehicles if they tried to enter certain streets, and residents used two-way radios as a means of calling up reinforcements if their defences were threatened or breached. The only true no-go area that Newcastle had ever known had been created in Paddy Conroy's name.

While in custody, Paddy had undergone an operation to remove a cataract from his eye. Shortly afterwards, he was taken under escort from HMP Durham to see an eye specialist, but while lying on a stretcher alone in a room he had struggled to sit up and fallen on the floor. The impact of his head hitting the floor burst the stitches in his eye, and the skill the surgeon had used during the operation was now undone. When the prison officers found Paddy, he was rushed to an operating theatre, where his eye was restitched under a local anaesthetic. The procedure was a success, but the specialist warned Paddy that his eye was now susceptible to haemorrhaging, which could result in him losing his sight. The point was stressed to Paddy and both of his escorts that he must attend the hospital every two weeks for an injection to lessen the risk of haemorrhaging.

A fortnight later, Paddy grew extremely concerned when officers failed to attend his cell in order to escort him to the hospital. Paddy demanded to be taken, but the staff members he asked claimed to know nothing about his appointment or passed the buck and sent him to see somebody else. That night, as Paddy lay in his cell, his eye haemorrhaged and tore the retina off the back of the inside of his eyeball. Unfortunately, such an injury cannot be repaired, and Paddy lost the sight in his eye. Behind his trademark patch, Paddy still has his eye, but it is a bloody mess, and so he chooses to cover it as a matter of courtesy for those he might meet.

The trouble on the streets of the West End meant that Northumbria Police had to divert much of its manpower away from regular duties, and this caused problems in other areas of the city. The authorities realised that the easiest way to resolve the civil disorder and cut their mounting costs of policing the streets was to grant Paddy bail. His solicitor was duly advised that if a bail application was made it wouldn't be opposed. However, if Paddy did inflame the tension on the streets further by taking part in protests or inciting others to do so he would be returned to prison forthwith. Paddy was grateful to be out. The people of the West End had, as always, stood by one of their own and on this occasion forced the authorities to secure his release.

Paddy knew that his freedom was only temporary. He still had to stand trial and convince a jury that the police were mistaken and that he, Paddy Conroy, a man with a string of criminal convictions, was being honest. There were only two hopes: Bob Hope and No Hope. But regardless of the odds he intended to fight his cause until the bitter end.

Paddy appeared at Newcastle Crown Court before Judge Percy in February 1989. The prosecution alleged that he had been arrested when a car in which he had been a passenger was stopped by police after being followed through Newcastle. It was accepted that Paddy had not been driving, and none of the other people in the car had been charged with any offence. The prosecution claimed that, when the vehicle had pulled up at the rear of Paddy's home, PC Middleton had arrested Tommy Findlay on suspicion of taking and driving the vehicle away. It was said that Paddy then grabbed PC Middleton from behind, struck him and proceeded to drag him off Findlay, who then managed to escape. Several officers claimed that during Paddy's struggle with PC Middleton they had seen a long-bladed knife fall from his jacket or waistband. Paddy nearly fell out of the dock with laughter when it was alleged that, while handcuffed, he had launched his own head through the police station window. Unfortunately, the jurors were not laughing with him. The looks on their faces told Paddy that they believed the police and were disgusted by such behaviour. Unsurprisingly, Paddy was convicted of wounding PC Middleton, possessing an offensive weapon and criminal damage but cleared of assaulting another officer.

If the shock of being wrongly convicted wasn't enough for Paddy, Judge Percy sentenced him to five years' imprisonment for wounding and eighteen months for possessing a knife. The shouting and stamping of feet as the Conroy family and their friends made their disapproval known drowned out the judge's words, and so Paddy was unable to hear what sentence he had received for the alleged kamikaze-style attack on the window with his head. After Paddy was led away to the cells to begin his sentence, his partner, Maureen, walked out of the court, whereupon Pinky, the police officer, sneered at her and said, 'What are you going to do for money now, Maureen?' Officers Pinky and Perky were loving every minute of Paddy's family's misery, and as Maureen turned away the sound of their laughter echoed through her ears.

Paddy's family and friends had arranged to go out after the trial to celebrate his acquittal, which, with the benefit of hindsight, may have been tempting fate. But Paddy felt he was genuinely innocent, and so he hadn't contemplated being found guilty. Nobody should ever take anything for granted in this world, especially when dealing with the police. As the prison van drove Paddy towards Durham jail, a fleet of taxis was taking his family and friends down the town. Instead of celebrating Paddy's release, they were now going to drown their sorrows. The end result of their pub crawl that night was always going to be the same, regardless of the outcome of Paddy's trial: the lads were going to get drunk out of their minds. They spent that evening visiting pub after pub, and when the pubs had closed they went to a nightclub called Zoot's before later moving on to a venue called Julie's.

At the door of this second venue stood Viv Graham, who was surrounded by a group of fellow scowling, steroid-bloated bouncers. Viv pointed out one or two of the lads and said that they were OK to go in, but he refused Paddy's brother Michael and others entry. Put out by Viv's blatant rebuke, Michael said to him, 'You're just a fucking copper.' Viv immediately pushed his chest out and flexed his enormous muscle-bound frame, but Michael, an extremely competent boxer, wasn't impressed or intimidated by his feather ruffling.

'If you're going to call me a copper, Michael, I will have to fight you,' Viv said.

'Well, let's get fucking started,' Michael replied.

Standing toe to toe, the two men exchanged a flurry of vicious blows. Every time Michael smashed Viv in the head, the bouncer dropped his guard and struggled to remain on his feet. Fearing he was going to be knocked out, Viv abandoned the use of his boxing skills, grabbed hold of Michael and began to wrestle with him. Few men could match the power of Viv Graham in such a situation, particularly if they had consumed as much alcohol as Michael had that night. Using just his sheer weight and size, Viv overpowered Michael and struck him twice in the face before leaping back into the doorway of the club. The end result of the brief encounter was that Michael suffered a broken jaw and

Viv Graham had been humiliated in front of his friends.

'No comebacks, Michael, no comebacks,' Viv shouted out as Michael walked away. 'It was the hardest fight I've ever had. Respect to you, Michael, but no comebacks.' Clearly concerned that Michael was going to confront him when sober, Viv was doing his sorry best to smooth the situation over. Across the road, a van full of police officers had watched the fight, and Viv went over to speak to them. Turning to Michael and his friends, Viv shouted out, 'Say goodnight to Number One, lads. Don't worry, nobody is getting nicked over this.' People can make their own minds up as to whether Viv was trying to impress the police by calling himself 'Number One' or trying to curry favour with Michael by saying that nobody would get arrested. What isn't in doubt is the fact that Michael Conroy wasn't the only person Viv had upset around Newcastle, and somebody somewhere was planning to have him removed.

Chapter Three

FUCK ROGER RABBIT

FOLLOWING PADDY CONROY'S conviction and imprisonment, a man nicknamed Willbow set up a 'Justice for Paddy Conroy' campaign and organised protest marches through the streets of Newcastle. Initially, the authorities did not take much notice, but as the numbers of those marching swelled, the chief of police called a meeting with Willbow and several others who were sympathetic to Conroy's plight. Willbow and Mickey Burke, who had hit the police officer with a lump of wood on the night Paddy had been arrested, were chosen by his supporters to represent them at the meeting. Fortunately for the chief of police and the other officers in attendance, Mickey chose to leave his lump of wood at home. After several heated exchanges between the protestors and the police, a route for the protest marches was agreed. The organisers were asked to give an undertaking to the police that all the marchers would be law-abiding and any demonstrations that they held would be peaceful.

Michael 'the Bull' Bullock, who could never be accused of being a conformist, broke this agreement on the very next march. A lorry adorned with banners proclaiming Paddy's innocence was to be driven along the agreed route, and the Bull, who didn't even possess a dog licence, never mind a driving licence, had volunteered to be behind the wheel. After just a few yards, he lost control of the large vehicle, mounted a pavement and narrowly avoided crushing a pedestrian, who fortunately managed to leap to safety. John Henry Sayers, who was one of those on the march, advised the Bull to stand down and suggested that it might be safer for everybody if he were to drive the vehicle instead. On the roof of the lorry that John Henry Sayers drove that day stood John and Geoffrey Harrison, whose family were feared throughout the West End. It's hard to believe that members of the Harrison and Sayers families united that day to support a Conroy, because events since have soured relations between them all. The only procession they would like to see one another on now would have to be led by a hearse.

Undeterred by his lack of driving skills and keen to play an active role in guaranteeing the demonstration's success, the Bull 'acquired' a 2.8-litre Granada, which he used to ferry people from around the city to the march. He was also stopping to distribute to protestors T-shirts with the slogan 'Fuck Roger Rabbit. Who framed Paddy Conroy?' and a cartoon rabbit emblazoned across the front and back. The T-shirts, which were snapped up by people who had not even intended to join the march, had been donated by a local businessman who said that he was 'troubled' by Paddy's conviction.

A vigilant police officer noticed that the vehicle the Bull was driving was untaxed and so attempted to stop him. The Bull, fearing that the fact that he didn't quite own the vehicle would be unearthed if he complied with the policeman's request, raced away in the opposite direction and abandoned the vehicle near the Tyne Bridge. The Bull was aware that the march was due to cross the famous Newcastle landmark, and so he began to climb the structure, which at its highest point stands 59 metres above the mighty River Tyne.

As the marchers, who by this time numbered more than 200, approached the bridge, the Bull was spotted by the police, who immediately stopped any traffic or pedestrians from proceeding. The senior officer on duty that day strode onto the bridge with the Bull's brother Billy following and pleaded with him to climb down before he fell down and killed himself, but the Bull refused. In desperation, the officer turned to Billy for help and asked him to appeal to his brother to apply some common sense, but when Billy refused to negotiate on behalf of the police he was promptly arrested for being drunk and disorderly. It was 10 a.m., and Billy hadn't even smelt a drink.

As Billy was led away protesting his innocence, the officer called up to the Bull and once more demanded that he come down. 'Fuck off,' the Bull replied. 'I am not going anywhere.' Realising the traffic chaos and the media attention the Bull's protest was now creating, two other lads,

Gary Baron and Joe Lowe, climbed up onto Scotswood Bridge, which also spans the River Tyne. Those concerned didn't appreciate just how cold it could be up on top of those huge structures. The wind whistled around their heads, and soon all three of them were shaking so violently that they were barely able to talk.

As the elements, rather than the efforts of the police, began to wear the three lads down, they decided to negotiate with the police and end their protest. 'You have caused traffic tailbacks for miles,' one officer shouted up at them through a loudhailer. 'The city of Newcastle is gridlocked; it's time for this to end. If you come down now, you will be charged with a relatively minor offence and granted bail immediately. If you don't come down now, you may be charged with a more serious matter and kept in custody until you appear in court.' It was Saturday, 1 April. No Geordie likes to miss his beer and football, and so the thought of spending an entire weekend in police cells was not one that they wished to contemplate.

The two lads on Scotswood Bridge came down first and were whisked away by the police to be charged. The Bull, suspicious of any deals, particularly those offered by irate policemen, remained on the bridge for a further four hours. When he could not stand the cold any more, he climbed down into the waiting arms of several pretty pissed-off police officers. Like King George V, who had opened the bridge in 1928, the Bull smiled and waved at the crowds who had gathered to greet and cheer him. Unlike King George V, the Bull's civic reception took place at the city's police station. He was charged with a public order offence, refused bail and thrown into a cell to await his court appearance on the Monday morning. To his surprise, he was not alone in the cells; the two lads who had scaled Scotswood Bridge were also in residence. 'I thought the police had promised you bail if you climbed down,' the Bull said.

'Yes, they did,' Joe Lowe replied, 'but when we were arrested they reminded us that it was in fact April Fool's Day.'

When the trio appeared in court, they were banned from going within 100 metres of the Tyne Bridge and bound over to keep the peace for a year. The first Paddy knew about the protest was when a prison officer in HMP Durham told him that presenters were discussing his case on the radio. Paddy immediately raced back to his cell and switched on a small transistor that he had. 'Three protestors have scaled two bridges in Newcastle, which police have now closed,' the newsreader announced. 'Traffic has been brought to a virtual standstill, and queues into the city are currently stretching back for up to 40 miles.' Paddy didn't know why, but he just knew that the Bull would be one of the men who had climbed the bridges. He felt extremely proud of all three men and of his community, who had turned out en masse to protest about his conviction. Their belief in Paddy's innocence gave him hope.

Paddy spent every day of his imprisonment poring over the evidence against him. He felt so aggrieved by his conviction, and by the length of his sentence, that he wrote to legal eagle Lord Gifford QC and pleaded with him to take on his case:

> I am currently serving a prison sentence of five years for something which I didn't do. I am totally innocent and feel confident that once you have read through the various documents you will accept that statement as fact. It is my firm belief that I was not given a fair trial . . . justice, in my case, quite blatantly was not seen to be done.

Lord Gifford QC agreed to represent Paddy, and 14 long months after his conviction he appeared at the High Court in London to have his appeal heard. One point of contention was the trial judge's decision to allow the prosecution to cross-examine Paddy about his criminal record, as he had recent convictions for dishonesty and violence, including previous assaults on police officers. In the 1980s, such information was normally kept from the jury so that their deliberations were not prejudiced. However, the prosecution argued that Paddy's allegations of police brutality meant that he was casting doubt upon the integrity of the police witnesses, and so he was putting his own character at issue.

Judge Percy's summing-up of the case also came in for severe criticism from Lord Gifford QC. In particular, he had failed to point out to the jury the primary issue: had it been proven beyond reasonable doubt that Paddy had caused PC Middleton's wound? Furthermore, the judge had failed to sum up evidence from a police officer that contradicted evidence given by his colleagues, and he had misdirected the jury on evidence relating to the knife. In addition, several months after Paddy's trial, PC Middleton's behaviour had been criticised by Mr Justice Potts, who was presiding over a case in the High Court in Newcastle. Mr

Justice Potts said that while arresting a man for having a stolen car the officer had gone 'too far' with behaviour 'wholly disproportionate' to the offence.

Paddy's convictions were quashed, but his joy was short-lived: the court refused to accept that he had not been in possession of the knife. With the benefit of hindsight, one can see why that decision may have been reached. It was a blow for Paddy, because with an absolute acquittal he would have been able to claim compensation for the 14 unnecessary months in jail. To add to Paddy's disappointment, the appeal judges said that, as it had been twelve months to the day since Paddy's conviction for the knife, he still had six months of his eighteen-month sentence to serve. Taking into account the mandatory time off for good behaviour that all prisoners are given, they said that he still had to serve a further five days, 'for the Queen'.

Outside the court, the Conroy family protested vehemently to Lord Gifford QC. They pointed out that Paddy had served 14 months and not 12, as the judges had indicated, and that he should therefore be released immediately. Moments later, Lord Gifford QC was down in the cell block ordering the prison officers to release Paddy at once. Before walking to freedom, Paddy thanked his legal team, who had never doubted his innocence throughout the case.

Lord Gifford went on to have a remarkable career as a pioneer in human rights and legal reform. He was chairman of the Broadwater Farm Riot Inquiry and the Liverpool 8 Inquiry, both of which looked at racism and discrimination. Lord Gifford represented the family of James Wray at the Bloody Sunday Inquiry and appeared for Gerry Hunter of the Birmingham Six and Paul Hill of the Guildford Four at their appeals. He is undoubtedly a remarkable man who has been driven to right some of the many wrongs that exist in the judicial system.

Paddy walked out of the court and into the arms of Maureen. 'I am absolutely overjoyed. My head is just dizzy,' Paddy told reporters from the *Newcastle Evening Chronicle*. 'It's great to be back out with my family. The judge's summing-up sent me away [to prison]. After the jury heard what he had said, there was no way I was coming out of that court. Even if I had been guilty, the sentence was ridiculous. The officer concerned had nothing more than a little cut, and I got five years.' A murky kind of justice had sort of prevailed.

The train journey home to Newcastle was made in high spirits. All of Paddy's family and friends gathered at the bar not just to celebrate his release but also to toast his brother Neil and his new bride, as they had married that very day. To Paddy's surprise, Paddy Cosgrove, the barrister who had appeared for the prosecution in his case, was also at the bar. Paddy did not bear him any malice – the man was only doing his job – and so he joined him for a drink. To avoid any embarrassing moments, Paddy didn't mention the case to him. Instead, they just indulged in small talk and chatted about matters in general. When Paddy arrived back in Newcastle, his brother's wedding reception had been turned into a joint celebration to incorporate his release. Paddy did not wish to sound ungrateful, because he was touched by the support his family, friends and the local community had given him, but he wasn't in the party mood. Paddy had been in prison for more than a year for something that he had not done, so he had a couple of drinks before heading home to Maureen.

Paddy had eight separate outstanding complaints against Northumbria Police for alleged harassment, and so he went to see a solicitor the following morning to ask if he could withdraw them. He wanted to forget the past and get on with his life. Paddy asked the solicitor if he would seek assurances from the police that, in return for his gesture of goodwill, he would be given a little breathing space so that he could get on with rebuilding his life. Later the same day, a police inspector rang Paddy at his home and said that if he kept out of trouble there would be no need for officers to contact him. The inspector explained that he was not in a position to do deals but that if Paddy did withdraw the complaints and kept out of trouble he would ensure that he would never hear from Northumbria Police again.

Paddy withdrew the complaints, but the very next morning his front door was kicked off its hinges by officers who said they had a warrant to search his home. Between 20 and 30 police officers had sealed the street off before storming the property. Paddy was out at the time, and so the first thing he knew about it was when Maureen rang him. Paddy raced back to his house and ran in, shouting, 'Get out of my fucking home!'

His old adversary Pinky stood beaming with delight in front of him. 'Not possible, Conroy,' he replied with a wry smile. 'We have a warrant to search this house.' He thrust the document in Paddy's face and strode off into the lounge.

Paddy was astounded when he read the warrant. It had clearly been issued to search number 115, and Paddy lived at number 113. Paddy's home was wrecked while the police were searching it. They pulled out all the drawers, tipped up beds and even unwrapped presents that he had bought for his children. The officers didn't find anything, but that didn't seem to matter to them. Paddy was given a half-hearted apology and a claim form for the damage, and the officers then went next door to search his neighbour's house. Paddy was fuming, but he told himself to remain calm. He knew that the police would want him to lose his temper so that he could be returned to prison. The very thought of Paddy being cleared of wounding a policeman and assaulting another was obviously troubling some officers.

Paddy too was troubled about past events. He hadn't forgotten that Pinky had been rude to Maureen outside the court on the day that he had been convicted. Paddy wanted to have words with him about it, but he knew that if he did so when Pinky wasn't alone he would be arrested for threatening behaviour. Pinky was always cruising around the West End, making a nuisance of himself, and so Paddy knew that it would be only a matter of time before their paths crossed.

One afternoon, Paddy was driving along Westmoreland Road when he saw Pinky parked up on the opposite side of the street. Paddy swerved across the carriageway in front of Pinky so that, when his vehicle came to a halt, he was sitting facing him. Paddy could see the blood draining from Pinky's face as Paddy went to get out of his car. Before Paddy could do so, Pinky had engaged reverse gear, accelerated and then sped away.

Paddy gave chase, and once he had caught up with Pinky he pulled alongside his vehicle and gestured for him to pull over. Instead of obeying Paddy's command, Pinky applied the handbrake, and his vehicle slewed across the road. Paddy braked hard to avoid colliding with Pinky and then immediately manoeuvred forward. A group of Paddy's friends happened to be travelling towards him in a car. They could see what was happening, and so they parked behind Pinky in order to block his escape route. Paddy got out of his vehicle and strode purposefully towards Pinky, who locked the doors and scrambled over the passenger seat in a vain effort to avoid him. Paddy managed to get his fingers into a gap in the window on the driver's side of the vehicle, and eventually he was able to pull it completely down. Paddy reached in to grab Pinky, but the officer curled up into a ball on the back seat, ensuring that he was way out of his grasp. 'You fucking maggot!' Paddy shouted. 'If you ever insult or even speak to my wife again, I will make sure that you regret the day that you were born.' Judging by the smell that was emanating from Pinky's car, Paddy was fairly certain that particular police vehicle would need cleaning. Pinky whimpered something that Paddy failed to understand, but he believed that he had understood his message.

A few days after he had confronted Pinky, there was a loud and insistent knock at Paddy's front door. Glancing quickly through the lounge window, Paddy saw that a police car was parked out in the street and that Pinky was sitting in it, staring directly at him. As Paddy flung the front door open to find out what Pinky wanted, he encountered the biggest police officer he had ever seen in his life. Before Paddy could say a word, the policeman blew a cloud of cigarette smoke into his face. 'Paddy Conroy, I assume,' he said. 'You think you're a fucking hard man, don't you?' He then turned, coughed up a mouthful of phlegm and spat it onto the bonnet of Paddy's car.

Paddy looked this mountain of a man up and down as feelings of utter contempt and hatred surged through his veins. 'So, who the fuck are you? The village idiot?' Paddy asked. 'Have you come to fight me? Let's fucking do it now then, you mug. Come through the house now, and we can sort this out in the back garden.'

Paddy could tell by the expression on the policeman's face that he hadn't expected him to go on the offensive. 'Calm down, Paddy,' he pleaded. 'I have only come here to talk to you.'

'Get in this house now, or get out of my fucking face,' Paddy roared. 'And take your fucking halfwit sidekick with you.' Paddy had really lost the plot by this stage and moved to grab the officer by the throat. The giant leapt backwards when Paddy lunged at him, then turned and ran towards the car, where his terrified colleague was revving the engine in readiness to escape. In his haste to flee, the giant had dropped a clipboard, which Paddy picked up and hurled at the vehicle as it disappeared amidst the sound of squealing tyres and a pall of blue smoke.

In an effort to instil some form of normality into his family's life, Paddy stopped going out down the town and for the umpteenth time threw himself once more into trying to earn a reasonably honest living. But, as always, Paddy could not control the will of others or the effect their actions had on him and his loved ones. The Sayers firm had become extremely influential in the West End during Paddy's absence. Their street credibility had been given a boost following John Henry's trial for a £750,000 armed robbery at a Post Office sorting depot in Sunderland. Masked men had threatened staff with shotguns and ordered them to hand over the cash before making their getaway. John Henry, who ran a fruit and vegetable shop at the time, was later arrested following a dawn raid at his home. Pleading his innocence, John Henry gave detectives investigating the case a perfect alibi. He said that at the time the robbery was committed he was being watched by members of the Regional Crime Squad. For reasons known only to the officers investigating the robbery, they refused to accept John Henry's story or the evidence of their colleagues in the Crime Squad, and so he was placed on an identity parade, where a witness named Sloane picked him out.

Nineteen-year-old John Sloane had earlier contacted the police from his cell at HMP Low Newton. It's not known if Sloane's public-spiritedness was rewarded, but his claim that he had seen a man who resembled John Henry in the vicinity of the sorting office on the day that the robbers struck turned out to be the best evidence that the police managed to gather. Sloane told detectives that he had seen a man with a mask pulled over his head sitting in a white van; he was also cradling a shotgun in his lap. Sloane said that moments later he had seen the man again. 'He came across the road and was smoking a pipe,' he said. 'He was dripping with sweat and was shaking so much that when he went to light his pipe the match went out.' Sloane assisted the police in producing an identikit picture of the man he claimed to have seen, and it bore a remarkable resemblance to John Henry Sayers. Having secured a positive identification from a not so squeaky-clean witness, the police charged John Henry and another man, named Kenneth Sandvid, with armed robbery.

At the trial of Sayers and Sandvid, which took place at Durham Crown Court, postal worker Frank Bell told how cash bags at the West Sunniside Post Office had just been loaded onto a trolley when a dark blue Range Rover smashed through the depot gates. A man had then appeared, levelled a shotgun at the postal workers and taken control of the trolley. When John Henry gave evidence, he told the jury about his alibi and called members of the Regional Crime Squad as witnesses to support his account. One would imagine that testimonies of serving police officers would be accepted by the prosecution, but they were not. The prosecution claimed that the officers must have been mistaken. However, when John Henry pointed out to the jury that he had never smoked in his life, the evidence of Sloane regarding the pipe-smoking robber was discredited and both Sayers and Sandvid were acquitted on the direction of the judge.

John Henry returned to the West End a conquering hero, and every wannabe gangster in the area made it his business to be somehow associated with him. Almost overnight, this legion of fools were claiming to be members of the Sayers firm and were stomping around the city dictating to everybody what they could and could not do. Everybody but the Conroys, that is. They were not prepared to be told, by anybody, what they could or could not do.

Young guys began appearing at Paddy's door complaining bitterly about unwritten rules and restrictions that were being imposed upon their criminal enterprises. 'We are being pushed out of business, Paddy, by this so-called firm, and there's nothing we can do about it,' they would say. People who broke these unwritten rules were being beaten, tortured and, in at least one case, hacked with blades.

The other 'problem' these feral youths imported into the West End was the sale of Class A drugs. The 1980s had seen a rise in the number of armed robberies being carried out in the UK. Several of these crimes reaped huge rewards for the villains involved. On Easter Monday 1983, a gang led by a 'toff' with a 'posh' accent carried out what came to be known as the Great Banknote Raid, in Shoreditch, east London. Six million pounds was taken from the Security Express headquarters in Curtain Road when half a dozen masked men burst in at 10.30 a.m. One of the guards was doused in petrol and warned that if he did not disclose the combination for the safe he would be set alight. The guards were then tied and blindfolded for the duration of the raid, which lasted a further five hours.

Within six months, the Security Express robbery had paled into insignificance. At 6.40 a.m. on 26 November 1983, £26 million worth of gold was taken from the Brinks-MAT warehouse on the Heathrow trading estate. Again, the guards were intimidated, and some were doused in petrol. One guard was even threatened with castration, and another was coshed and punched until he handed a set of keys over. The gang drove off with 6,400 bars of gold.

These two robberies alone netted £32 million, but their success created huge problems for the perpetrators. How were they ever going to 'clean' so much money? They could not give up their council flats, park up the old Ford Escort and suddenly start purchasing mansions, Rolls-Royces and private jets, because the authorities would want to know where they had acquired their new-found wealth. The obvious answer to their problem was to invest their ill-gotten gains in another criminal enterprise. Unfortunately for the British public, the only enterprise that ticked all the required boxes happened to be drugs. As a direct result of the robbers' successes, the late 1980s witnessed the arrival of the rave culture, which was fuelled and enjoyed by revellers high on the 'love drug' Ecstasy. Instead of youngsters getting drunk and fighting one another, they were soon popping pills and embracing both friends and strangers.

The general consensus was that cannabis and Ecstasy were harmless social drugs rather than dangerous, habit-forming substances. However, there was so much illegal money swilling around the world of drugs that it wasn't long before cocaine and heroin were also flooding the streets at knock-down prices. As the rave scene began creeping into the north-east, an avalanche of illegal drugs quickly followed. Cannabis, amphetamines, Ecstasy, cocaine and heroin were on sale at prices even the unemployed could afford. This influx of drugs into the area signalled the bitter end for old-school characters like Viv Graham. Drugs such as cocaine gave fools confidence, but the fools still couldn't fight, and so they armed themselves instead. Gentlemanly conduct was pronounced dead upon the arrival of rave.

In one incident where old-school values clashed ith new, drug-induced thinking, Billy Robinson was shot. Billy, who had employed Paddy Conroy, John Henry Sayers and Viv Graham as doormen, was socialising one evening at Bentleys nightclub with friends. There he encountered a man named Alan Swindon, who, Billy had heard, was guilty of harassing a female member of the Robinson family. A quiet word was all that was needed, but Swindon, bolstered by drugs, refused to listen to Billy's reasonable request and began issuing threats. Billy, who was more than capable of resolving the issue with a single punch, did not wish to cause trouble in the nightclub, and so he ignored Swindon's rant and hoped he would walk away before he had to be carried out.

When Bentleys closed, Billy and his friends went to a house party in the Felling area of Gateshead. A short while later, a man approached Billy with a shotgun and opened fire. Rather wisely, Billy and others sought cover, but Billy's leg was trapped in a door that other revellers were trying to slam shut. The gunman blasted the door, causing extensive injury to Billy's exposed leg and minor injury to the foot and leg of another reveller. The police arrested Swindon for the double shooting, but Robinson refused to assist the police and the case was dropped but not forgotten.

Some time later, Swindon and a male friend were in Rockshots, a gay bar in Newcastle that was equally popular with heterosexuals. Both men were stabbed; both survived. The police were called, but they were unable to find out who was responsible, as anybody who may have witnessed the incident suffered bouts of amnesia. A trivial dispute had resulted in two people being shot and two stabbed.

The demand from revellers for illicit drugs gave criminals in the north-east a huge financial incentive to supply. Not only was the old-school rulebook concerning fighting torn up, but the edition concerning not grassing was also rendered redundant. As Stephen Sayers and his associates Alan 'Fish' Tams and David Lancaster boarded an aeroplane at Newcastle airport in April 1989, little did they know that another associate was on the phone to the police. They were informed that Sayers and Tams were in possession of a large number of Ecstasy pills, which they intended to sell in Tenerife. When the men arrived at the popular holiday destination, local police swooped before they had even left the airport. When they were searched, just a small amount of cannabis and a few pills, which were for their own personal use, were found. Nevertheless, they were arrested and remanded in custody to the not so plush Granadilla Detention Centre. They had clearly upset somebody in Newcastle, and the aggrieved had hit back by doing the previously unthinkable: he had informed on them to the police. All three were eventually released and returned to England.

As the rave scene grew increasingly lucrative for those involved in the supply of drugs, the city of Newcastle found itself besieged by villains eager to take control. They were not only selling Ecstasy. The low cost and availability of cocaine and heroin meant that they could almost afford to give these vile drugs away in the hope of saddling potential long-term customers with an addiction. As the various gangs flexed their muscles, the violence meted out was of a nature and ferocity the police had never previously known.

A popular rave club in Sunderland called the Blue Monkey was brought to the attention of a gang of drug dealers from Newcastle. An age-old rivalry exists between Geordies and Mackems, as people from Sunderland are known. It was decided, therefore, that the Geordies would take over the lucrative drug-dealing operation at the club by ousting their Mackem counterparts, but things didn't quite go according to plan. The Geordies were forced to retreat from the club after a vicious fight, but they vowed to return. If they couldn't control the club, then nobody would.

A few days later, the Geordies stormed the Blue Monkey club and snatched 19-year-old Darren Poole, who had been alone decorating the premises. The building was doused in petrol before being set alight. Mr Poole, who was handcuffed, watched as his handiwork went up in flames, but as the fire took hold he was bundled into a waiting vehicle and driven ten miles before being dumped. Speaking to the *Newcastle Evening Chronicle* newspaper, Mr Poole said of his ordeal:

> I thought I was going to be burnt alive or shot. I have never been so frightened in my life. These two men suddenly appeared. One pulled out a revolver, pointed it at my head and threatened to shoot me. They then handcuffed my hands behind my back and ushered me into the main area of the club. They then handcuffed me to a railing and started dousing petrol both upstairs and downstairs. They used matches and a lighter to set it alight, and I thought they were going to leave me there. They then untied me from the railing and handcuffed my hands behind my back. They pushed me onto a car seat and one of the men sat on top of me. They were threatening

me all of the time and telling me not to say anything about what
had happened to the police. I am still shaking. I really thought that
I was going to die.

When the club eventually reopened, the gang violence continued, and
when a man was murdered outside, the owners decided to employ a
legendary fighter from Sunderland named Ernie Berwick to provide
security. Following the trouble with gangs from Newcastle, Berwick
was rightly cautious of anybody trying to enter the club who was not
from the Sunderland area.

One evening, Billy Robinson arrived at the Blue Monkey with a group
of men in tow. Berwick said that they would all have to pay to get in, to
which one of Billy's entourage replied, 'Do you know who you're talking
to?' Berwick explained that it was irrelevant to him who he was talking to,
because the rules would remain the same: if people were not prepared to
pay to get in, they would not get in. Words were exchanged between Billy
and Berwick before Billy slapped him hard across the face. Berwick
lunged at Billy, who tried to punch him, but Berwick ducked the incoming
fist and landed a punch of his own, which knocked Billy over.

A few months later, Berwick was asked if he would have a 'straightener'
– that is, an old-school fight, man to man, with no weapons involved –
with Billy, and he agreed. The fight was arranged to take place at a gym
in Jesmond that was owned by former Mr Great Britain Andy Webb.
On the day of the fight, Berwick arrived at the gym alone and found Viv
Graham and several others waiting for him. They seemed surprised
that a Mackem would have the audacity to turn up alone for a fight in
Newcastle. Viv immediately telephoned Billy to say that Berwick had
arrived. Two hours later, Billy walked into the gym and shook Berwick's
hand. Always the gentleman, Billy said, 'I want to shake your hand
before this fight, and I want to shake it afterwards.'

With the formalities over, Billy, who was much larger than Berwick,
took up a boxer's stance. Berwick was aware of Billy's punching power,
and so he elected to wear him out by moving around and then, when
Billy tired, going in for the kill. For the first few minutes, Berwick flicked
punches at Billy, egging him on to come forward. Billy responded by
throwing knockout punches that Berwick ducked and weaved to avoid.
At one stage, Billy managed to grip Berwick in a headlock and rained

sickening punches down upon his head. However, Berwick managed to struggle free and move around while composing himself. After hitting Billy with a barrage of right hooks, Berwick was stunned by an uppercut that put him down on one knee. Fearing Billy would begin kicking him, Berwick leapt to his feet and ran at his opponent screaming, 'Come on!' The Queensberry Rules were forgotten as Berwick attacked Billy in a fit of deranged temper. Viv Graham separated the fighters and grabbed Berwick while shouting, 'Howay, Ernie, howay.'

The fight was over, but Berwick was unsure as to who had been declared the winner. Billy, true to his word, shook Berwick's hand and hugged him. That, as far as he was concerned, was the end of the matter. As Berwick walked out of the gym, he saw Viv Graham sitting on a bench. He was quite surprised and confused when Viv began saying, 'I don't want any trouble with you . . .'

When they had both been amateur boxers, Berwick had fought and beaten Viv in the ring. That was the only 'trouble' they had ever had. Berwick genuinely had no idea what Viv was on about, and so he shook his hand and left. As Berwick was getting into his car, one of the men who had watched the fight said, 'Viv shouldn't have stuck that sly punch on you.' It was then that Berwick realised that it wasn't Billy who had delivered the devastating uppercut that had dropped him to his knees.

Berwick walked straight back into the gym, and when Viv saw him he said, 'Billy was like a dad to me. He brought me up really. I am sorry I hit you.'

Berwick thought for a moment before replying, 'It was only a daft punch. Forget about it.' In keeping with the old-school tradition, the matter was then closed.

Despite the number of power-crazed wannabes and gangs that had emerged around Newcastle in the hope of controlling the drug trade, only the 'Sayers-backed firm' appeared to be untouchable. Flat caps and whippets had been in vogue when Paddy Conroy was sent to prison, but by the time he was released thieving smackheads and young girls on the game trying to earn money for their filthy habits were almost fashionable. Heroin is the scourge of the modern world. It turns decent young people into rodents who scavenge and steal from their own mothers to feed their disgusting habits.

'Skinny' Gary Thompson, who had so fiercely protested against

Paddy's arrest for allegedly wounding PC Middleton, became a victim of the heroin dealers, and the drug soon turned a once decent man into a zombie who had lost his soul and the control of his own mind. While suffering from the effects of his addiction, Thompson broke into the home of a 90-year-old war veteran named Ernest Hall. Thompson tied the elderly gentleman to a chair, gagged him, beat him and robbed him of his meagre possessions just so that he could feed his addiction. Before leaving the helpless old man, Thompson, for reasons known only to himself, turned off the central-heating system in the house. The following morning, Ernest Hall was found in freezing-cold conditions. Eleven days later, he died in hospital of pneumonia.

Thompson had been a decent sort when Paddy had known him, but heroin had poisoned his mind and the craving for that vile drug had made him commit this terrible, inhumane crime. If anybody wants to know why Paddy Conroy hates addictive drugs being sold to members of his community, they should ask themselves why a brave man like Ernest Hall had to die in such an undignified manner. Shame? It's a fucking scandal, and anybody involved in the sale of heroin shoulders some of the blame for the diabolical crimes that their customers go on to commit.

Paddy knew the true strength of the Sayers family; he had grown up on the same streets as John Henry and his brothers Michael and Stephen. Paddy did not believe for one moment that they would be party to some of the crimes that were being committed using their name, particularly the sale of heroin, and so he decided to talk to them about what he had heard. He believed that they might listen to him and distance themselves from the numerous hangers-on that they had attracted. Paddy also believed that he owed his community a debt for the loyalty they had shown him when he was in prison. He felt that he could not stand by and allow people to sell their sons and daughters shit like heroin, and so he went to a hostel that was owned by the Sayers family, initially to speak to their father.

When Paddy knocked on the door, John Sayers senior stepped outside and asked him what it was he wanted. Paddy asked John if he would have a word with 'his lads', because people around them were getting involved 'in shit', which, in the long term, would cause problems for all decent people living in the West End and beyond. John Sayers senior looked at Paddy as if he were stupid. He then shook his head and walked back inside the hostel without saying a word. Stupid or not, Paddy was not going to stand by and allow people to sell heroin on the streets where his own children were growing up. Realising John Sayers senior wasn't interested in the problem, Paddy decided to talk directly to his sons about the situation. It's not known what was said when they met, but an understanding was reached before the parties went their separate ways.

As far as Paddy was concerned, the sale of heroin was no longer to be tolerated on the streets of the West End, and that was the end of the matter. However confident Paddy may have felt about the outcome of the talks with the Sayers brothers, he should have known that they, like him, would not be dictated to by anybody. On the tranquil streets of Newcastle, a storm was brewing, but neither side could possibly have foreseen the impact that conflict would have on all concerned.

In 1989, the Sayers firm was dealt a huge blow when John Henry was convicted of masterminding a terrifying armed raid on the Pritchard's security depot in Gateshead. Security-office staff, mainly women, were compiling wage packets for the following day when the six-man armed gang smashed its way in with sledgehammers. The terrified staff were herded into a back room and forced to lie on the floor as the gang ransacked the premises. A security guard who had driven into the yard during the raid had his windscreen smashed with a sawn-off shotgun. He was then dragged from his vehicle and forced to remain on the floor while a gun was pointed at his head. When he heard an order from one of the robbers to a gunman to blow off his legs, he managed to roll to safety under a van, where he remained until all of the cash was loaded.

Their work complete, the robbers sped off in two stolen vehicles towards the East End of Newcastle, where they switched vehicles while threatening passers-by at gunpoint. They eventually arrived at a 'safe house' in Heaton, Newcastle, where the up-until-then perfectly executed plan began to fall apart. An empty flat had been carefully chosen to store the money until the dust settled. However, the daughter of the flat's owner happened to walk past the following night and, seeing lights on in the flat, thought that it was being burgled and telephoned the police. When uniformed officers attended expecting to find squatters in the empty premises, they couldn't quite believe their luck when they discovered £350,000 in cash, two sawn-off shotguns and a machine gun. Two men, Alan Minniken and Surtees Fisher, were arrested nearby after a brief chase. Both denied any knowledge of the money and firearms in the flat.

It was, at that time, the biggest wages robbery ever carried out in the north-east. Inquiries spanning ten months took detectives to Yorkshire, Scotland and Liverpool. Eventually, John Henry Sayers, George McFadyen, Alan Minniken, Geoffrey Whelans and Surtees Fisher were all charged and later convicted of involvement in the armed raid. Sayers and McFadyen were each sentenced to serve fifteen years' imprisonment, Minniken and Whelans thirteen years, and Fisher three years. Not all the gang members were caught. A few years later, Alan Minniken's brother Chris 'Kicker' Minniken disappeared from his home without a trace. It is rumoured on Tyneside that Kicker was a member of the robbery team and that not all the gang's money had been recovered by the police. Kicker has been missing for more than a decade now, and the police are in no doubt that he has been murdered by persons unknown.

The West End community breathed a huge sigh of relief when they learned of John Henry's imprisonment, because they believed that an all-out war with the Conroys had been averted. 'Temporarily postponed' may have been a more accurate description of the situation, as neither party was of a forgiving nature. However, John Henry's imprisonment did take the sting out of the situation, and the families went from being on red alert to amber. Family members would see one another in the street, but little was said, although in time they did begin to exchange strained pleasantries.

In the late '80s and early '90s, there was a huge rise in the number of counterfeit goods being produced in the north-east of England, and it wasn't just T-shirts and handbags that were being made. Booze, cigarettes and even car parts were being imported and relabelled as the genuine item. Some items were mass-produced locally in small factories and warehouses. Scottish & Newcastle Breweries were forced to reduce their staff following a significant fall in sales in 1998, and this was accredited solely to the activities of bootleggers earlier in the decade. The manufacturing, sale and purchasing of counterfeit goods became extremely popular, simply because people did not consider them to be real crimes. The huge corporations whose goods were being reproduced were, it was felt, already making more than enough money from the public, and so taking a little back would not do them any harm. They were, of course, wrong. Both the music industry and the film industry have had to totally rethink how to market their products, because in recent years they have lost millions of pounds in revenue to the bootleggers.

Never one to miss a business opportunity, Paddy decided to look into the production and distribution of fake designer T-shirts. A man named Tommy Cowan was flooding the north-east with fake Newcastle United football shirts, and so Paddy went to him for advice. Unbeknown to Paddy at the time, Tommy and a man named John Lee had become the new owners of the Hydraulic Crane pub. When Paddy first approached Tommy, Tommy said that he didn't wish to have any involvement with him or his business ventures, as he was well aware of his reputation. However, Paddy did manage to get the first batch of T-shirts made via Tommy after sending a third party to him with his order.

Once the garments had been delivered and Tommy had been paid, Paddy visited him once more. Paddy explained that the T-shirts that he had recently made had in fact been for him. Tommy had been paid in full, there had been no problems and, therefore, after much deliberation, Paddy was able to persuade Tommy to sell him the fake T-shirts in bulk on a regular basis. After a month or two, Paddy received a visit from a man named Dickey Ford, who said that he shouldn't be doing business with Tommy because he was a police informant. 'Rip him off,' Ford urged Paddy. 'It's all the fucking grass deserves.'

'Who said he is a police informant?' Paddy replied. 'I don't listen to rumours. If he is a grass, I want to see proof.'

The next time Paddy saw Dickey, he asked him if he had the paperwork that would prove to him that Tommy was a grass. Rather meekly, Dickey replied, 'A man named John Lee had it, but he has had to give it back to the policeman he got it from.' Paddy didn't mention the fact that he now knew John Lee was Tommy Cowan's partner in the Hydraulic Crane, but he did ask how Lee had managed to acquire sensitive paperwork from a policeman. 'John Lee's sister goes out with a policeman, and he got the information from the police computer,' Dickey replied. 'Because he had to enter his name and badge number in order to access the information, he insisted that John give the paperwork back to him once he had read it.'

Paddy told Dickey that the first thing he ought to do was to go to see John Lee and ask him what he thought he was doing sitting down having cosy chats with a policeman. Paddy then advised Dickey to ask his friend why a policeman would be feeding him such sensitive information if he wasn't getting anything back in return. Dickey seemed troubled by Paddy's response and left without saying another word. Paddy chose not to say anything to Tommy about his partner's betrayal or about the allegations that people were making. As far as Paddy was concerned, there was no evidence to suggest the man was an informant, and so he would continue to do business with him as normal.

About a month later, Michael and Stephen Sayers knocked on Paddy's door and said they had heard he was interested in purchasing an embroidery machine. Paddy had been watching how Tommy produced the fake garments. It appeared to be none too complicated a procedure, and so he had made enquiries about obtaining a machine for himself. Paddy was told that a large embroidery machine would cost in the region of £12,000, and so he decided to seek out a heavily discounted one via his criminal associates. Moments after answering the door, Paddy was in a car with the Sayers brothers heading towards a rendezvous with a person who had such an item for sale. When they pulled up outside the Hydraulic Crane pub, Paddy had a good idea who he was going to be introduced to.

John Lee shook Paddy's hand warmly when the Sayers brothers introduced him, and said he had heard that Paddy wished to purchase a cheap embroidery machine. Paddy didn't know if Lee was aware that he knew he was Tommy's partner or if he knew that he had spoken to Dickey Ford about his allegations, but his demeanour and the conversation suggested that he was oblivious to both facts. Lee described the machine and told Paddy the address where it could be found, which, of course, was Tommy's house. 'That's your partner's address, isn't it?' Paddy asked. Stuttering and mumbling, Lee was unable to give a satisfactory answer or explanation, and so Paddy walked back out of the pub, leaving Lee and the Sayers brothers behind.

FUCK ROGER RABBIT

The next time Paddy visited Tommy to collect his T-shirts, he sat him down and told him what had been going on behind his back. 'Have you got problems with these people, Tommy?' Paddy asked. Hesitating at first, Tommy began to tell Paddy about a campaign of intense bullying and harassment by his partner and others to get him out of the pub. The Enterprise Zone had attracted lots of new businesses whose employees were frequenting the Hydraulic Crane at lunchtimes, and it was growing into a very successful business.

'They are demanding to buy me out, Paddy. What can I do?' Tommy asked, almost in desperation. Paddy knew exactly what Lee, Ford and their friends the Sayers were up to. They were trying to force Tommy out of the pub so that they could take over a lucrative business for peanuts. Paddy told Tommy that he still had enough money to buy a share of the pub from him and mentioned that if he did become involved in the business once more nobody would dare to try to intimidate him.

The following day, Paddy handed over £10,000 in cash and became partners in the pub with not only Tommy but also John Lee. The atmosphere between Lee and Paddy could at best be described as dire, and Paddy ensured that it remained that way for several weeks, until Lee suggested that he wanted to sell his share of the business. After handing over another £20,000 in cash, Paddy became the joint owner of the Hydraulic Crane with Tommy, and the business went from strength to strength thereafter. To prevent objections from the police, Paddy was essentially a silent partner, but everybody knew that the pub was his concern.

During the day, they served food for office staff and general workers, and by 6 p.m. the locals would begin to arrive. The pub was always busy with the type of people who were not afraid to spend their money, and Paddy's presence ensured that there was never any trouble. For the first time in his life, Paddy Conroy genuinely believed that he was finally going to be able to settle down to living some form of normal existence with his family. But, as always, fate was waiting in the wings, preparing to knock him back down with the cruellest of blows.

Chapter Four

IN THE NAME OF HIS FATHER

THE BULL WAS arrested after a trail of stolen goods that had been taken during ram raids led the police to the Conroys' front door. Nobody was surprised. The police, however incompetent you may think they are, always get you one way or another. A prison sentence looked inevitable, and so the Bull decided to postpone his free holiday within the confines of one of Her Majesty's Victorian retreats to go on the run. It's inconceivable that the Bull imagined he was going to evade capture for all time. No doubt he had made prior arrangements that clashed with Northumbria Police's plans for him, and so he had chosen to delay the justice that awaited him. Unfortunately for all of the Conroy family, a much darker cloud loomed on the horizon. In the absence of the Bull, Paddy's mother had gathered all her children in the front room and broken the terrible news that their father had been diagnosed with terminal cancer.

The Conroy family was naturally devastated, but, true to form, their father, Leonard, refused to let them show him any sympathy or concern for his fate. Leonard simply told his children that he didn't want any fuss – what will be, will be – and that they should continue living their lives as before. As soon as the Bull heard about Leonard's condition, he handed himself in to the police and explained that he had done so in order to be there for the Conroy family. Unfortunately, the police failed to reciprocate the Bull's humane good intent and asked magistrates to remand him in custody to await trial. They, of course, duly obliged.

It was the Bull's first time in prison, and, coupled with the knowledge of Leonard's deteriorating health, he found it extremely difficult to cope with. Leonard had been the Bull's father in every way but name, and the Conroy children's feelings of despair and sadness were no greater than his. When rumours began to circulate about protest marches being organised throughout the West End to highlight the lack of compassion being shown to the Bull, the authorities' ice-cold attitude began to thaw, and when the Bull reapplied for bail it was granted. For nine long months, Leonard Conroy followed the advice that he had given to his family and got on with his life. He drank with his friends and went about his business as if there was nothing wrong with him.

When the disease did eventually overcome Leonard, he lay on his deathbed struggling to breathe. A doctor was called, and he suggested performing a tracheotomy, a procedure whereby a tube is inserted into the patient's throat to make good his airway. The doctor explained that Leonard was near death but that a tracheotomy might prolong his life for a few more days. Shaking his head, Leonard glared at the well-meaning doctor and indicated that he was refusing any further treatment. He had lived his life with his head held high, and he wanted it to end with dignity. It was hard for the Conroy family to let Leonard go sooner than they should have had to, but none of them was going to argue with him. Not long after, a paramedic arrived at the Conroy home and tried to intervene, but Leonard's brother Billy grabbed hold of him and bundled him outside the front door. With his family standing proud and as one around him, Leonard Conroy closed his eyes and passed away peacefully shortly afterwards. It was the only fight that Leonard had ever lost in his life. He was a real man's man, a gentleman, and his children were very proud to have called him Father.

Leonard's funeral was the largest gangland funeral the north-east had ever known. Everybody turned out to pay their respects to him. Paddy, on the other hand, tried hard to pretend that the funeral wasn't happening. He refused to look at all the mourners. Instead, he sat in a car at the head of the funeral cortège with his head bowed, just staring at the floor. After Leonard's death, the Bull appeared in court and was sentenced to serve a short prison sentence, Neil kept the residents of the West End of Newcastle stocked up with electrical goods from his ram raids and Paddy continued to strive to make an almost honest living.

* * *

Upon the Bull's release from prison, he and Neil were asked to frequent the Green Tree pub in Benwell Village by the owner, Harry Perry. In his prime, Perry had been one of the guv'nors in Newcastle, but age and injuries received from being shot had convinced him that it was time to take a back seat. The Green Tree pub had been attracting an undesirable element of late, and Perry thought that the presence of the Bull and Neil on the premises would deter people from causing trouble. For their services, the Bull and Neil were paid a small wage and were given free access to the bar. After several weeks and as many bloody battles, the Bull and Neil had cleared the pub of urban warriors, but Harry Perry had failed to pay them. Despite the messages the Bull and Neil left with the bar staff about their overdue wages, Perry refused to contact them, and so one evening they decided to wait in the pub for him to arrive.

The Bull and Neil were playing pool and enjoying a drink when Perry eventually walked into the bar. Trying to keep relations amicable, the Bull politely reminded Perry that they had not been paid, and Perry replied, 'Come and see me upstairs in a few minutes, and I will sort that out for you both.' When they had finished playing their game, the Bull and Neil went upstairs to a dining area, which they discovered was empty except for their once infamous employer, who was propping up the bar. As they approached him, Perry pulled out a revolver from the inside pocket of his jacket and said, 'There you go, lads. You can have this gun instead of your wages.'

Neil laughed, grabbed the revolver and immediately pointed it at the Bull, who pushed his hand away and said, 'Don't be fucking stupid.'

Neil looked at the chamber of the revolver, saw that it was empty, put the gun to his head and said, 'Look, man, it's fucking empty.' They were the last words Neil ever spoke.

The Bull tried in vain to snatch the gun from him, but before he could do so Neil had squeezed the trigger and a loud explosion filled the room. When the bullet entered Neil's head, he immediately crumpled to the floor. As Neil's lifeblood poured from a gaping wound, the Bull knelt down beside him and tried to administer first aid. 'Get a fucking ambulance, Harry,' the Bull shouted. 'Get a fucking ambulance now.' Instead of doing what he was told, Harry Perry kept asking the Bull where the gun was. 'Here is the gun,' the Bull replied. 'Take the fucking thing.' As soon as Perry had taken possession of the weapon, he fled from the pub with it and left the Bull cradling Neil.

The gunshot had been heard by a resident in an old people's home next door, and they had telephoned the emergency services. Within minutes, ambulancemen, firemen and police officers were rushing into the pub to go to Neil's aid. The Bull was still holding his stricken friend, who was alive but unconscious, when firemen first burst into the room. They physically lifted the Bull up and carried him away from Neil, who was then left alone in a pool of his own blood. The Bull was arrested by the police on suspicion of attempted murder, and Neil was rushed to Newcastle General Hospital.

As soon as Perry had stopped running in the opposite direction of the incident and composed himself, he telephoned a senior police officer he was acquainted with and said that he needed to talk with him urgently because something had gone terribly wrong. The first Paddy heard about his brother Neil being injured was when a police officer rang him and said that he should attend the hospital, as his brother had been hurt. The officer added that he did not know what had happened to Neil or if his life was in danger. When Paddy arrived at the hospital, he was told that Neil was in the operating theatre and that he would be informed of any news in due course. As Paddy paced up and down the waiting room, two surly-looking detectives approached him and identified themselves as the officers who had telephoned him. 'How did you get my phone number?' Paddy asked.

'Your friend Michael Bullock gave it to us,' one of the detectives replied. 'He is in a lot of trouble, Mr Conroy, and is asking to see you.' When Paddy asked the detectives why the Bull was in trouble, they told him that Neil had died and the Bull had been arrested for shooting him.

Paddy was in deep shock, but his instincts told him that he had to stay calm and keep his head. Paddy could not do anything for his brother, but he knew that he could help the Bull, and so he rushed to the police station, where a senior detective was waiting for him in the reception area. The detective offered Paddy his condolences, but he was not interested in fake sentiments and so demanded to see the Bull. The detective looked shocked and said that Michael Bullock was the man that police believed had murdered Paddy's brother. 'And what is the

Bull saying about your belief?' Paddy asked the detective.

'He has been questioned and has said that the shooting was a terrible accident,' replied the detective.

'Let me talk to the lad,' Paddy said. 'I will know as soon as he looks at me if he intended to shoot my brother.'

When Paddy walked into the interview room, the Bull was slumped at the table. Paddy saw before him a broken man. He knew in his heart that the Bull could never intentionally hurt his brother or any of his family, but he had to ask the question. 'Well, Bull, what happened?' Paddy asked.

Looking directly at Paddy, the Bull replied, 'It was an accident. Neil was messing about with . . .'

'Hold it there,' Paddy said. 'Sit there and don't say another fucking word to anybody until I tell you to, and I mean *anybody*.'

Paddy knew that Neil would not want his best friend to spend one minute in jail for his own stupidity, and so his job now was to ensure that did not happen. The police, never ones to allow the truth to get in the way of what they believed, charged the Bull with Neil's murder, and, despite Paddy's pleadings with the magistrates to grant him bail, the Bull was remanded in custody to HMP Durham to await trial.

An air of suspicion hung heavy over Neil's death, because the Bull had refused to say where the gun had come from and where it had gone after the shooting. Because the weapon was not found at the scene, the police were confident that somebody other than the Bull had been present during the incident. To make matters worse for the investigating officers, who clearly had their own theories, when the forensic scientists and the pathologist concluded their investigations, there seemed to be little doubt that the Bull had in fact told the truth about Neil's death. Reluctantly, detectives visited him in prison and explained that if he wanted the murder charge dropped he would need to cooperate by at least telling them where they could find the gun, so that ballistic tests could be done to support his account of the incident. Despite the fact that the Bull was facing a murder charge and the possibility he might have to serve life imprisonment, he still refused to cooperate with the police.

The senior officer Harry Perry had called straight after the shooting rang Paddy one day and said that he would like to talk to him face to face. Wary but equally curious as to why a policeman would wish to speak to him, Paddy declined the offer of a meeting but agreed to listen to anything that he had to say. 'It's like this, Paddy,' the policeman said. 'If your brother's death was an accident, we need the gun to prove that fact. Today is Friday. If we are given the weapon today, for instance, it could be tested by the ballistic guys by Monday or Tuesday. Your friend Bullock is back in court on Thursday, and so he could have the murder charge dropped if he is telling the truth. If he has done no wrong, he has nothing to fear.'

As soon as the officer had finished talking, Paddy replied, 'I will see what I can do.' Paddy then hung up the telephone before the officer had a chance to continue the conversation.

It didn't take Paddy long to locate Harry Perry, and when he found himself sitting face to face with him it was hard to contain his anger. Perry began warbling on about how sorry he was, but Paddy made it blatantly obvious to him that he wasn't interested in how he felt. Paddy told Perry that the only thing he wanted from him was the gun, adding, 'Not next week, not tomorrow, but today.'

A few hours later, Paddy received a call requesting that he drive to a certain car park and wait. Sitting alone, Paddy watched intently as a vehicle circled the perimeter before pulling up alongside him. The driver's window opened and a shoebox wrapped in newspaper was thrust towards Paddy. He grabbed the parcel and threw it onto the passenger seat before driving to his local pub, the Grainger.

Once there, Paddy asked two local lads to take the box, put it in a bin cupboard at a nearby house and then ring the police to tell them it was there. Sitting in the bar of the Grainger, Paddy watched through the window as the two lads did as he asked. Paddy was expecting a police car to pull up, check the cupboard, find the parcel and drive away, so one can imagine his shock when the bomb disposal squad arrived and cordoned off the street. After two or three hours, they established that the parcel was not an explosive device. It was then removed from the bin cupboard, and the gun was later identified as the one that had taken Neil's life.

The Bull's relief at being released from custody and having the murder charge dropped was short-lived, as the gun turned out to have been stolen. Both he and Harry Perry were arrested and taken to the police station. As usual, the Bull refused to answer police questions, but Harry Perry requested to speak to his friend the senior police officer. It's not known what was said, but neither man was charged, and after three weeks the police informed them both that the matter was now closed. The death of Neil Conroy had a devastating effect on all of his family, but the Bull in particular suffered badly. To this day, a part of him has never fully recovered from what happened that terrible night.

The Harrisons were a large, powerful family who struck fear into the hearts of many in the West End of Newcastle. Their notoriety was such that investigative journalist Roger Cook dedicated an entire episode of his television series *The Cook Report* to their tyranny and drug-dealing activities. There were eight brothers, ranging in age from their early teens to their late twenties. They lived in a block of flats that became known locally as 'Fort Harrison'. If a stranger dared to approach the premises, it was more than likely that a gun would be aimed at them from one of the upstairs windows, which were always manned.

A man in his early twenties named Darren Vent became embroiled in a dispute with a member of the Harrison family, and in an effort to resolve the issue the two men agreed to have a straightener. When the pair fought, Vent soon got the better of Harrison and began beating him to a pulp. That was until an onlooker passed Harrison a knife, which he plunged into his opponent. Vent was not seriously injured, nor was he defeated. As he was helped away from the scene of the fight by friends, Vent vowed to take on Harrison again just as soon as he had recovered from his gaping stab injury. When Vent was once more fighting fit, he not only beat Harrison badly with his fists but also stabbed him in revenge for the knife wound that he had suffered.

The Conroys were unaware of the trouble between Vent and Harrison until one night when Paddy was in the Grainger pub having a drink. Paddy heard sirens approaching, and moments later the interior of the bar was illuminated by blue flashing lights as a fire engine flashed past in the road outside. In the West End, there were no strangers, and so anything that affected one family had an effect on them all. Paddy was concerned, therefore, when the fire engine braked and turned into the road next to his home. Somebody close to Paddy was clearly in need. Turning to the Bull, Paddy said, 'Go and find out what that's all about.'

Shortly afterwards, Paddy was told that the Harrisons had petrol bombed a flat belonging to a girl named Debbie Cronin. As the flames engulfed the front door and threatened to cut off Cronin's escape route, she had grabbed her daughter from a blazing bedroom and run through the inferno. Cronin suffered terrible burns to her arms, but fortunately her child escaped unscathed. Word soon spread around the West End that Cronin was in a relationship with Vent and that this cowardly attack on a woman and her child was allegedly in retaliation for him stabbing Harrison. Paddy couldn't have cared less if they had shot, stabbed or crucified Vent, but he failed to see how the Harrisons could justify petrol bombing the home of a young mother and her daughter. It's fair to say that he and many others were absolutely disgusted and incensed by the Harrisons' behaviour.

A few weeks later, the Harrisons' father, Duncan, and two of his sons entered the Hydraulic Crane. The moment Paddy set eyes on them, he walked over and sat down at their table. 'What the fuck do you think you're doing petrol bombing women and children?' Paddy said. 'You're so fucking out of order.' Maybe Paddy was being naive, because he was expecting an answer, but in retrospect how could any man defend such a cowardly and despicable act? Quite rightly ashamed, the Harrisons slunk out of the pub without even finishing their drinks.

Before the situation could escalate between Vent and the Harrisons, Vent was permanently removed from the situation by his own actions. He and another man, Lee Cockburn, had visited the home of a drug dealer named Michael McHugh. Both men felt that they had justified grievances with McHugh. Vent thought that McHugh had insulted a female friend of his, and Cockburn believed that he had been ripped off in a drug deal. In the violent fracas that followed, McHugh was stabbed. He died of his injuries shortly afterwards. Both Vent and Cockburn were convicted of murder and sentenced to serve life imprisonment.

The weekend after Paddy had spoken to the Harrisons in the Hydraulic Crane, his nephews were enjoying an evening out with their friends at a pub called the Hawthorns. The Harrison boys swaggered in, saw members of the Conroy family and immediately attacked them. Petrol bombing women and children is foolish, but attacking a Conroy for no reason at all is fucking suicidal. Paddy's eldest brother, Lenny, went in search of the Harrisons as soon as he heard what had happened to his sons and beat them all around the car park of a pub. Fearing a tit-for-tat war was about to break out between the Conroy and Harrison families, Duncan Harrison contacted Paddy and said that any issues should be resolved by having a straightener. 'Lenny can fight one of my sons,' Duncan said. 'And one of Lenny's sons can fight another of my sons around the same age.'

The Conroys have never walked away from any man or gang, and so Duncan Harrison's offer was readily accepted. When the day of the proposed fight arrived, the Harrisons appeared to have backed down, because they replaced one of their men with a man named Paddy Summerville, who was going to fight Lenny, and their other fighter failed to materialise. Despite Lenny's opponent being a big, fit man and Lenny being older and certainly past his best, he still accepted Summerville's challenge. The venue for the fight was the car park of the local Presto store, which adjoined Lenny's home. It was agreed that only two people could be present during the fight, which would prevent others from getting involved and things getting out of hand, and so Paddy and Duncan Harrison volunteered.

Nothing can be taken away from Paddy Summerville. He knocked Lenny Conroy over as soon as the fight started. As Lenny fell to the floor, Summerville began kicking him, even though Lenny had made it clear that he had accepted defeat. There was no way that Paddy was going to stand by and watch his own flesh and blood be kicked to a pulp, and so he grabbed Summerville by the hair and began pounding his face with his fists. Four members of the Harrison family came running from nearby bushes, where they had been hiding, wielding bricks, sticks and a cricket bat. Despite being greatly outnumbered, Paddy stood his ground until eventually the Harrisons backed off and then ran away. Paddy had suffered a few cuts and bruises, but apart from a deep gash in his mouth, where he had been hit by a brick, he was OK. Lenny remained motionless, curled up on the floor. 'Come on Lenny,' Paddy said. 'Let's get cleaned up. This doesn't end here.'

Paddy walked with Lenny to his home, and once his brother was safely inside Paddy made his way to the local hospital, where he had five stitches to his mouth. Paddy's wounds were relatively minor, but the damage to the Conroy family pride was considered to be major. When Paddy arrived home, the only thing he could think about was the best way of hitting back at the Harrisons.

Before Paddy had a chance to wreak his revenge, the Harrisons struck again. The Bull was filling his car up at a garage when three of their gang pulled up alongside him on the forecourt in a van. They knew the Bull was a Conroy in everything but name, and so one of the Harrisons pulled out an Irish shillelagh, crept up behind him and brought the hammer-like weapon crashing down onto his head. Until this incident, Paddy had been unaware of the Bull's interest in American sports, but it just so happened that a heavy baseball bat that he had recently purchased was still in his car. Staggering back towards his vehicle in order to retrieve the bat, the Bull saw that the other two Harrisons were armed with bottles and blocking his route. In desperation, the Bull picked up sections of a stack of metal shelves that were displaying fancy goods and began hurling them at his attackers. The Bull in a rage and swinging a weapon in your direction is not a pretty sight to behold, and so, rather wisely, the Harrisons ran back to their van, jumped in and sped away.

Pauline Patton, one of the Bull's cousins, was at that time living with Trevor Harrison, one of the three men who had attacked him at the garage. The Bull 'retired' his new baseball bat, because he deemed it unsuitable for the task ahead, and instead acquired a samurai sword. He then asked his cousin Pauline to arrange a 'meeting' for him with the Harrison brothers. When the time and location had been agreed by both parties, the Bull arrived in a taxi with his samurai sword lying across the back seat. 'Give me two minutes,' he told the driver. 'I just have to pop in and see my cousin.' When Trevor Harrison answered the door, the Bull hit him with a barrage of questions: 'What the fuck was all that about? Your problem is with Paddy and Lenny. It has nothing to do with me. Why was I attacked by a group of you? Aren't you man enough to take me on alone?' Unable to offer any sort of rational explanation, Trevor Harrison told the Bull to fuck off or he would sort him out. Laughing sarcastically, the Bull informed Harrison that he wasn't going anywhere and so he had better carry out his threat. Harrison walked out of his house and into the street, where he and the Bull began to fight.

The Bull lived only a stone's throw from his cousin Pauline's home. It was important to him, therefore, to resolve any issue that the Harrisons might have had with him. The last thing he wanted was to walk home every night looking over his shoulder. As soon as the Bull started to get the better of Trevor Harrison, a transit van sped into the street and screeched to a halt. The side door flew open, and the Harrison gang spilt out onto the street like a pack of rabid dogs. Brave but not stupid, the Bull considered running to the taxi to retrieve his sword, but after glancing at just how far away it was he ran for his life in the opposite direction. Fearing he would be caught by the Harrisons, the Bull decided to seek refuge in his own flat.

As he sprinted down the street at the speed of an Olympic athlete, the Bull could see his stepson standing outside his home, and so he called out to him to open the security door. The boy ran and began shouting into the intercom for his mother, Margaret, to operate the door-release button. By now, the Bull had reached a gate that led into the flats, but as he tried to climb over it he was hacked across the back of his neck and shoulder with a sword. Doctors have since said that had his assailant struck him cleanly across the neck instead of catching his shoulder he would have been beheaded. Falling to the pavement with blood gushing out of a gaping open wound, the Bull saw to his horror that the Harrisons were not quite finished with him just yet. 'Kill the fucking pig bastard! Kill the fucking pig bastard!' Duncan Harrison shouted. As his sons dutifully attempted to carry out their father's command, others loyal to the Harrisons kicked and hacked at the Bull with a variety of weapons.

One person who witnessed the attack later told the police that the Bull's attackers looked like wild animals engaged in a feeding frenzy. As the violence continued, the sword was thrust firmly into the left side of the Bull's chest, just a quarter of an inch from his heart. The tip of the blade poked precariously out of his back. Instinctively, the Bull gripped the sword with both hands to prevent the weapon being used against him again, but his assailants were equally determined to achieve their aim. Deep lacerations appeared in the Bull's hands as he fought to keep control of the sword. He knew that if he dared to let go it would cost him his life. 'I'm done. I'm done,' he called out. 'What more do you fuckers want?' The Bull was unable to protect himself, because his hands were gripping the sword, but the Harrisons replied to his pleas for mercy by repeatedly smashing him in the face.

A woman who unwittingly happened upon the slaughter as she left the flats began screaming hysterically, and this brought a degree of sanity back to the bloodthirsty mob. The attack stopped, and the Harrisons gathered up their weapons and ran back to their van. Getting to his feet, the Bull managed to pull the sword out of his body before staggering into the safety of the flats. 'I am OK. I am OK,' the Bull mumbled before collapsing in a pool of his own blood. The Bull's partner, Margaret, had witnessed what had happened and had called for an ambulance before the attack had finished. By the time she had run down the stairs and begun to comfort the Bull, the ambulance had arrived. She begged the Bull to allow her to accompany him to the hospital, but he was having none of it. 'You stay here and look after the kids. I can look after myself,' he said.

The Bull didn't know it at the time, but the sword had punctured his lung and he was losing a life-threatening amount of blood. As the Bull started to lose consciousness, Margaret began to scream and the paramedic kept saying, 'Stay awake, lad, or you might never wake up.' As the ambulance disappeared up the street with its blue lights flashing and sirens wailing, Margaret sank to her knees and sobbed her heart out. As soon as Paddy heard about the attack, he began to plan a bloody reprisal. There was no way back for the Harrisons now. The Conroys were going to hit back and hit back fucking hard.

David Glover junior, who as a child had terrorised the West End of Newcastle, had his own chew (trouble) with the Harrison family at this time. It wasn't surprising, therefore, when he turned up at the hospital to visit the Bull and ask if there was anything that he could do. The Conroys were not involved with Glover at that time, and they certainly did not trust him, because he was quite an unpredictable person. Glover had been in secure homes since the age of nine for committing robberies and attacking other children. On his 15th birthday, he had graduated to a young offenders institute, from which he had managed to escape no fewer than 15 times. Paddy had lived with Glover in the past – Paddy's partner, Maureen, was Glover's aunt – and so he was practically family, but his sudden interest in the Conroys' problems with the Harrisons did set alarm bells ringing. Everything about Glover appeared to spell trouble.

When Glover's father, David Glover senior, had been serving a seven-year prison sentence for his part in a conspiracy to supply £180,000 worth of cannabis, he had almost managed to get Paddy locked up. Long-term prisoners are allowed to 'accumulate visits' if they are serving a sentence in a jail that causes hardship for their loved ones to get to. Instead of their families trekking the length and breadth of Britain once a month for a one-hour visit, the inmate can save up six or seven visits and then get transferred to a local jail for a week so that all the visits can take place on consecutive days.

David Glover senior was serving his sentence in HMP Acklington, in Northumberland, and had successfully applied to have a series of accumulated visits at HMP Frankland, in County Durham. Two guards and a driver were assigned to get Glover safely to his destination, but on the way he somehow talked them into stopping off in Newcastle for some lunch. Paddy had to look two or three times before he was sure who it actually was when Glover and the three prison officers walked into the Hydraulic Crane.

Moments later, David Glover junior walked into the pub, 'quite by chance', and joined them. Fearing the local constabulary might pop their heads around the door to check on his clientele, Paddy chaperoned Glover's party into a discreet corner and sent them over complimentary food and drink. After half an hour or so, David Glover junior slipped out of the pub. He was later arrested for an armed robbery that had been commmitted just down the street. When he was questioned about his whereabouts at the time the robbery took place, Glover junior told detectives that he had been in Paddy's pub with his father.

Two days later, the head barman informed Paddy that earlier that morning, while he had been out, two detectives had been in the pub looking for him. 'David Glover junior has been arrested for armed robbery, and he has claimed that he was in here drinking with his father and three prison officers,' he said.

'No, no, no,' Paddy groaned. 'What the fucking hell is he thinking of?' If Paddy supported Glover's alibi, the prison officers might have faced prosecution, but if he didn't Glover might have been charged with armed robbery and faced a lengthy prison sentence. Paddy had no choice: he had to support Glover's alibi and say that he had been in the pub throughout the relevant time with his father and the three prison officers.

When the detectives began to take a closer look at all the individuals concerned, they soon discovered that the prison officers' drinking partner, Glover senior, was supposed to be behind bars – but not the type that sell alcohol. The incident was reported in all the national newspapers, and Glover escaped prosecution, but the three officers were sacked for gross misconduct. With far more pressing problems, concerning the Harrisons, to contend with, Paddy didn't forget David Glover junior completely, but rather foolishly he did put Glover's eagerness to involve himself in his affairs to the back of his mind.

Paddy contacted a relative of the Harrisons and asked him to accompany him to the hospital to visit the Bull. In the intensive care unit, Paddy and the man stood at the Bull's bedside watching as he gasped for oxygen. 'He is my friend,' Paddy said. 'Tell the Harrison boys that I want to talk to them about this. They can bring as many men as they can muster. There will be just me and my brothers, and we will be waiting in the Gold Cup pub tomorrow at 2 p.m.' The man simply nodded before turning and walking away.

Paddy Conroy is many things, but stupid isn't one of them. Paddy knew that if the Harrison firm did turn up they would be mob-handed and they would all be armed. Paddy rang his friends and associates from all over Newcastle and told them to meet him at the Gold Cup pub at midday the following day. 'Don't hang about outside,' he warned them. 'Let the Harrison mob turn up at 2 p.m. thinking there's just a few of us. They will then unwittingly walk into a fucking massacre, and we can do the lot of them.' Approximately 150 men loyal to the Conroy family arrived at the pub the following morning. The pub was so packed that 20 or 30 men had to stand outside in the back courtyard. The Harrisons never did show – no doubt they got to hear about the reception party that awaited their arrival.

At 3 p.m., Paddy went for a drink in his local pub, the Grainger. Most of his friends had gone home, but 50 or so had stayed out for a drink. Just as it was getting dark, a man came into the pub and called Paddy to one side. 'Be on your guard, Paddy,' he said. 'Somebody has riddled Duncan Harrison's mobile home with bullets, and there's bound to be a comeback.' Paddy instinctively knew who had done this, but in order to protect the guilty he refused to name him. Paddy was aware that the actions of his trigger-happy associate would provoke a response from the Harrisons, and he didn't want to sit at home with his family waiting to find out the severity of their reprisal.

The best form of defence is undoubtedly attack, and so that night allies of the Conroy family lay in wait for the Harrisons to emerge from Fort Harrison. In the early hours of the morning, two or three members of the Harrison family walked out in the company of one of the Bull's cousins. They were chased, but with fear on their side they soon managed to lose their pursuers. Later that day, however, the Bull's cousin was seen walking along the street. A car pulled up, and a group of men jumped out. The Bull's cousin was grabbed and forced into the boot at gunpoint before the vehicle sped away. The terrified man was taken to an alleyway at the side of the Grainger pub, where his abductors attempted to break his arms and legs with crowbars and a hammer. They were partially successful: both of his arms were broken, and his legs were so badly beaten that it was some time before he could walk again without the aid of a stick.

Ironically, the Bull's cousin ended up on the same hospital ward as the Bull, which caused the doctors and nurses a great deal of concern. The police had warned hospital staff that each side involved in the feud would be more than happy to carry out further attacks on their opponents as they lay in their beds. Extra security had been drafted in to watch the hospital entrances, but that didn't prevent the Bull from staggering from his own bed to confront his cousin. 'If I find out you were involved in the attack on me,' the Bull said, 'you won't be in here for much longer. You will be downstairs in the morgue.' As soon as the Bull's cousin was discharged from the hospital, he hobbled to the airport and waved goodbye to Newcastle forever. Nobody has seen or heard from him since.

* * *

It was not all one-way traffic, though. The Harrisons were equally competent at serving up violence. Twenty-five-year-old Patrick Kirby, an associate of the Conroys, was gunned down outside Paddy's Happy House. Kirby left a trail of blood as he staggered from the scene of the shooting, which nearly claimed his life. Geoffrey Harrison, aged 21, and Paul Benson, aged 19, were charged with attempted murder, wounding with intent and violent disorder, but both were cleared of all charges. Although he was cleared of the shooting, Geoffrey Harrison was given a total of 30 months in prison for firearms offences.

On another occasion, Paddy was at home when Maureen called to him and said that four of the Harrison gang had just pulled up outside in a car. Grabbing a handgun, Paddy rushed out into the street to confront them before they could alight from their vehicle. Only the driver was unarmed. Two of his passengers were brandishing shotguns, and a third had a handgun. Before they had a chance to point the weapons in Paddy's direction, he was on them. 'What do you fucking want?' Paddy asked as he leant into the car. The man nearest to Paddy put his hand up as if to protect his head and then began pleading with him not to shoot him. Suddenly, a shot rang out, and Paddy jumped back. The man in the passenger seat, on the far side of the car, had fired his handgun into the air. As Paddy moved away from the vehicle, he gave the occupants enough time to train their guns on him and open fire. As bullets and shotgun pellets whistled past him, Paddy attempted to return fire, but his weapon had jammed. Paddy turned, ran to his house and took cover behind a brick parapet that supported the front door. When the bullets continued to fly in his direction, Paddy kicked the door closed in the hope that the shooting would stop, but a more sustained hail of gunfire began, which blew all the glass out and sent bullets whizzing down the hall. Maureen and her daughter were in the kitchen, which faced the front door, and so Paddy dashed along the hallway shouting for them to take cover. As Paddy did so, he felt a bullet smash into his back, but he continued running until he was in the kitchen and sure that his family was safe.

When the guns fell silent, Paddy waited a few minutes before peering down the hall. The front door had been obliterated, and there were bullet holes in the walls. Maureen looked at Paddy and shook her head in dismay. Paddy knew what this meant. He had only one course of action open to him: he was going to have to redecorate. 'Check my back,

Maureen,' Paddy said. 'I think I've been shot.' Paddy could feel pain, but there didn't appear to be any blood. When Maureen inspected Paddy's back for bullet holes, she could see that there were marks and abrasions but that the skin had not been broken. Paddy later discovered that a large piece of concrete lintel had been shot away above the front door. The bullet that hit it must have ricocheted off a wall or the ceiling before striking him.

The following night, the Happy House was petrol bombed. One of Paddy's tenants on the lower floor was watching television when his window exploded and the room was engulfed in flames. Fortunately, he escaped the fire unscathed and damage was minimal. Paddy did have to move the tenant to the top floor, as he said he no longer felt safe in that particular room. The Harrisons had broken the criminal code: they had endangered non-combatants, and they had previously involved a woman and child in a feud. As far as Paddy was concerned, the rulebook had to be discarded. He wanted the Harrisons struck down; he wanted them terminated like vermin.

Less than 12 hours after the attack on the Happy House, Duncan Harrison's son Joseph looked nervously around before getting out of his car. Despite his vigilance, he failed to see a man hiding in bushes nearby. Once Joseph was out and away from his vehicle, the man strode purposefully towards him, pulled a gun out from his jacket and shot him in the face. At the hospital, Joseph's injuries were described as not life-threatening, but this incident brought about an escalation in violence that undoubtedly was. Both sides began purchasing caches of firearms and wearing bulletproof vests every time they dared to venture out of their homes. Life in the wild West End of Newcastle began to compare with life in west Beirut.

The only people who benefited from the volatile situation were the members of the Grainger pub darts team. Notoriously poor players, they were competing against another local pub team one night when the Harrisons pulled up outside the Grainger and opened fire. All the windows were shot out as everybody dived for cover. When the sound of squealing tyres indicated that the Harrisons had sped away, people got up off the floor and continued drinking. However, one member of the visiting darts team remained motionless where he had fallen during the attack. Initially, it was thought the man might have stopped a bullet, but it was soon discovered that he had passed out through fear. Sitting him on a stool, the landlord tried to reassure the man that everything was going to be OK. Trembling and weeping, the man, who had soiled himself, begged to be taken home. His equally terrified teammates, huddled in the corner of the pub, unanimously agreed it was time to leave and declared the Grainger team winners by default. Whether this is true or not, it is said by the Grainger regulars to be the only darts match that their team has ever won.

Soon after the Grainger pub was shot up, the Happy House was petrol bombed again. On this occasion, the front door and one of the first-floor bedsits were set on fire. Collecting the rent from his not so Happy House tenants became somewhat embarrassing for Paddy. He tried to laugh off the attacks by saying that there would be no additional charge for the heating the fires were generating, but it's unlikely that his tenants ever did see the funny side of it.

Shortly after the Bull's release from hospital, he was once more removed from 'active service' when officers from the Metropolitan Police and Northumbria Police raided a house in order to rescue two men who had earlier been kidnapped in London – and found the Bull. It was alleged that the cockneys had taken payment for a delivery of fake perfume but that the goods had failed to arrive on Tyneside. The Bull and others, according to the police, had travelled to London in a transit van and kidnapped the men. They had allegedly said that they would release them only when they were given the perfume or had their cash returned. To be honest, the whole case stank – if you'll pardon the pun. The cockneys who were found in the house with the Bull and others said that they had no idea who had abducted them, as their kidnappers had been wearing ski masks. The Bull protested his innocence, but the police were far from convinced, and so he was charged with kidnap and remanded in custody to await trial.

Just after the Bull was locked up, the feud with the Harrisons reached its peak, or lowest point, depending on your outlook. One of their number had the audacity to desecrate the grave of Leonard and Neil Conroy. They smashed the headstone and, a few days later, threw the pieces at Michael Conroy's front door. In the weeks that followed this barbaric act, there were 22 separate attacks on the Harrison firm, during which numerous people received gunshot wounds.

In one incident, Alan Harrison, aged 20, and his brother Charles, aged 18, were out walking their Rottweiler in Rye Hill, in the West End. A man approached the brothers and words were exchanged, but before a fight could break out the man pulled out a gun and shot the dog in the head and the brothers multiple times in the legs. Charles was so badly injured that he ended up in intensive care fighting for his life on a ventilator. As well as 'successful hits' such as this, there were many occasions when gunmen simply missed their intended victims, and others in which vehicles and property were the targets.

It was David Glover junior who came to break the news to Paddy about his family's grave being desecrated. Paddy couldn't accept that anybody would stoop that low, and so initially he refused to believe what he was told. Glover said that a friend of the Harrisons named Billy Collier had been seen in the Blue Man pub wearing a bulletproof vest and brandishing a shotgun while bragging about the crime. Glover said that Collier had claimed that he had since been offered £5,000 to dig up Leonard Conroy's corpse and throw body parts through the front window of a member of the Conroy family. Paddy kept telling himself that this vile act could be a ploy to lead him into a trap or to make him do something irrational. 'Keep your head, Paddy,' he kept telling himself. 'Keep your head until you know for sure that it is true.'

Walking down the street, trying to rationalise all that he had just been told, Paddy bumped into a man he knew. The man was not involved in any type of criminality and so had no reason to lie to Paddy regarding anybody involved in the feud. This man frequented the Blue Man pub, and so Paddy asked him if he had seen Collier drinking in there. The man told Paddy how Collier had been boasting in the pub about the Conroy headstone being smashed and the fact that he was being offered money to dig up Leonard's body. Paddy knew at once that Glover had been telling the truth and that, in the name of his father, he would have to have his revenge.

The following evening, a member of the Harrison family was confronted by a gunman and shot five times in the legs. In addition, Duncan Harrison's mobile home, on the Oakwellgate site, in Gateshead, was riddled with bullets and blasted with a shotgun, but, fortunately for him, he happened to be elsewhere at the time.

An hour after the attack on the caravan, Joseph Harrison opened the letterbox of the Happy House lodgings and tried to pour petrol inside. Unfortunately for Joseph, someone was lying in wait for him. It was almost as if it had been second-guessed that the Harrisons would attack the Happy House if their father's caravan was trashed. As the silhouette of Joseph Harrison appeared in the frosted glass, a gunman took aim with a shotgun and fired from the other side of the door. The blast hit Joseph in the face and chest and threw him to the floor. The gunman fired again, hitting him in the face once more. As Joseph's accomplices began to run, the gunman took aim again and fired, hitting one of them in the back. During the gun battle that followed, a child in the street ran for cover and an innocent motorist caught in the crossfire had to crawl to safety as his vehicle was sprayed with bullets and shotgun pellets.

When the police arrived, the gunman and the Harrison firm were nowhere to be seen, but a telltale trail of blood led officers to 'Fort Harrison'. The police arrested the three Harrison brothers and charged them with conspiracy to set fire to the Happy House and two offences of possessing firearms with intent to endanger life. The police alleged that sawn-off shotguns, pump-action rifles and a revolver had been used during the incident. Three days later, the police raided the Happy House and found guns that had been hidden in the loft. However, because the property had numerous residents, the police were unable to establish who actually owned the firearms. No doubt officers had their suspicions, and they didn't concern the elderly lady in room seven.

Everybody associated with the Conroy family refused to assist the police when asked to make statements against the Harrisons, but Terry Nordman, a close friend of the Harrisons who had been present when the Conroys' grave was desecrated, turned supergrass against his friends in an exchange for a new identity. It's fair to say Nordman knew that if the Harrisons were locked up he would be left out on the streets with little or no backup against the Conroys. It wasn't the type of future any man would relish, especially one who had been placed in the top three of a gunman's most-wanted list. To save himself, Nordman took the police's offer of a new identity in exchange for giving the evidence that would deprive his former friends of their liberty.

Prior to the trial, members of the Harrison and Conroy families found themselves at Newcastle Magistrates' Court, for unrelated matters. It's never been established who did what to instigate what followed, but up to 20 people ended up brawling in the waiting room. Both men and women were involved in the fighting, and horrified members of the public reported seeing clumps of hair, a lump of flesh and blood 'spattered everywhere' at the scene. When the fighting broke out, a court clerk had to press a panic button to summon extra police. Twelve officers entered the waiting room to separate the warring factions, and others threw a cordon around the building to stop people loyal to the Conroy family from entering. A female was arrested, but she was later released without charge.

A few months later, Andrew, James and Joseph Harrison all pleaded not guilty to the attack on the Happy House and elected to stand trial at York Crown Court after their defence team had successfully argued that a trial held in Newcastle would be prejudicial because of their notoriety. Terry Nordman told the jury that he had been with the Harrison brothers when their father phoned to say his caravan had been blasted by a shotgun. Nordman said that the Harrison brothers had then planned a revenge firebomb attack on Conroy's Happy House bedsit premises, as they believed that he was responsible for the caravan shooting. Nordman said that the Harrisons had marched up to the Happy House hooded and armed. Fifteen shots were fired before Joseph Harrison returned home injured and was taken to hospital.

The brothers were convicted of conspiracy to cause arson with intent to endanger life and two offences of possessing firearms. They were sentenced to ten years' imprisonment for each offence. After the case, Detective Superintendent John Renwick said, 'The sentence serves as a warning to anyone intent on using weapons to carry out criminal activity. They do so at their cost. This was a very difficult case to bring to court because of the reluctance of some people to give evidence for fear of reprisals. Three people did give evidence, and they have been put on the Northumbria Police witness-protection scheme. They had the courage to help police in this case and they have been given a new identity and have been rehoused outside the force area.'

It was reported that two of the Harrisons wept when the judge passed sentence on them. They were big enough to try to burn down a house full of innocent people, and big enough to order the desecration of a grave, but it appears they couldn't face serving a few years behind bars.

Chapter Five

VIV NO MORE IN '94

ON TYNESIDE, A romanticism surrounds the name and deeds of Viv Graham. He is remembered by the majority of Geordies as the fourth emergency service or as a swashbuckling Robin Hood-type gentleman. However, there are some who hold a conflicting view. To them, Viv Graham was little more than an egotistical bully.

In February 1988, Viv was involved in an attack on a man named Carl Wattler that, by any man's standards, can only be described as pretty disgusting. According to several witnesses, Viv had been working at a bar called Baxter's and had ordered Wattler to drink up at closing time. Wattler had failed to do so fast enough for Viv's liking and so suffered a crushing blow to the face. It is unclear what happened after that, but Wattler was seen shortly afterwards waiting for Viv by the exit doors. A fight broke out, and Wattler appeared to be getting the better of Viv when out of the shadows stepped one of Viv's doormen, who smashed Wattler over the head with an iron bar. Carl Wattler was later found lying unconscious in the street. He was rushed to hospital, where a CT scan revealed that a large blood clot had formed at the base of his skull. Wattler underwent emergency surgery and then spent a considerable length of time in intensive care, where a ventilator was used to assist him with his breathing.

Shortly after the attack on Wattler, 'Skinny' Gary Thompson, who had been charged with a number of offences following the 'Free Paddy Conroy' marches and subsequent riots, was alleged to have tried to shoot Viv. Some say it was a revenge attack because of what had happened to Wattler; others say Thompson was just a typical West

Ender venting his anger because he had had enough of Viv Graham's bullying behaviour.

One morning in the early hours, as Viv and his friend Rob Armstrong walked from the Quayside towards Manhattan's nightclub, they failed to notice a black Nissan vehicle that was shadowing them. When the vehicle suddenly accelerated past Viv and Armstrong, they thought that it was just another boy racer showing off to friends. That was until the driver jumped on the brakes and a gunman blew out the back window and opened fire with a pump-action shotgun. Armstrong shouted at Viv to move, but he appeared to be rooted to the spot with fear. Armstrong, who had his back to the gunman, dived on Viv, and both men fell to the floor. His act of undoubted heroism came with a price. Armstrong was shot in the back and shot again as he lay on top of Viv on the ground. An innocent bystander also suffered facial injuries after being struck by stray shotgun pellets. The incident was over as soon as it had begun. All the victims later recovered from their injuries, and 'Skinny' Gary Thompson, who had been arrested for the shooting, was released without charge.

When Viv appeared in court and pleaded guilty to the attack on Wattler, many expected him to be sent to prison for a number of years. Wattler had survived the assault, but he had suffered permanent injury: he walked with a limp, endured regular and severe migraines and had sustained nerve damage that caused blurred vision in one eye. In his defence, Viv claimed that he was sorry and that, upon reflection, he might have acted 'a bit hastily'. Judge Angus Stroyan sentenced Viv to 18 months' imprisonment, which was suspended for 18 months. He was also ordered to pay a rather insulting £500 in compensation to his victim. Little wonder Viv was punching the air and laughing when he left the court building.

On 22 August 1988, a man named Robert Bell spent the night drinking in Newcastle city centre. The Bigg Market is an area awash with pubs, clubs and restaurants, and Bell had arrived there just before closing time. It remains unclear exactly what happened, but at some stage Bell and others began fighting with a 24-year-old man named Peter Donnelly. Three people were arrested for public order offences, but Bell and Donnelly were allowed to walk away. According to eyewitnesses, Bell had got the better of Donnelly, who was less than happy about the situation.

Bloodied and bruised, Donnelly decided to go home and get changed. It had been his intention to remain at home, but he was simply not prepared to lose face. Just after midnight, armed with a shotgun and a knife, Donnelly returned to Newcastle city centre, where he eventually found Bell sitting at a table in Santino's restaurant with Viv Graham. An unidentified accomplice of Donnelly stood at the entrance to the restaurant with a knife as Donnelly approached Bell's table armed with the shotgun. When Bell looked up from what could have been his last supper, he saw that the barrels of a shotgun were just inches from his face. Viv Graham snatched the weapon and threw it against the wall before Donnelly was able to squeeze the trigger.

A confusing but extremely violent fight broke out, and diners began to run and scream in terror. The unidentified man who had been guarding the door came forward and held his knife to the stomach of Bell's younger brother Ian. Somebody else ran up behind the knifeman and brought a chair crashing down upon his head. He immediately collapsed and lay motionless. Bell and Donnelly somehow ended up brawling in the back alley of Santino's. As the two men traded punches, Bell suddenly fell back. He had been stabbed in the shoulder and heart. As blood pumped out of Bell's chest, he screamed for assistance and Viv was soon on hand to help him once more. Viv punched Donnelly, breaking his jaw, and then began to administer first aid to the dying man.

Miraculously, the knife had not penetrated deep into Bell's heart, and Viv was able to stem the flow of blood until an ambulance arrived. From his hospital bed, Bell named Donnelly as his attacker. Both his brother Ian and Viv Graham also made statements telling police what they had witnessed. Donnelly was charged with attempted murder, wounding with intent, possessing a firearm with intent of endangering life and possessing a firearm without a firearm licence. He was remanded in custody to await trial.

It is rumoured on Tyneside that Bell was financially compensated on the condition that he did not implicate Donnelly at the trial. Whatever the truth may be, when Bell entered the witness box he suffered a bout of acute amnesia. He could not remember what had happened that night or who had attacked him. Bell's amnesia proved to be extremely contagious, because not only his brother but also Viv Graham suffered from it too. The jury unsurprisingly found Peter Donnelly not guilty of all charges, and the judge ordered his immediate release.

A few months after Viv had displayed the type of behaviour that has led many Geordies to believe he was a hero, he was involved in yet another cowardly attack on an innocent person. It is alleged that Stephen Sayers had been refused entry at a nightclub in Newcastle called Hobo's. Stuart Watson, the head doorman at the venue, had made it known that he didn't want the Sayers brothers or their firm frequenting the club, because, according to him, they had no respect for the other customers and treated the place as if they owned it. Stephen Sayers had tried to square up to Watson when he was refused entry, but Watson had stood his ground and Sayers was forced to walk away. It is said that, that same week, Sayers met Viv and falsely claimed that Watson had broken the jaws of two young lads while ejecting them from Hobo's. Sayers knew that Viv objected to this type of behaviour by door staff and so added that he had remonstrated with Watson, who had allegedly told him that he wasn't afraid of the Sayers family, nor did he care what Viv Graham thought about the way he did his job.

Viv's ego was as big as his biceps, and so he was easily wound up by this comment. Together with Alan 'Fish' Tams, David Lancaster, Rob Armstrong, John Thompson and Stephen Sayers, Viv made his way to Hobo's and asked the receptionist to fetch Stuart Watson. Rather than comply with Viv's request, the receptionist fled upstairs and telephoned the police. Moments later, Watson appeared in the reception area and Viv began to punch him repeatedly in the face. In fairness to Watson, he was struck at least 20 times by Viv and never went down. In fact, he parried many of the punches and made no effort whatsoever to hit back. It is accepted that Watson didn't hit back because he was, understandably, scared. Watson had seen who had attended to back Viv up and rather wisely realised that if he did fight back they were more than likely to join in.

After throwing an array of ineffective punches, Viv began to tire, and so he resorted to grabbing Watson and throwing him about like a rag doll. To this day, CCTV footage of the attack captured by the nightclub's security system can be viewed on the website YouTube. The assault looks a lot worse than it actually was. Watson appears to have been knocked all over the place, but if you look closely you will see that it is his oversized jacket that is moving rather than anything else. Watson was quite right to assume that he would have been in a more dangerous situation if he had fought back, because as the brawl spilt out onto the dance floor Sayers and others began kicking him, although he still refused to go down.

It later emerged that a male and a female police officer had witnessed the attack. Working undercover, they had been assigned to attend the club to gather intelligence about a suspected drug dealer. One would assume that police officers present during the attack of an innocent man would be duty-bound to intervene or at least to alert their colleagues, but Viv seemed to enjoy a special relationship with some members of Northumbria Police. When the gang walked out of Hobo's nightclub, Watson was bleeding profusely, but he was still on his feet. The police did eventually arrive, but Watson refused to assist them. For a time, it looked as if Viv was going to escape justice, but when all the other gang members were identified from the CCTV footage the police felt compelled to act.

In July 1990, Watson's attackers appeared in court before Judge Mary MacMurray to face charges of violent disorder and wounding. All pleaded guilty, and they were sentenced to a total of fourteen years and two months' imprisonment. Lancaster, Armstrong, Tams and Sayers received two and a half years each; Thompson was sentenced to four months; and Viv was sentenced to three years, plus the remaining ten months of his suspended sentence, which had been imposed for the attack on Wattler.

Viv, having acquired a criminal record for assaulting Wattler and having then been sent to prison for the cowardly attack on Watson, should have been banned from working on the doors of pubs and nightclubs according to regulations that were implemented under the Door Supervisors Registration Scheme in May 1992. For reasons known only to Viv and Northumbria Police, a blind eye was turned and he was permitted to be excluded from the scheme and do as he wished. There are some who believe that he was the eyes and ears of the police and that it was important to them that he should be allowed to mingle with and befriend the criminal fraternity that frequented clubland.

A short while after Viv was released from prison, he confronted

Michael Sayers in a Newcastle nightclub. Eyewitnesses described Sayers as 'cowering with fear' when Viv accused him of trying to distribute drugs on the premises. A minor scuffle ensued, and Sayers left the club via a fire exit, with Viv in hot pursuit. Sayers suffered only minor physical injuries, but his ego was severely dented. Viv may have got away with assaulting the likes of Carl Wattler, but he had also assaulted Michael Conroy the night that Paddy had been sentenced to five years' imprisonment and had now assaulted a member of the Sayers family. For at least one of those attacks, somebody somewhere was bound to make him pay.

Viv's biggest problem was that he was a loner operating in a city steeped in family history and deep-seated loyalties. The Conroy and the Sayers families had fathers, sons and brothers who were villains, and each of those family members had numerous friends who were fiercely loyal to them. Viv had little more than casual acquaintances he had made in bars, nightclubs or the gym. He had given these fair-weather friends jobs working on the doors of various clubs, and in return they had pledged their allegiance to him. Such people inevitably lack that unique commitment created by strong family ties.

Whichever way you look at it, Viv Graham's actions were going to get him killed, and there is evidence to suggest that he knew it. He often told his partner, Anna Connelly, that he would never reach 40 years of age. Anna's brother Peter Connelly had once asked Viv who he thought would be most likely to shoot him, and without hesitation he had replied that it would be one of the Sayers firm.

On Christmas Eve 1993, Paddy Conroy went to the Rob Paul jeweller's shop in Newcastle with a friend, Dave Garside. Paddy had to pick up a Christmas present that he had chosen for his partner, Maureen, the week before. The shop was packed with Christmas shoppers, and, just to make Paddy's journey to the counter more difficult, two enormous men stood directly in front of him and blocked his view of the sales assistants. Paddy leant around one of the men to catch the proprietor's attention. 'Have you got Maureen's chain?' Paddy asked when the manager, whom he had known for a number of years, finally saw him.

'There you go,' the manager replied as he handed Paddy the gold chain. 'I'm rushed off my feet at the moment, so pop back in next week and pay me for it.'

Paddy thanked the manager, wished him and his staff a Merry Christmas and then left the shop with Garside. As Paddy and Garside walked back to their car, the two huge men who had been in the jeweller's came bounding towards them calling out Paddy's name. Paddy did not recognise the men, and the blank expression on his face must have made that fact obvious to them. 'It's me. Viv. You know me, Paddy. I'm Viv Graham,' one of the men said. Paddy exchanged pleasantries with Viv and introduced him and his friend to Garside. All the men shook hands. Paddy didn't really want anything to do with Viv, because he had fought his brother Michael, but being rude isn't his style. As Paddy turned to walk away, Viv said, 'Here, Paddy, I am told that the Sayers firm and the Conroys are coming down the town tonight to take over my doors.'

'Who told you that shite?' Paddy replied. 'If the Conroys were going to do anything, you would see or feel it, not hear about it.' Viv appeared unsure as to how to take Paddy's remark, and so he said that it was just a rumour he had heard and that he wanted to know if it was true. 'Put it this way, Viv,' Paddy said. 'If people do cause trouble with you tonight, do what you have to do, because there will be no Conroy men there.'

Viv's reaction was comical. He did a kind of war dance with his arms raised high above his head. 'Yes, yes, yes,' he shouted. 'Bring it on.'

That night, members of the Sayers firm went to the club where Viv was working, and a fight broke out. Viv smashed one of the firm repeatedly and broke his jaw; the rest were chased down the street. Viv Graham didn't know it, but, deeper and deeper, he was digging his own grave.

As the clock struck 12 a.m. on Saturday, 1 January 1994, a lot of Geordies were celebrating something other than the start of a new year. 'Viv no more in '94!' they chanted as the champagne corks popped. The news that Viv Graham had died after being gunned down in cold blood spread through Newcastle like wildfire and created a carnival atmosphere. Twelve hours earlier, Viv had been at home with his partner, Anna Connelly, before going to visit his parents and a childhood sweetheart named Gillian Lowes. He had wished his family and friend a Happy New Year before returning to Anna to spend what would be his last few hours on earth with her.

While researching this book, the author asked Anna Connelly if she would meet with him so that he could ask her in detail about events that day. Anna agreed, and in November 2008 the author met her at the Ship Inn, which is situated beneath Byker Bridge in the East End of Newcastle. Nearly 15 years had passed since Viv's murder, but Anna's love and passion for her man had more than stood the test of time. She told the author that she had initially hated those who had taken Viv's life but she now felt sorry for them. The following is Anna's version of events concerning the day that Viv Graham met his death: 'The night before Viv died, he had been at home with me. My sister was due to fly to Tenerife the following morning, and he had agreed to take her to Newcastle airport. Viv had told me before he left that once he had dropped my sister off he was going to call in at a friend's and his parents' house. Once he had wished them all a Happy New Year, he was then going to return home. I cannot now recall the time that he arrived back at our house, but I do remember that we laid out all of the clothes that we were going to wear that night on the bed. We always dressed smartly, and so getting ready to go out was a bit of a ritual, as we both liked everything to be just so. We had planned to have a drink with friends in Newcastle and then welcome in the New Year at a pub in Wallsend High Street.

'Before getting dressed, Viv said that he had to go down the town to check if everything was in order at the numerous venues where his door staff worked. Shortly after he had left the house, I received several silent phone calls. I was not unduly worried at the time. I thought that it was probably some drunken idiot playing a prank, but following Viv's murder it dawned on me that it was probably his killers trying to find out if he was home. I was tempted to stop answering the phone, but as it was New Year's Eve I thought I had better, just in case friends or family were trying to contact me.

'Viv had gone for a drink at a pub called the New Anchor in Wallsend High Street. Whilst there, the landlord had called Viv over to the bar, passed him a phone and said, "It's for you." As soon as Viv had hung up the phone, he told the landlord that he had just received a death threat. Witnesses later told the police that Viv had tried to disguise his fear but they had noticed that he did look troubled by the call. About an hour after Viv had left me, he rang to ask if I had received any "funny phone calls". He said that he had received a number of calls from a man with a

Geordie accent who was saying that he was going to be shot. The calls were threatening rather than well-meaning. Viv did not seem too concerned, but, knowing him as I did, I think it would have certainly made him more vigilant that night. That is what I do not understand about the way in which he was murdered. He was always so alert, expecting and ready for the unexpected to happen. This may sound odd, but Viv knew that he was going to die young; he used to say to me, "I will never see my 40th birthday." Something was obviously going on in his head. Something or somebody was warning him, and he clearly believed them. Sadly, he was right to do so.

'Viv was just 34 years old when he met his death in the street that night. He had been told on numerous occasions by friends that if he should ever return to his car and see that a tyre was flat or a window had been broken he should run. Apparently, would-be assassins do things like that so that their intended target is distracted and they can get in close to carry out their cowardly deed. After receiving the threatening phone calls, Viv would have undoubtedly been suspicious of everybody and everything around him. I have since been told that his drink was spiked, which made him sluggish. I don't know if it's true. I personally doubt it. In my opinion, his killers just got lucky. Before ending the call, I asked Viv if he would buy me some cigarettes and our dog some food, and he replied, "No problem. I will be home soon." At 4.15 p.m., Viv left the New Anchor and walked a few metres to the Queen's Head Hotel. I have no idea if his killers were watching him, but as far as I know he didn't receive any more calls and he remained in the Queen's Head until 6.05 p.m.

'Shortly after speaking to Viv, a man named Terry Scott came to my house and asked where Viv was. I thought that it was odd, because Viv's car was not outside and so Terry would have known that he wasn't home. Terry had Viv's mobile phone number, and so I don't understand why he hadn't called him directly rather than coming to the house to look for him. It has been suggested to me that Terry, who was considered by Viv to be a friend, might have been trying to locate him so that he could pass the information on to others, but I do not believe that this is true.

'When Viv left the Queen's Head, he had stopped at a corner shop which was en route to his car. He had wished the proprietor a Happy

New Year, and after paying for my cigarettes and the dog food he had given a young girl a handful of change. Viv was like that; he would always look after young children and the elderly. I find comfort in the fact that his last gesture on this earth was one of kindness. Moments later, Viv had walked through the shop door and out onto the street. The young girl had followed him. Less than ten seconds after leaving the shop, Viv was standing beside his car. It was dark, and he was concentrating on selecting his car key when he noticed that somebody had smashed a window in his vehicle. As he stood inspecting the damage, somebody had called out, "Happy fucking New Year, Viv."

'The young girl who had followed Viv out of the corner shop later told police that she saw that Viv had turned to see who was calling him and then she heard three loud explosions. Viv had then crumpled to the floor. The shopkeeper also heard the loud bangs and saw Viv crawling along the street. As the shopkeeper rushed outside to assist Viv, he saw that Terry Scott had run out of the Queen's Head and appeared to be chasing somebody. Scott had clearly found Viv after leaving my house. When Scott returned to assist Viv, he leant over him and tried to lift him back onto his feet. "I am going. I am going," Viv had said. A taxi driver stopped and also ran to Viv's aid. He later said that Viv had kept pulling his shirt down to cover his wound and was saying, "Get me up onto my feet. Don't let people see me like this. I do not want anybody to see me down." As Viv tried to grab what remained of his shirt, he could feel the gaping wounds in his body and said, "Oh, they have done it this time. Look after Anna, my mother and father and the kids, because I am going." Some of the people who were trying to help Viv did try to do as he asked and get him to his feet, but the massive holes that the powerful 3.57 Magnum bullets had punched through his body prevented him from remaining upright. It was as if he had been blown almost in half.

'As I continued to get ready at home, I received a phone call from my uncle, who is employed as a taxi driver. He said that he had been dropping customers off in Wallsend High Street and he had heard that there had been some sort of incident there. "I think it's your Viv that's involved, and I think that he has been shot," he said.

'"It couldn't be Viv. I only spoke to him a few minutes ago," I replied.

'As we were talking, Viv's friend Bopper came to the house, and he appeared to be extremely upset. Bopper didn't knock the door as normal; he just appeared in my front room, which really alarmed me. I was sitting on the sofa in my pyjamas, and so I asked him what he thought he was doing barging into my home. "Your Viv's been shot, Anna. Get yourself ready quickly, and I will take you to the hospital," he replied. I am uncertain of much of the content of any conversations that I had thereafter. My mind was racing, but everything around me appeared to be happening in slow motion.

'"What do you think, Bopper? Is Viv going to be OK?" I asked.

'"I think . . . I think . . . I don't know what I think," he blurted out. "Let's just get you to the hospital."

'When we arrived, the ambulance transporting Viv had not yet reached the accident and emergency department. I later learned that a police officer who travelled with Viv was talking to him in an effort to gather evidence and keep him conscious. Leaning over Viv, the officer had said, "You saw who it was, Viv, because they didn't have masks on. Just give me a name." The officer knew the men had not tried to hide their identities, because the young girl who Viv had earlier given money to had described seeing three unmasked men lurking near the crime scene before she went into the shop. Viv had looked up at the officer through his dying eyes, but he did not answer. He appeared to be calm, the officer said later, "concentrating on his fight to remain alive rather than wanting to answer my questions".

'Pacing nervously around the entrance to the accident and emergency department, I could see that a team of medics were eagerly waiting just inside a pair of clear plastic doors. Minutes felt like hours as we all waited, but then all of a sudden the medical team began talking loudly to one another as an ambulance backed up to the doors and Viv emerged on a stretcher. I felt relieved, because I could see that he was alive. He was conscious and looking all around. I was so overcome by emotion that I burst out crying and called out his name. Looking up at me, Viv forced a smile and told me to dry my eyes, before being whisked away to an operating theatre. I tried hard, but I was unable to do as Viv had asked, and so my tears continued to flow as I stared at the operating theatre doors waiting for somebody with news to emerge. A police officer sat down next to me and tried to reassure me by saying,

"Don't worry, Anna. Viv is a big, strong lad. He will be OK."

'A few minutes later, a surgeon came out of the operating theatre and ushered me into a small office. "His heart stopped twice on the way here. He is still fighting hard for his life. There is a hole the size of a melon in his back, and so it is a miracle that he is still with us," he said. The hospital waiting room was packed with Viv's friends. They all offered words of comfort and support, but I wasn't listening. My eyes were fixed firmly on the doors behind which I knew my Viv was lying. Terry Scott appeared in the waiting room and began running up and down, punching the walls and shouting. I really didn't know what to make of his behaviour. It was disturbing to say the least. I had telephoned Viv's parents and other family members, and when they arrived we sat huddled together in an effort to comfort one another.

'After what felt like an age, Viv's father, my father and me were eventually called and taken into a small room by a grave-faced surgeon. He didn't need to speak. I just knew what he was going to say. I just had the most awful feeling in my heart imaginable. When we entered the room, we were invited to sit down, and five members of the medical team stood before us. As soon as they said, "We have tried our best, but . . ." we all broke down. A surgeon held my arm and said to me, "Please do not think for one moment that we did not do all we could have done to save Viv's life. I assure you that we fought on even when we realised that all hope had gone." The surgeon's words were sincere, and I found them really comforting. At least Viv died in the company of people that cared, rather than instantly, which would have meant his last contact would have been with animals full of hate.

'Forty pints of blood were used to try to save Viv, but the medical team explained that it was pouring out of his body quicker than they could pump it into him. Nearly four hours after being shot, my brave and gentle Viv had conceded defeat for the first and last time in his life. I honestly cannot remember too much after his death was announced, because I was beside myself with grief. I did ask if I could go to Viv, as I felt an overwhelming need to be close to him. I was led into a side room and left alone with Viv, who lay beneath a white sheet on a hospital trolley.

'I used to work in nursing homes and have had the misfortune of seeing several deceased people. They had all remained warm for some time after death, but when I held Viv to cuddle him he felt unusually cold. I don't know if I am right or wrong, but I formed the opinion that he had been dead for some time. Perhaps his body felt so cold because of the massive blood loss that he had suffered, or perhaps the police did not want to announce his death straight away, because it could have sparked trouble in the town. All of the people that Viv had excluded from pubs and clubs over the years might have heard about his death and returned en masse to the various venues, and the police might not have had the manpower to deal with such an event.

'I honestly don't know what I was thinking that night. Irrelevant events came flooding back to me as if they were important, and relevant events, such as the threatening phone calls, somehow seemed trivial. The medical people could see the effect the news was having on me, and so I was given a sedative and taken home. I have five brothers and three sisters, and I can recall them being there for me in the days and weeks that followed. I thank God that I had them; they really did help me through the darkest times, of which there were many.

'The presence of the police at my home became an everyday fact of life. They sifted through all of Viv's possessions, scrutinised every note that he had ever written and asked me repeatedly about who he knew, how he got on with them, where he went and why. It was an upsetting, tiring and very emotional time, but I kept telling myself that I had to go through with it for Viv, his parents, his children and the love we had shared, and so I bit my lip and persevered. I did go to the mortuary to say my goodbyes to Viv, but I found it to be an extremely distressing experience. The procedures that the pathologists had to carry out in order to perform the autopsy had dramatically altered his handsome features. I knew in my heart that Viv had gone to another place, and so I left the mortuary and I grieved for the man I loved in the house of God, where I knew he would be. I am a deeply religious person, and my faith has undoubtedly brought me a lot of comfort throughout this terrible ordeal.

'The police have told me that they believe that Viv was murdered simply because he refused to let a major drug gang in the city sell their vile wares in the premises where he ran security. One thousand people have been interviewed regarding Viv's murder. Five hundred homes have been visited, but nobody has been charged. Initially, every little villain in the north-east bragged about being involved in the shooting, but as they have grown older and wiser one by one they have changed their stories and denied knowing anything. So many people still claim to know the identity of Viv's killers. They accuse and blame one another, but when I ask for proof none is forthcoming. I actually carry a Bible in my bag to this day and ask people to take an oath before they utter another word about Viv's death. Most think that I am joking, but when I persevere few do as I ask.

'I must admit that I do have a fear that somebody claiming to be a friend of mine or somebody who may sit in my company could have played a part in the killing. I am in no doubt that the truth will come out one day, because the police have never given up investigating the case, and they assure me that as allegiances change and people grow older somebody somewhere will talk. Recently, a man who claimed to be very close to the killers was facing a lengthy prison sentence and described what had happened to the police in an off-the-record interview in the hope that he would secure a reduced sentence. I am not privy to exactly what was said, nor do I know his identity, but I do know that the police were on the verge of a breakthrough. I don't know if the man concerned is still going to go through with telling all he knows. I have simply been informed that he is considering his options.

'At first, I was full of hatred for Viv's killers, and I do not mind admitting that I felt that they should suffer a similar fate. I do not feel that way any more. They have to live with what they have done, and they will face justice one day, whether that is here on earth or when they pass away. If they are reading this, I would like to say that I cannot understand why you did such a thing. Why would you take another human being's life away, regardless of what they may or may not have said or done to you? Viv was not a danger to you or anybody else. He was simply doing his job by stopping you from selling drugs, which is an abhorrent trade in any event, because it claims lives and destroys families. In many ways, I feel pity for you. The cowardly act you have committed is nothing to boast about or be proud of; in fact, you should hang your heads in shame. Viv Graham was more of a man than any of you will ever be. I know that, and you know that, which is why you were not men enough to face him.'

Detective Chief Superintendent Barry Stewart, who was head of

Northumbria Police CID, took charge of the murder inquiry. With such a high-profile victim, known to every member of the criminal fraternity in the north-east, it was inevitable that the investigation was going to be burdened with fruitless leads and speculation. The police did establish that a stolen blue Ford Escort, registration number G668 DTF, had been seen in the vicinity of the murder at the relevant time. It had been parked in a dark back lane close to where Viv regularly parked his car. A man had also been seen leaving the Queen's Head Hotel shortly before Viv. Described as being approximately 5 ft 2 in. tall with mousey hair, this man had walked in the direction of Viv's car and may have been alerting his co-conspirators that their target was on his way.

After the killers had struck, they sped away from the scene to Simonside Terrace, in Heaton, where the blue Escort was found burned out. A blonde woman had also been seen hanging around near the spot where Viv was shot. One eyewitness claimed that this mystery woman had actually gone over to look at Viv as he lay dying in the street. Considering Wallsend High Street is, as it suggests, a main shopping thoroughfare, it is hardly surprising that various individuals were strolling up and down it, seemingly doing nothing other than looking.

Within a month of the murder, Northumbria Police arrested five suspects in dawn raids. Alan Wheat, an ex-boxer from Cheshire, and Karen Young, Alan Young, Darren Arnold and Brian Tait, all from Wallsend, were kept at separate police stations, questioned and released on bail. The police seemed to think that these locals had recruited their friend from Cheshire to dispose of Viv simply because he had been throwing his weight around in the pubs around Wallsend.

In March 1994, two other men, from the West End of Newcastle, were arrested for the murder in dawn raids. They were questioned throughout the day at Wallsend Police Station, and one of them, Michael Sayers, was bailed pending further inquiries the following afternoon. The other man, Lee Watson, who gave his address as the Ord Arms pub, in Newcastle, was found to have outstanding warrants for assaulting police officers and driving with excess alcohol. As well as these warrants, Watson had an outstanding extradition warrant, which the Swiss police had applied for in August 1993 following a £300,000 robbery at a jeweller's in Zurich. Watson was therefore refused bail and transferred to Gateshead, where he appeared in court.

The magistrates adjourned the case for three months and ordered that Watson be taken to Bow Street Court, in London, for the extradition process to begin. Clearly upset by this decision, Watson stunned the court by shouting a tirade of foul-mouthed abuse and boasting, 'You couldn't catch us for the shooting of Viv Graham.' When questioned by detectives about his claim, Watson would only say that he had been given information by his underworld associates about who was behind the murder. He did add that he wasn't prepared to say if he was involved in the shooting in any way, 'on the grounds that I might incriminate myself'. Watson was eventually extradited to Switzerland, where he was sentenced to seven and a half years' imprisonment.

By April 1994, the murder inquiry appeared to be going nowhere. The volume of information that the police had received was unprecedented, but the vast majority of it was based on myth, lies or hearsay. Viv Graham's reputation had served him well in life, but in death it was depriving him of justice. Following Viv's murder, Michael Sayers began to call at Paddy Conroy's home, which somewhat surprised Paddy. Michael didn't appear to want anything in particular and Paddy did not wish to appear rude, and so they sat and chatted about everyday events. Occasionally, they would have a drink together or drive around the neighbourhood, visiting mutual friends. Paddy believed that the friendship was beneficial to both families, because it would ensure that the peace was kept between them.

One afternoon, Michael Sayers called at Paddy's house saying that he had been arrested for some misdemeanour or other and that, while in the police station, Paddy's old adversary DC Perky had told Michael that Paddy was a grass. 'I am not saying that you are, Paddy. I am just warning you about what this particular officer is saying,' Michael said.

Paddy immediately drove down to the police station and demanded to see DC Perky. The desk sergeant informed Paddy that he was not on duty, and so Paddy asked him to pass on a message word for word. 'Tell Perky that when I see him he is fucking dead,' Paddy said.

The following morning, Paddy went to a flower shop owned by a lady named Ella Knights and ordered a wreath for DC Perky with his name, address and condolences written on the greeting card. Later that day, Ella's son Freddie delivered the wreath to the police station. Paddy never did get a thank-you call from DC Perky, but the image of Freddie Knights walking into a police station with a funeral wreath in his hands has never left him.

Chapter Six

THE ENEMY WITHIN

ON THURSDAY, 16 July 1992, an incident occurred at the Oz nightclub in South Shields. A gang that included David Glover junior, Dave Garside and a man named Scott Waters entered the nightclub at approximately 11 p.m. A notorious Newcastle villain named Philip Abadom immediately left the premises at speed and was pursued by the group. Minutes later, Abadom was found unconscious outside a nearby public house. He was taken to hospital, where he remained for several days in a serious condition. The head of South Shields CID, Detective Inspector Ian Smith, led the investigation into the incident and soon arrested ten men, who had been captured on CCTV entering the club. Those arrested, interviewed and bailed pending further inquiries included Glover, Garside and Waters.

Soon after being bailed, Glover was arrested in relation to another matter and remanded in custody to await trial. When Glover appeared at South Shields Magistrates' Court, an officer named DCI Felton attended in the hope that he could interview him further about the attack on Abadom. Before DCI Felton could do so, he received a message from Glover stating that he wanted to see him alone and stressing that he did not want his solicitor to know. DCI Felton spoke to Glover briefly in an interview room, and Glover said that he had information he would like to give to the police in exchange for certain matters, which he refused to elaborate upon. Glover said that it was vitally important that his solicitor must not know about his offer to inform, as he represented some of the people whom he wished to give information about. DCI Felton told Glover that he would have to be interviewed about the assault on Abadom in front of his solicitor but that if he was charged and wished to talk again afterwards then that could be arranged.

Following a six-minute interview, Glover was subsequently charged with assaulting Abadom. After his solicitor had departed, Glover was returned to the interview room to talk to DCI Felton alone. Glover offered to give information about the importation and distribution of large quantities of drugs, which he alleged that the Conroy family, Dave Garside, Michael Bullock, Scott Waters and a man named John Chisholm were responsible for. Glover spoke for 45 minutes, while DCI Felton took notes. At the end of the conversation, Glover agreed to become a registered police informant and was given the pseudonym Adrian Scott. Before they parted company, Glover promised DCI Felton that he would relate to the police 'any information' he became aware of about 'the activities of the Conroy family'.

All registered police informants are given false names. Self-proclaimed cockney 'gangster' Dave Courtney was given the name Tommy Mack when he registered as an informant with the Metropolitan Police, and Darren Nicholls, who informed on the men convicted of the 1995 Rettendon Range Rover murders, was given the name Ken Rugby by Essex Police. Informants are given these pseudonyms to prevent their true identity and treachery being discovered by people who may eavesdrop on conversations or catch sight of names on paperwork that they were not meant to see. It is a seedy and rather abhorrent way to live one's life. Little wonder Judas Iscariot went out to hang himself after betraying Jesus Christ. It's a pity his modern-day counterparts aren't man enough to do the same.

Glover appeared to believe that he was a law unto himself after being given the status of police informant. He realised that if he got caught doing anything illegal all he would have to do to avoid justice would be to claim that somebody else had committed a more heinous crime, the details of which he would then trade for immunity from prosecution. In effect, he had a licence to break the law without any fear of retribution or penalty. After pledging his allegiance to Northumbria Police, Glover was granted bail and DCI Felton obtained permission from his superiors to allow Glover to deliver a huge parcel of drugs to an address on Tyneside that was allegedly linked to the Conroy family. This plot to incarcerate the Conroys failed miserably, but Glover, despite his incompetence, was kept on the police payroll. Paddy didn't discover the full extent of Glover's treachery until several years later, when it turned out to be too late. In the interim period, Paddy foolishly allowed Glover into his company, where he was was secretly conspiring against him, inventing stories and fabricating scenarios.

The war that had waged on Tyneside between the Conroys and the Harrisons had been an opportunity for other members of the criminal fraternity to vent their anger upon their enemies without fear of detection. Every incident involving guns or knives was linked by the media and the police to 'the ongoing feud involving the Conroys'. It would be naive to suggest that the Harrisons and the Conroys were totally innocent, but they and those loyal to them were certainly not responsible for every casualty during those troubled times.

The Harrisons' uncle Jimmy 'Psycho' Summerville was drinking with two friends in the Star Inn in Newcastle city centre one evening when gunmen walked in and blasted them with shotguns. All three men survived, but two of them suffered injuries that were so severe that they each lost a leg. Witnesses to the shooting described the scene as a bloodbath. After seeing the horrific injuries the gunshots had caused, one barmaid was taken to hospital suffering from shock. Despite the fact that it was a member of the Harrison family who had been shot, nobody could say with any certainty that it was a Conroy who was responsible. One man who undoubtedly was a victim of the Conroy firm was Billy Collier.

He was rumoured to have desecrated the Conroy family grave. Collier had been arrested alongside the Harrisons for allegedly being involved in battles during the bloody feud but had been released without charge before their trial and subsequent imprisonment. Paddy made it known that he was looking for Collier. He also told his associates that if Collier had any sense he would leave the north-east and never return. Unfortunately for Billy Collier, he didn't possess any sense.

It's important that people understand the type of individuals the Conroys were up against in this feud. In 1988, Collier had been imprisoned for three years after being convicted of mugging a frail seventy-four-year-old woman. Walking home, the pensioner was finding her way in the November darkness with a torch. She was also clutching a panic alarm. Collier, who was 17 at the time, pushed this lady to the ground and tried grabbing her handbag. As the shrieks from the lady and her personal alarm filled Collier's ears, he panicked and became more violent in his effort to snatch the bag. When he finally walked away with the pensioner's meagre possessions in his grubby hands, she was left lying on the pavement with a broken arm and pelvis. Traumatised by the cowardly attack that had been carried out on her, the lady no longer felt safe being on her own, and so she sold her home to go to live with a family member.

Collier's other achievements in life include convictions for theft, going equipped for theft, stealing cars, driving while disqualified and burglary. Paddy Conroy had been wrongly convicted and given a five-year prison sentence for hitting an able-bodied policeman, while Collier had got three years for robbing a pensioner and breaking her arm and pelvis. Justice? Don't make me laugh. That's not justice; that's an insult to Collier's frail and elderly victim. One can begin to understand why people like the Conroys never involve the police and prefer to serve up their own brand of justice.

On Sunday, 13 March 1994, 23-year-old Billy Collier and his girlfriend, Michelle Mathews, took a mid-morning stroll to a local convenience store in order to purchase cigarettes. These days, every packet carries a government health warning about the damage smoking can cause, but I very much doubt that Collier had any idea just how much damage his habit was about to cause him. Dean Afzel, who was working at the John and Sons store on Elswick Road that day, later told police, 'At about noon, Billy Collier was in the shop with his girlfriend. I was sitting at the till with my back to the shop door. Billy and Michelle were both leaning against the freezer in the centre of the shop talking to me. After approximately ten minutes, I suddenly became aware of a male entering the shop and grabbing hold of me. My first thought was that I was being robbed. My instincts took over, and I managed to break free. I ran along the side of the freezers and straight out into the back of the shop, where I locked myself in the storage area. After ten minutes, I unlocked the door and made my way back into the shop. Both Billy Collier and his girlfriend had disappeared.'

According to Collier, when Afzel had sought refuge at the rear of his shop, three or four men had grabbed him. One of these men was David Glover junior; the two others were Scott Waters and Paddy Conroy. Struggling and shouting for help, Collier was dragged out of the shop and forced into the back of a red Range Rover. Moments later, Northumbria Police received a frantic call from Collier's mother:

Q: Hello, police control room, can I help you?
A: Aye, Mrs Collier here. My son, Billy Collier . . . erm . . . a lad called Davy Glover and his mates have just took him away.
Q: Right, do you know where they are taking him?
A: They are taking him to do him over. I don't know where they are taking him.

When the vehicle pulled away, Collier was systematically kicked and punched. After five or ten minutes, the vehicle pulled up outside Glover's house, in Chesterfield Road, and Collier was then led into a neighbour's backyard. Blood was pouring from his nose and several superficial wounds to his face. Collier says that, once his kidnappers were all in the yard, he was ordered to sit on the floor but refused, and so two men forced him down. Collier was then beaten repeatedly across the legs with a 6-ft long stick. He was screaming and shouting about being unable to feel his legs, but this did not stop the man who was wielding the weapon from thrashing him. In fact, the man stopped beating Collier only after the stick had snapped on two separate occasions. Collier claimed that the man was Paddy Conroy and that, as Paddy stood back after administering that beating, David Glover picked up a heavy Calor gas bottle, raised it above his head and then smashed it down onto his legs. When Collier screamed in pain, Glover is said to have picked up the gas bottle again and brought it down on Collier's legs four more times. Collier was sobbing and pleading for his life, but he claimed Paddy and Glover refused to show him any mercy. According to Collier, the attack then continued. He said that his head was kicked and punched like a football and his blood was splashed up the walls.

It was alleged that, during the beating, somebody repeatedly shouted, 'You're going to get it, you little bastard, Billy. You're going to get it.' If somebody had been shouting such a thing, it was a naive comment to make, because, by anybody's standards, Billy Collier was already 'getting it'. After approximately 15 minutes, Collier appeared to be losing consciousness, and so the assault ceased and he was ordered to get to his feet. Collier, barely able to see because of the mask of blood that covered what had once been his face, tried to stand up, but he just kept collapsing in a heap. 'I cannot get up. I cannot get up. There is no feeling in my legs', he whined. As he continued to plead to be spared further punishment, Collier was dragged back out of the yard and bundled once more into the Range Rover.

Moments after Collier's mother had telephoned the police, they had received a second call:

> Q: Hello, police emergency, can I help you?
> A: Hello, there's some people beating up somebody at Chesterfield Road.
> Q: At the West End?
> A: Yeah, the corner house. It's in the backyard. They have got a big canister, and they are beating somebody with it, and somebody's screaming.
> Q: What's your name?
> A: I don't really want to give my name.

Somebody being assaulted in the West End of Newcastle was hardly going to result in all police leave being cancelled, but, coupled with the fact Mrs Collier had reported an abduction, officers on patrol were asked to be extra vigilant.

As Collier was driven around the West End, he was repeatedly stamped on and punched in the face and upper torso. When the Range Rover eventually came to a halt, two pillowcases were placed over Collier's blood-soaked head and he was dragged along the ground to a house in Westmoreland Road. Once inside, the pillowcases were removed. Collier was then handcuffed, his legs were tied up with rope and he was subjected to yet another wave of flaying fists and boots. Because Collier's hands were manacled behind his back and his knees were secured in the foetal position, he was unable to protect his head and upper body during this attack. It was clear to everybody present that Collier was not going to remain conscious for much longer, and so he was left to try to compose himself.

It is alleged by those who were present that during the beatings Collier admitted that he had been paid £5,000 to dig up Leonard Conroy's corpse, mutilate it and throw body parts through the windows of a family member's home. At that point, Paddy claims that he told Collier that he wanted him to repeat the story to his brother Michael. Collier agreed, and so Paddy drove him to a flat belonging to one of Glover's friends and told him to wait there while he fetched his brother. According to Paddy Conroy, it was while he was away fetching his brother that Billy Collier was tortured.

Collier later told police, 'A man who the others referred to as Scott was coming towards me with a pair of pliers. I was not struggling because I thought if I had a chance of living through this it would be better to accept the punishment. Scott put the pliers to the right-hand side of my nose and nipped them together. He then pulled them off my nose in the closed position. The pain was unbelievable. I couldn't stand much more. He then put the pliers on the flap of cartilage between my nostrils and squeezed them into the closed position. He then twisted the pliers and tore my septum out. I was screaming in agony but they were just laughing at me. Scott then put the pliers in my mouth and gripped one of my front teeth. I could feel the tooth cracking and snapping as Scott applied more pressure. He did this to another tooth before twisting it and ripping it from my mouth; again, the pain was immense. A piece of my right ear was then severed using the pliers. I thought they had torn the whole ear off, there was so much blood. I cannot express the trauma that these acts caused me. I felt sick, dizzy and all the emotions one associates with extreme and prolonged pain. Those present continued to laugh or kick me like a football, as if it were some sort of game.

'I was then left in the room on my own. I was in extreme pain, there was blood everywhere and I was violently sick. I was sure that when they returned they would finish me off. I mean kill me. I heard the front door close, which suggested to me that the men had left the house. About five minutes later, I noticed that the pliers had been left on a desk, and so I rolled over, picked them up and after a bit of a struggle I managed to free myself from the rope around my legs. I got to my feet, sat on the windowsill and somehow managed to open the window. I had no idea where I was at this stage. Directly below the window was an area of grass with a blue fence. I could also see houses. I tried to make my escape through the window, but I was still handcuffed. I managed to get halfway out of the window when a man I know named Paul "Peachy" Poland arrived and pushed me back inside. Peachy then climbed in through the window himself and closed it. It was then that Peachy told me that Paddy Conroy had already been arrested for assaulting me. Peachy told me that I had to go to the police station and tell them it wasn't Paddy but make up another story of events. I would then be left alone for good. I was so relieved I could not believe it. I honestly thought that they were going to kill me. I agreed to Peachy's request simply because I did not want to die. I had endured enough punishment, and I feared for my family.'

When Paddy left the flat of Glover's friend, he had gone to his brother's house before returning to his own home to wash Collier's blood off his face. While Paddy had been extracting the truth from Collier about the desecration of his family's grave, Collier had been crying and had sprayed or spat specks of blood all over him. Collier was a heroin addict, and the very thought of his bodily fluids being around Paddy's mouth sickened him. That is why Paddy felt it important that he should return home to get washed and changed. Once Paddy had cleaned himself up, he drove over to the flat, where he had last seen Collier, but the owner told him that Glover and Collier had begun fighting in the bathroom and so had been ordered to leave. Paddy was told that before Glover had departed he had left a message for Paddy to meet him at a house in Westmoreland Road.

When Paddy arrived, Glover had already left, and only Collier and Glover's friend remained. When Paddy saw what had been done to Collier, he dragged Glover's friend out of the flat, sat him in the car and asked him why they had given Collier a complimentary nose job and dentistry. 'It wasn't intended,' Glover's friend replied. 'We only meant to frighten him by putting the pliers on his tooth, but it crumbled.' The use of heroin does cause teeth to become brittle, and so it seemed like a feasible explanation, but no explanation was forthcoming regarding Collier's other missing body parts. While Paddy was remonstrating with Glover's associate, a police car arrived in the street. The driver glared at Paddy and then accelerated away out of sight.

A few moments later, the police car returned and pulled into a communal parking area, where the driver had a clear view of Paddy's Range Rover. Paddy told Glover's friend to get out of his car and then started the engine and drove out of the street. As Paddy did so, he saw that Glover was heading back towards the flat. Paddy had no idea if Glover could see him, because Glover was looking in the direction of the police car. As Glover drew level with the vehicle, he waved at the officer inside and the officer waved back. Paddy stopped his vehicle, and when Glover did eventually make eye contact with him Paddy wound down the window to talk to him. 'Be careful, Paddy,' Glover said. 'There is a policeman parked just behind me.'

'I know. I've already seen him,' Paddy replied, before accelerating away.

PC Noble, the officer in the police vehicle, immediately began to pursue him. After a few hundred yards, Paddy noticed that PC Noble had been joined by colleagues in another vehicle, and so he pulled over. As the two police cars parked alongside the Range Rover, Paddy wound down the window. 'Conroy . . .' PC Noble began, but before he could say another word Paddy interrupted by saying, 'Fuck off you pair of daft bastards.' He then slammed his vehicle into gear and sped away.

For the next 15 minutes, Paddy was chased at speed by several police vehicles and a police helicopter around the Scotswood, Benwell and Elswick areas of Newcastle. Paddy knew that he didn't have a chance of outrunning the police, but he had no intention of making their job easy. When Paddy had grown tired of the cat-and-mouse game, he drove on to a grassed area behind the Noble Street flats and stepped out of his vehicle with his hands raised. Paddy was then arrested on suspicion of abduction and taken to Newcastle City West Police Station, where he was informed that he would also be charged with dangerous driving.

When Peachy and Collier arrived at the police station, Peachy sat in the waiting area and Collier went to the front desk, where he demanded to speak to the officers involved in the case. Collier was taken to an isolated room on the second floor, where he was seen by DS Thomas and DC Gallagher. Collier told the detectives that he owed money to people from Gateshead but he did not wish to name them. He said that he had been taken by five or six of these men and beaten. Collier was adamant that Paddy had not been involved in his abduction or assault. The detectives refused to believe Collier and urged him to tell the truth.

However, Collier refused to be swayed and said that if the police refused to let him leave the station he would jump out of the window and onto the ground, some 25 ft below. Shortly after Collier had left the police station (via the front door), Paddy was released.

Two days later, on Tuesday, 15 March 1994, Collier was walking near his home when he saw a white motor vehicle pull up approximately twenty yards from him. A man wearing a cap leant out of the window and pointed a gun directly at his head. As he turned to run, Collier heard two loud explosions, but fortunately the gunman had missed him. Later that day, in fear of his life, Collier contacted the police and asked for protection. When asked why he might need protecting, Collier blurted out a story about the attempt on his life being linked to his kidnap and torture. It's not difficult to imagine the smiles on the faces of some of the police officers when Collier agreed to make a statement implicating Paddy Conroy. They arrested Glover two days later, and Peachy was taken into custody soon afterwards.

Paddy was told about the arrests, and he warned Scott Waters that he too might have been implicated by Collier. Two weeks after Collier had walked back into the police station, Waters was arrested. Paddy continued to go about his everyday business as normal, but he knew that it was only a matter of time before the police would swoop on him. The day after Waters' arrest, Paddy travelled to Leeds to meet a friend at the Stakis Windmill Hotel. He could sense that something was not quite right as soon as he arrived. Shortly after Paddy had gone to his room, there was a knock at his door, and when he opened it officers from the Drug Squad and the Regional Crime Squad burst in, waving guns and shouting that he was under arrest. Paddy was taken back to Newcastle, interviewed and charged with several offences relating to Collier. When he appeared in court the following morning, he was remanded in custody with his co-accused to await trial.

While Paddy and Glover were on remand at HMP Holme House, in Durham, Glover talked of little other than escaping. He had managed to break free from captivity several times in the past and told Paddy just how easy it could be. At first, Paddy was sceptical, but the more Glover talked the more he realised that freedom was an option.

On Wednesday, 27 April 1994, Paddy and Glover were due to appear at Newcastle Magistrates' Court for a pre-trial review. On previous occasions they had appeared at court, Paddy and Glover had been transported in a minibus taxi and handcuffed to burly prison officers. This was because they were the only prisoners in HMP Holme House who were having a case heard in Newcastle, and it wasn't cost-effective to send two prisoners there in a large prison van. Glover has extremely large, thick wrists, and he told Paddy that handcuffs didn't fit him very well and so he was often able to slip them off. In order to make his task even easier, Glover had filled an empty peanut packet with washing-up liquid, which he secreted between the cheeks of his backside. The pair thought that they would be handcuffed together, which had been the case on previous occasions, but for reasons never explained they were manacled to two separate prison officers. Glover's basic but admittedly feasible plan was in tatters.

The place Glover had chosen to make the escape bid was along the Felling Bypass, a section of road that adjoins Newcastle and Gateshead and which was heavily congested at the time owing to ongoing roadworks. Two cars containing the associates of Paddy and Glover would be shadowing the taxi. A BMW was to transport the duo away from the scene, and a Range Rover containing four burly men was to ensure that if anybody intervened during the escape they could be dealt with. As the taxi neared the roadworks, Paddy looked out of the window and alongside saw the two cars full of his co-conspirators. Paddy nodded at the man in the front passenger seat of one vehicle, and he acknowledged him by smiling. Glover, who was sitting directly in front of Paddy, kept turning around and grimacing, as if to say, 'Do something.' Because both men were handcuffed to different prison officers and were seated apart in the taxi, Paddy didn't for one moment believe that Glover was going to go through with his attempt to escape.

They were still travelling at approximately 70 mph when Glover suddenly stood up and roared, 'We have got fucking help! We have got fucking help!' Glover then grabbed the handbrake with his free hand, and the minibus lurched across the carriageway before spinning round and round. After what seemed like an age but was probably just a matter of seconds, the minibus came to rest on the hard shoulder facing the wrong way up the road. The unsuspecting prison officers had been tossed around the taxi like rag dolls after Glover had pulled on the handbrake, and so they were still disorientated when the vehicle eventually stopped. Glover punched one of the officers in the face and shouted, 'Get my fucking cuffs off!' a request the stunned man felt more than obliged to comply with. The officer was assaulted again and suffered a broken arm. A female prison officer was struck on the head. Once free, Glover leapt out of the minibus, just as the getaway car pulled up next to him. People at the scene later told the police that the men in the car were armed with shotguns.

Paddy was convinced that Glover was going to save himself and leave him shackled to a prison officer. Glover stopped suddenly and, almost as an afterthought, returned to the taxi and shouted at the officer to release Paddy. The prison officer who was handcuffed to Paddy glanced down at their wrists and then back at his keys. Paddy knew that he wasn't going to resist, and so he raised his hands for the officer to release him. As soon as Paddy was free, he ran to the getaway car and jumped in. Glover grabbed a briefcase that was on the front passenger seat of the taxi before joining Paddy and their associates in the car. After the ambush, the prison officers ran into a nearby petrol station to call for help. The cashier later told police, 'The female officer was shaking terribly and couldn't talk coherently, she was so scared. At first I didn't know who she was, but then I saw a badge on her shoulder and she said that she had been held up by a gang with shotguns and knives.'

As the getaway vehicle roared down the road towards Newcastle, Glover opened the briefcase that he had stolen and pulled out a brown envelope, which contained £2,200 of Paddy's private cash. It had been in the vehicle because the Prison Service is obliged to take all inmates' personal possessions to each court hearing, just in case they are released. 'Fucking hell! Two grand,' Glover said as he tore open the envelope.

'I'll have that, thanks. It's mine,' Paddy said, snatching the wad of cash from Glover's grasp. As the getaway vehicle continued to make its way through the roadworks, a steady stream of police cars travelling in the opposite direction flashed past, with sirens blaring. The fugitives were left in no doubt that their audacious escape had now been reported. The speeding car entered Newcastle by driving over the swing bridge that spans the Tyne, before making its way down to the Quayside. Because progress was slowed to walking pace by the early-morning traffic, Paddy opened the car door and jumped out. 'I will see you lads

Ronnie Kray (second from left) at the Mayfair Club, Newcastle. (© John Carter)

Leonard Conroy is arrested on the pitch at St James' Park in the 1974 FA Cup quarter-final between Newcastle and Nottingham Forest. (courtesy of the author)

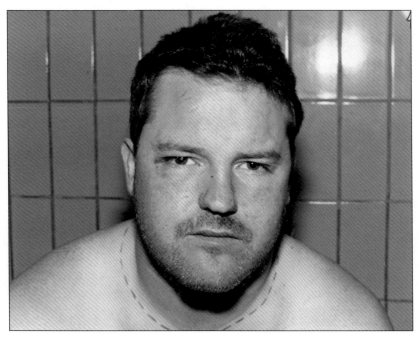

Paddy Conroy following his arrest for allegedly assaulting
two police officers. (courtesy of the author)

Residents in the West End of Newcastle protesting against
Paddy Conroy's arrest and treatment. (courtesy of the author)

The lorry originally driven by Michael 'the Bull' Bullock on the protest.
In this photo, John Henry Sayers is at the wheel. Among those on the
roof are members of the Harrison family. (courtesy of the author)

Legendary Tyneside fighter Billy Robinson (© Brian Anderson)

Viv Graham, Newcastle's fourth
emergency service. (© Anna Connelly)

'Geordie Mafia' member Kenneth
'Panda' Anderson. (© Brian Anderson)

Bernard O'Mahoney and Stuart Watson. (© Brian Anderson)

From left to right:
Alan 'Fish' Tams,
Bernard O'Mahoney
and Stephen Sayers.
(© Brian Anderson)

Paddy Conroy has
changed the company
he keeps since his
release from prison.
(© Brian Anderson)

David Glover and Bernard O'Mahoney. (© Brian Anderson)

From left to right: Lenny Conroy, Paddy Conroy, Vinney King and Michael 'the Bull' Bullock. (courtesy of the author)

Paddy Conroy enjoying freedom and the sun in Spain
following his daring escape. (courtesy of the author)

Bernard O'Mahoney and Brian 'the Tax Man' Cockerill. (© Brian Anderson)

John Henry Sayers. (courtesy of the author)

Murder victim Freddie Knights. (courtesy of the author)

later,' he said before disappearing into the crowds of commuters and shoppers.

Paddy walked to a nearby scrapyard, owned by a friend of his, but the friend did not appear to be on site. Paddy waved down a vehicle that was leaving the yard and said that he had broken down and needed a lift to the home of the owner of the scrapyard as he had important business with him. The lift cost Paddy £40, but it was money well spent, because it got him out of the city centre and into the suburbs. 'What the fuck are you doing here?' the scrapyard owner said when Paddy knocked on his door. 'You're supposed to be in jail.'

'The less you know the better,' Paddy replied. 'I need a lift to Scotland.'

Later that night, Paddy was sitting in the home of a Glasgow acquaintance celebrating his freedom with an ice-cold glass of beer. The escape was the leading story on the news that night, and a police spokesman claimed that Paddy was now the most wanted man in Britain. Paddy's host looked at the television, looked at Paddy and burst out laughing. 'Fucking hell,' he said. 'I thought you said it was nothing serious?'

The following morning, a press conference was held at Felling Police Station, in Gateshead. Alistair Papps, the manager of the Prison Service in the north-east, said, 'We regret this incident very much, but we cannot always get it right. Given an open chequebook, we would always play safe on every occasion. Clearly, when we have high-risk prisoners, we use special secure vehicles. But it would just be too expensive to transfer all prisoners, regardless of their security risk, in secure vehicles.' A spokesman for the Prison Officers Association added, 'It is the government's obsession with cost which is to blame, and the safety of the public and health and safety of our members is being put on the line by what is calculated neglect.' A spokeswoman for Northumbria Police urged members of the public not to approach the escaped men. 'They are considered to be extremely dangerous, and anyone seeing them should contact us,' she said. Later that day, Frank Cook MP demanded a full inquiry into the Prison Service policy of using private vehicles to transport dangerous criminals around Britain. 'It is nothing short of a national scandal,' he said. 'If we continue to expose our prison staff to appalling risks like this, we will before long have a tragedy on our hands.'

When the furore surrounding the escape had died down, Paddy arranged for one of his friends to pick him up in Glasgow and take him to Gateshead, on the opposite bank of the River Tyne from Newcastle. Bensham is a run-down district of Gateshead inhabited by a large community of Jews and other assorted immigrants. Numerous bedsits and flats are always readily available to rent at generally low rates. In the area, few people know their neighbours or their business, and those that do pretend that they don't. Bensham was the ideal location for Paddy to lie low. He knew that he could not stay there indefinitely, but until a more safe and permanent location could be found it would suit his needs ideally.

While Paddy was hiding from the authorities in Gateshead, Willbow, who had organised the 'Free Paddy Conroy' marches in the West End, went to see him and said that he could get him out of the country. Paddy had no idea how Willbow knew where he was living, and so he was extremely suspicious of his intentions. Paddy asked Willbow how he had found him when every policeman in the country had failed to do so, but he never did get a suitable answer. A lorry was due to board a North Sea ferry to the continent, and Willbow explained that he could arrange for Paddy to be smuggled out of the country in the back of it. Customs officers rarely search vehicles that are leaving these shores, because their main purpose is to prevent people from importing rather than exporting illicit cargo. Paddy told Willbow that he was interested in his offer, but as soon as Willbow had left to arrange everything Paddy began packing his possessions. Ten minutes after his departure, Paddy was driving towards the Scottish border, where he knew that there were people he could trust.

Shortly before the feud with the Harrisons had erupted, Dave Garside, whom Paddy considered to be a true friend, had become embroiled in a dispute with a man mountain from Middlesbrough named Brian 'the Taxman' Cockerill. During the 1990s, Cockerill made a name for himself in the north-east by robbing – or taxing, as he preferred to call it – drug dealers. Cockerill was an awesome fighter who few would even contemplate taking on. His sheer size deterred most hopefuls. It has to be said that Garside was no mug either. He had fought 45 professional fights in the ring, which included a British heavyweight title fight at

Wembley and two British cruiserweight title fights. He had been present the night Abadom had been assaulted at the Oz nightclub, in South Shields, the very incident that had led to Glover being recruited by the police as an informant.

One night, Cockerill had 'taxed' a drug dealer in a Middlesbrough nightclub who was friends with Garside. A few weeks later, Cockerill went out clubbing, and by his own admission he consumed ridiculous amounts of Bacardi and Coke and popped more than 20 Ecstasy pills over a long weekend. At 9 a.m. on the Sunday morning, Cockerill decided that the party was over and headed home. As he walked towards the door of the club he had spent the night in, a member of the door staff warned him that Garside was waiting for him outside with 'two or three cars full of lads with hammers and bars'. To Cockerill's credit, he refused to run or hide and walked out of the club alone into the morning sunlight and extreme danger.

As soon as Garside saw Cockerill, he said, 'We want the fucking money that you took off the lad.' Dazed and confused by the drink, drugs and daylight, Cockerill was struggling to focus. Garside was standing side-on to Cockerill, and it looked as if he was preparing to land one of his powerful punches that had brought him so much success in the ring. Before Garside could do so, Cockerill head-butted him three times full in the face. To everybody's amazement, including Cockerill's, Garside staggered back and appeared to be out cold on his feet.

'I've beaten you! Look at you!' Cockerill shouted. As Garside began to fall to the floor, he made a last-ditch attempt to stay on his feet and grabbed hold of Cockerill. The two giants began to wrestle, and after a couple of minutes Cockerill threw Garside over his back and he crashed to the floor. Pulling Garside to his feet and throwing him against a wall, Cockerill sank his teeth into an ear and spat out a lobe. Then, locked in a bear hug, Cockerill and Garside fell struggling to the floor. Cockerill managed to get his opponent in a headlock and applied his vice-like grip to his throat. Bystanders soon began screaming, 'Let go, Brian! Let go! You've killed him!'

When Cockerill released Garside's seemingly lifeless body, he got up and leant on the roof of a taxi, gasping for breath. To everybody's astonishment, Garside picked himself up off the ground, walked up behind Cockerill and landed a devastating punch that broke his ribs. Cockerill didn't even turn around. He just slumped to the floor, barely able to breathe. As Cockerill fought to compose himself, Garside began to kick him in the head and upper torso. Cockerill, still suffering from a weekend of excessive alcohol and drug abuse, had no more to give, and so he remained on one knee rather than getting to his feet to continue the fight. When Garside realised that the battle was over, he began jumping in the air and shouting, 'I am the daddy! I am the daddy!'

Following the fight, for reasons known only to himself, David Glover contacted Cockerill and his associates, saying that he 'and others' were going to kill him. Rather than respond to Glover's threats, Cockerill threw himself into a rigorous training regime and vowed to revisit Garside when he was fighting fit. When Cockerill felt the time was right to take on Garside again, he arrived at a club in Newcastle with a gang of about 50 men in tow. Garside had been warned that Cockerill was looking for him, and so he had recruited approximately 50 men from as far afield as Manchester and Liverpool. Paddy Conroy, who knew Cockerill and who also happened to be in that particular club that night, was asked if a fight could be arranged with a £20,000 purse for the winner, but Garside declined, saying that he had not trained. As far as Paddy was concerned, that was the end of the matter. He certainly had no further involvement in their feud.

The following night, Cockerill and up to 70 men armed with shotguns, handguns, machetes and baseball bats went to a rave club where Garside was working on the door. Instead of storming the front doors, they went to a rear door and used bolt cutters to gain entry. As his men kept the door staff at bay, Cockerill went to a small office, where he found Garside. According to Cockerill, one punch floored Garside, and he then began to kick and stamp on him without mercy. When Cockerill stepped back to admire his handiwork, Garside had suffered numerous injuries, including a broken nose, a broken cheekbone and a broken jaw. Everybody thought that would be the end of the matter, but both men had egos as big as their hulk-like frames.

Tommy Harrison (unrelated to the Harrisons involved in the Conroy feud) is a legendary figure in the Teesside underworld. Men who live in the area, like Cockerill, have nothing but the utmost respect for him.

When Harrison phoned Cockerill one evening and invited him to his home, Cockerill accepted and walked like a lamb to the slaughter. Unbeknown to Cockerill, Harrison had been forced to make the phone call, which was luring Cockerill into a trap, while staring down the barrel of a loaded shotgun. As soon as Cockerill knocked on Harrison's door, a man from Newcastle answered and invited him in. As Cockerill stepped into the lounge, a dozen men pounced on him with a variety of weapons. Like a pack of wild animals, they hacked, chopped and stabbed Cockerill before leaving him for dead. The room resembled an abattoir. Blood had even splashed onto the ceiling.

As the men made good their escape, Harrison and his son bundled Cockerill into a car and rushed him to hospital. In his own words, Cockerill was sewn up by the doctors 'like an old three-piece suite'. He had been repeatedly stabbed, an iron bar had been used to try to break his jaw and one of his legs, and his other leg had been hacked with a machete so badly that it was almost severed. Despite his life-threatening injuries, Brian Cockerill refused to assist the police, but others couldn't wait to implicate people in the murderous attack. Paddy Conroy did not know it at the time, but David Glover made a statement blaming him. Paddy was arrested, charged and remanded in custody, but Cockerill came forward and exonerated him. It was a man named Phil Berriman, from Garside's home town of Hartlepool, who had alerted Cockerill to Paddy's plight by showing him David Glover's statement concerning the attack on him. Berriman was well known amongst the criminal fraternity in the north-east, as he was often used by them to smuggle 'various commodities' from Europe into the UK. After helping Paddy in one incident, Berriman went on to be instrumental in almost sending him to prison for life.

After spending three weeks on the run around the Scottish borders, Paddy once more returned to the Bensham area of Gateshead, where he rented out another flat. It had been ten long months since his escape from custody, and he had rarely ventured outside. Paddy was beginning to feel claustrophobic, and the monotony of his existence was making him restless and agitated. Dave Garside had visited him one night and said that his friend Phil Berriman was sailing to Spain the following morning. If Paddy wanted a lift out of the country, Garside could arrange it. Paddy trusted Berriman, as he had assisted him indirectly in the matter concerning Cockerill, so his reponse was unsurprising: 'Fucking right I want a lift, and Spain will do nicely.'

Paddy was advised to meet Berriman at a harbour near Hartlepool early the following morning, where he assumed that he would be boarding a boat bound for Spain. When Paddy arrived, the crew were still preparing the vessel for its journey. Paddy was disappointed to say the least, but Berriman explained that when the vessel did eventually sail from the north-east it would be docking in Torquay before setting off on the main leg of its journey. The voyage from Hartlepool to Torquay would take approximately two days, so, rather than spend forty-eight hours bobbing about on the ocean waves in a boat, Berriman and Paddy agreed that they would drive down in his car. Paddy stayed at Berriman's home that night, and as the sun was rising the following morning they set off for Torquay. Paddy didn't know it at that time, but customs officers had Berriman under surveillance, and they were photographing everybody he came into contact with.

Chapter Seven

Y VIVA ESPAÑA

PADDY CONROY FELT relief as he watched the English coastline fade on the horizon, but a sense of sadness engulfed him when it had totally disappeared from view. Maureen and his children were back in that green and pleasant land, and he had no idea when he would see them again. Paddy had secured his freedom, but at what price?

Prior to Collier's abduction, Paddy had filled out the forms to apply for a new passport. For one reason or another, he had failed to post it, but after he went on the run Maureen had decided to do so. Paddy had warned her that it was a pointless exercise, because the authorities would never issue a passport to a person they were claiming was the most wanted man in Britain, but to Paddy's surprise that is exactly what happened. Before heading for Spain, Berriman made a detour to Brest, in France, where he met up with two people he said he had to 'discuss business with'. They were from the Newcastle area, and Maureen had asked one of them to give Paddy his new passport.

After completing their business in France, they set sail for the Bay of Biscay. Paddy may have been in a few scary situations in his life, but the night Berriman sailed into the eye of a storm would undoubtedly have been one of the most terrifying. Waves rising 40 ft above the small craft crashed down and tossed it around the ocean like a ball bearing being fired around a pinball machine. Berriman gave up trying to steer the boat and advised all on board to get below deck and hang on for dear life. All the lights went out on the vessel, and the occupants were smashed around the head and body by flying pots, pans and personal effects. The night air was freezing. Everybody was drenched in sea water, and the cold sweat of fear was pouring down their faces.

Before embarking on the voyage, Berriman had shown Paddy two survival suits that he had purchased from an oil-rig worker. These one-piece suits inflated when in water, keeping the people wearing them warm. They also had distress lights and whistles attached in order to attract would-be rescuers. There was a total of five men on Berriman's boat, which meant three would be without survival suits if the vessel ran into difficulties. Paddy had made his mind up as to who would be wearing one of them if the vessel did sink.

As the boat soared to meet yet another huge wave, Paddy let go of the rope that he had been hanging on to and ran towards the steps that led into the hold. *Crash!* A wave broke on the deck, throwing the boat to one side and throwing Paddy down the steps. 'Paddy, Paddy, are you OK?' shouted Berriman.

A few minutes later, Paddy staggered up the steps from the hold dressed in one of the survival suits. 'I'm OK now,' he said, smiling. Berriman and the crew looked at Paddy, looked at one another and stampeded towards the hold in search of the other suit. From amidst the melee that followed, it was Berriman who emerged triumphantly, wearing the only other available survival aid. Berriman and Conroy stood in the galley beaming at their ingenuity while the rest of the crew grimaced and prayed that the storm would soon subside.

The following morning, the sun beamed down on the boat and the sea was as flat as a sheet of glass. Sitting out on the deck, Paddy watched as five or six disorientated racing pigeons swirled and tumbled in the sky above. Clearly exhausted after being caught in the storm, they landed on the deck of the boat when Paddy put bread out for them. The pigeons were so tired, in fact, that Paddy was able to pick them up and put them in a box, which he decided to keep them in until he reached dry land. Later that day, Paddy could see a coastline on the horizon, and so he asked Berriman where they were. 'That's Bilbao. We're not far from our destination, now,' Berriman replied.

'Fuck your destination,' Paddy said. 'Get me off this boat now!'

As soon as the boat had docked in Bilbao, Paddy released the pigeons, grabbed his bag and headed for the nearest airport. Berriman was keen to remain in his company, for some reason, and volunteered to fly down to southern Spain with him. 'The crew can sail the boat from here,' Berriman said. 'We will meet them down there.' Thinking nothing of it at the time, Paddy agreed to let Berriman tag along.

When the pair arrived at the local airport, they booked themselves onto a small 30-seater plane that was bound for an airfield near Benalmadena. During the flight, Paddy noticed that the stewardess was walking up and down the aisle waving what appeared to be a P45 certificate. 'Has anybody dropped this?' she called out in both English and Spanish. Berriman, who had been in the toilet, emerged and took it from her. When he returned to his seat, Paddy snatched the certificate from Berriman and asked him what he was doing with a P45. When Paddy looked at it, he saw that the form was in fact a Crown Court expenses receipt. 'What the fuck is this?' Paddy asked. 'Who have you been grassing up?' Berriman bleated about things not being as they might appear, but when Paddy pressed him he admitted that he had given evidence in court on behalf of the police.

The rest of the journey was made in complete silence. When they reached Benalmadena, Paddy invited himself to a meeting between Berriman and his business associates. Paddy ordered Berriman to sit down and told him to explain to everybody who was present what he had done. The room had fallen silent by the time Berriman had finished telling everybody about the assistance that he had given to the authorities. 'Would you inform on anybody again?' Paddy asked Berriman.

'If it was a choice between me and them going to prison, then yes, I would,' Berriman replied. Before walking out of the room, Paddy dropped the Crown Court expenses form on the table and told all those present that they should have nothing further to do with Berriman.

After a few days in Benalmadena, Paddy rang home to ask a trusted friend if he had heard anything about his case on the news. Paddy was simply curious to know if the police were aware that he had left England. While talking to his friend, Paddy mentioned the names of some of the people on Berriman's boat who had been kind enough to help him. Paddy was told that one of the men he mentioned, whom I shall call Patrick, was a good man, a genuine friend, and that Paddy was to ensure that he didn't get involved with whatever Berriman was up to. Later that evening, Paddy took Patrick to one side and asked him what he was planning to do with Berriman. 'He is smuggling nearly four tonnes of cannabis into England on his boat, and I am sailing it,' Patrick replied.

Paddy told Patrick about the Crown Court expenses form and explained that he was risking everything by getting involved with Berriman. 'Do yourself a favour and keep off that boat, or you're going to spend the next decade behind bars,' Paddy said.

The following morning, Patrick had left Spain, leaving Berriman without anybody to sail his boat back to England. Paddy, who was by now extremely suspicious of Berriman's intentions, decided to keep a close eye on him and so suggested that they rent an apartment together. It was nothing too lavish, a simple two-bedroom property that overlooked the high street. Across the road was a café that was run by an English gangster's-moll type and her Spanish boyfriend. The proprietor's bleached blonde hair, waxed long legs and extra-large fake silicon breasts ensured that the numerous English villains in the town congregated there. Common sense told Paddy that if the police were trying to gather information about the criminal fraternity in exile then this was the place for them, and so he deliberately avoided it.

Every few weeks, Dave Garside and his girlfriend would visit Paddy in Spain to tell him what, if anything, was happening back in Newcastle. On one such visit, Paddy was talking to Garside's girlfriend, who said that she had spent the previous evening in the café opposite his apartment, where an ex-Scotland Yard policeman had been flirting with her. She said that he had been buying her drinks all night and was claiming that he was on holiday. 'What are you thinking, accepting drinks from a policeman?' Paddy asked. In an attempt to laugh off an incident that she realised had disgusted Paddy, Garside's embarrassed girlfriend rattled off some excuse about her being drunk and the entire evening being nothing but harmless fun.

A few days later, Paddy had a yearning for a traditional English breakfast. It was early, and he could see from his balcony that the café was empty. Paddy reasoned that it would do no harm to go in there while it was quiet, and so he rang Garside and arranged to meet him and his girlfriend at the café. They sat out on the veranda talking while they waited for their order to arrive. To their left was an old lady sipping orange juice, and to their right was a middle-aged man who seemed more interested in Paddy than his double egg on toast. Paddy watched Garside's girlfriend as she looked around the café. There was no reaction when she looked at the old lady, but she sat back in her chair when she made eye contact with the man. 'Was it in this café that the policeman was buying you drinks?' Paddy asked.

'Yes, yes,' she replied. 'But it was nothing serious, just a giggle, Paddy.'

Paddy asked her to look to her right and confirm that the man sitting at the table was the very same policeman. Feigning shock, Garside's girlfriend confirmed that it was. As Paddy turned to look at the policeman, he got up from his table and walked away from the café. Paddy threw a handful of pesetas on the table, made his excuses to Garside and went in pursuit of the man. As Paddy turned the street corner, the policeman was walking towards a car park at the rear of Paddy's apartment. Following him at a discreet distance, Paddy watched in horror as a motorbike pulled up and the two men astride it began talking to the policeman. The policeman pointed back towards the café. Paddy didn't need to hear his words to know that he was talking about him. Paddy rang Garside and told him to fetch his car, before running back to his apartment to pack his bags. Fifteen minutes later, Paddy was driving out of Benalmadena and heading for a small resort approximately twenty miles away, where he rented a new apartment.

From that day forth, Paddy made a conscious effort to avoid contact, if possible, with anybody who looked remotely British. He would spend his days on the beach lounging in the sun and the evenings in his room watching endless Spanish television programmes that he couldn't understand. Dave Garside continued to fly over from England to spend time with Paddy and help break up the monotony of his increasingly boring existence. Paddy thought nothing of it, therefore, when Garside said that he was coming over to see him one weekend and suggested that he meet him at the airport. Paddy was not prepared to go into the airport terminal building for fear of being recognised, but he did agree to wait for Garside outside in his car.

On the day of Garside's arrival, Paddy drove to the airport and found a space in the middle of the main car park where he could wait for his friend. As soon as Paddy had switched off his engine, a car pulled up in front of him. It then reversed back until it was approximately a pace away from his front bumper. 'Here we fucking go,' Paddy thought. 'If anybody pulls up behind me now, I am trapped.' Seconds later, a car coasted up behind Paddy's vehicle and parked inches from the bumper. 'Out, out, get out of the fucking car. We are Interpol. We are Interpol,' the plain-clothes policemen shouted as they leapt from their vehicles and trained their guns on Paddy. Lying on the hot tarmac with the Spanish sun beating down on him, Paddy knew that his days on the run were over. Paddy was handcuffed and helped to his feet while being informed in broken English that he was now under arrest.

When Paddy appeared in court, the magistrate ordered that he should be remanded in custody to Malaga Prison to await extradition back to the UK. Paddy had no experience of Spanish prisons, but he thought they could not be much worse than the penal dustbins that he had been incarcerated in back home. How very wrong he was. The special unit that Paddy was put into within the main prison was unfit to house dogs, the food he was served crawled around the dirty tin plate that it was on, and the prison officers shouted and spat at him as they walked past his cell. English citizens don't have the best of reputations on the continent, but this was more than banter: Paddy's fellow inmates appeared to genuinely hate him. Unable to speak the language and determine the reason for such deep-seated animosity, Paddy asked in pidgin Spanish to speak to anybody who shared his native tongue.

A day later, an Algerian man who worked in the prison kitchen was escorted to Paddy's cell. The Algerian's grasp of the English language wasn't great, but Paddy did manage to converse with him by talking slowly, mouthing words and indulging in bizarre hand signals that reminded him of the game charades. Paddy asked why he was the focal point of so much hatred and abuse from the prison staff and inmates. 'You are a very bad man, a very bad man,' the Algerian replied. 'You kidnap your victims, you torture them and then you rape them.'

'Fucking rape? Fucking rape?' Paddy shouted. 'I wouldn't dream of raping anybody!' It soon became apparent to the prison officers that Paddy was on the verge of exploding into a rage, and so he was ushered back into his cell and the door was locked.

The following morning, an English-language newspaper from

Gibraltar was pushed under Paddy's cell door. Paddy's photograph appeared on the front page, and the accompanying headline claimed that he was wanted in the UK for kidnap, torture and rape. Little wonder the entire prison population was out to make his life as difficult as possible.

When Paddy went out into the exercise yard for the first time, he was glared at by every single inmate. In one corner of the yard, a group of men were lifting weights, but they stopped as soon as they saw him. All around the perimeter of the yard, different ethnic gangs huddled in groups, whispering and pointing. Paddy knew what was coming, but he had no idea from which quarter it would come. As Paddy walked back to the main building, he was struck from behind, and so he immediately turned and launched himself at his attackers. Prison officers streamed out of the main building and began cracking people's heads with their batons. Paddy stood his ground, and the fight was over almost as soon as it had begun.

Paddy wasn't physically injured, but the stress of the allegation that he was a rapist did cause him a lot of mental harm. Paddy's once thick hair began to fall out in clumps, and he was rarely able to sleep or relax, through fear of attack. Whenever he saw somebody approaching him, Paddy was up on his feet preparing for yet another fight. He lost count of the number of battles that he had in the first few weeks of his imprisonment.

Paddy was told, rightly or wrongly, that 28 per cent of prisoners within that particular establishment had HIV. As Paddy was in no doubt that he was going to be engaged in regular close combat with his fellow inmates, he asked his partner Maureen to send him a pair of elbow-length leather gauntlets. He wanted to ensure that no opponents could bite or scratch him, just in case they were infected with a contagious and deadly disease. In the searing heat, Paddy would stomp around the exercise yard in his heavy leather gauntlets, growling at anybody who dared even to look at him.

After a week of watching this fearsome Geordie marauding around the prison, the governor ordered that Paddy be taken to the medical centre, where he would have to undergo a mental-health assessment. 'I'm not fucking mad,' Paddy protested. 'I'm wearing the gloves to prevent me from catching Aids.' Paddy later learned that several UK nationals had previously tried to feign madness in an attempt to avoid extradition, and that the Spanish authorities believed his unorthodox behaviour indicated that he was attempting to follow suit. Paddy was able to convince the doctors that he was as sane as the next man, but trying to prove to the other prisoners that he was not a rapist was hopeless, because they refused even to acknowledge him. To make matters worse, a radio station in Gibraltar was broadcasting the allegation and the newspapers were repeating it. They had even claimed on television that Paddy was a rapist.

Paddy contacted a friend named Bobby and asked him to visit as soon as possible. A few days later, Bobby arrived in Spain with the Bull and a few other lads in tow. 'The media are calling me a fucking rapist, and I am going to end up getting killed in here,' Paddy told his friends when they visited him. They looked at Paddy in astonishment and then burst out laughing. Pleading with Bobby to take him seriously, Paddy said, 'It's not fucking funny. These people honestly believe that I kidnap, torture and then rape people. They're calling me "the beast from the north-east".'

Bobby assured Paddy that he would sort the matter out, and after leaving the prison he drove down to Gibraltar with the other men. Barging past the security guard at the main door of the radio station, they demanded to see the news editor. The receptionist asked them what they wanted, and when they explained the purpose of their visit she claimed that they were at the wrong radio station and directed them elsewhere. When Bobby and the others descended upon the radio station the receptionist had redirected them to, it soon became apparent that they had been duped. 'When we get back there, don't bother talking to the receptionist this time. I will deal with this,' Bobby told the others.

After they had pulled up outside the radio station for the second time, Bobby kicked the front door open and shoved the security guard to one side. The receptionist started screaming something in Spanish, but Bobby ignored her and walked into the studio, where a presenter was broadcasting live. Grabbing the startled man by his lapels, Bobby ordered him to say that Paddy Conroy was wanted in the UK for escaping not raping. The terrified presenter repeatedly blurted out Bobby's request over the airwaves until he was finally released.

Although Bobby's attempt to set the record straight was admirable, the story that Paddy was a rapist was already in the public domain, and those who heard the presenter broadcast Bobby's demand were in a minority. Paddy's treatment, therefore, did not improve, and so he recruited an American man mountain as his friend and bodyguard.

The American was a muscle-bound monster who oozed brutality. He was from the State of Illinois, and he told Paddy that he was a Mafia enforcer awaiting extradition on charges of extortion and murder. He was one of the few English-speaking inmates, and so, somewhat inevitably, Paddy got to know him quite well. After Paddy explained his predicament to the American, he agreed that any battles Paddy had to fight would become his battles too. Towering over every other man in the prison, Paddy's American Mafia friend struck terror into the heart of anybody who attempted to cause him problems. Within a week, Paddy had abandoned his gauntlets and was walking around the prison without fear of attack.

When Bobby returned to Newcastle, he contacted the BBC World Service and asked them to look into the vile allegations that had been broadcast in error about Paddy. A BBC journalist contacted a police officer involved in Paddy's case, and he claimed that it had all been a terrible misunderstanding. 'I told the Spanish police that Conroy was an escapee not a rapist. Perhaps they misheard or misunderstood me,' the officer said. Perhaps they did misunderstand the officer; a cynic, however, might think that the error was in fact deliberate and designed to cause Paddy as much unnecessary hardship as possible.

The news that was filtering back to Paddy from England about his case filled him with a sense of hope. The Bull had told Paddy that Billy Collier's brother Terry had been asking him to attend a meeting, because Collier did not want to go to court to give evidence. Terry had informed the Bull that after Paddy's arrest the police had given his brother Billy and his family new identities and moved them to a safe house in Grantham, Lincolnshire. Two detectives from Newcastle had been appointed as Billy's liaison officers, and they had assisted him and his family with moving in and settling down. Unfortunately for the police, their efforts 'to protect and hide Billy' from whatever danger they believed he faced were in vain. Billy's drug habit meant that he could not adjust to a life of normality, and so he encouraged his brother Terry and others to build bridges with Paddy so that he could return to Newcastle. The Bull was pestered with olive branches in various guises, and so in the end Paddy told him to agree to listen to what Terry Collier had to say.

Terry Collier met the Bull at Newcastle Central Station and told him that his brother was willing to withdraw his evidence if Paddy paid him £15,000. The very thought of funding a junkie's habit was bad enough, but to compensate a junkie who had desecrated the Conroy family grave made Paddy's stomach churn, and so he passed a message back telling Collier to stick his offer where the sun don't shine. A few days later, Paddy was made a second offer. This time the asking fee was £10,000, but Paddy's response was exactly the same.

After failing to buy Paddy's friendship, Billy began to change the statements that he had made to the police. One day, he was claiming that Paddy had tortured him, and the following day he was saying that Paddy wasn't even present when he had been assaulted. Collier then employed his own mother to contact the Bull and assure him that all the conflicting statements should be ignored. Mrs Collier told the Bull that when her son did attend court he was going to tell the truth and so Paddy would be cleared of torturing him. Just after Mrs Collier had relayed her son's message to the Bull, he received a call from Billy, who confirmed that he wished to tell the truth and that he was willing to do everything in his power to put things right. The Bull asked Billy if he would be willing to make a full and frank statement about all that had occurred on the day he was abducted, and he agreed. 'Tell Paddy that I'm sorry,' Billy said. 'I am willing to make amends for all of the trouble I have caused him.'

The police had discovered that Terry Collier had been 'speaking to the Conroys' on his brother's behalf, and so they immediately moved Billy and his family to another safe house, this time in Peterborough. The last thing the police wanted was the torture victim admitting that Paddy Conroy had nothing to do with such a heinous crime. Despite the best efforts of the police to gag Billy, he once more contacted the Bull and asked to meet him in Newcastle so that he could attend a solicitor's office and make a fresh statement. When Billy arrived in the city, he was naturally nervous, until the Bull explained that the last person Paddy wanted to see hurt was him. 'Paddy knows that if anything ever happens to you the truth might never come out,' the Bull said. 'And so you have absolutely nothing to worry about.' This seemed to relax Billy, and he asked the Bull to accompany him to a solicitor's where he could 'sort this mess out'.

Unfortunately, the statement Billy did eventually make that day, which exonerated Paddy of any involvement in his torture, was deemed inadmissible by Paddy's legal team, because he had simply written it out himself and asked a solicitor to witness him signing it. When Paddy informed the Bull, he once more contacted Billy, who returned to Newcastle to make a sworn statement in an acceptable format. When Billy arrived, he wasn't in any rush to go to a solicitor's office. He told the Bull that his partner had been 'doing his head in' while they had been in hiding and that he wanted to enjoy himself. The pair went for a drink, and Billy ended up taking the Bull to the flat of a female friend in Wallsend, where he spent the night.

The following morning, they didn't bother travelling back into Newcastle. Instead, they attended a local solicitor's office. Fearing Billy might later allege that he had been forced into making the statement, the Bull waited in a nearby café while Billy went into the solicitor's office alone. Billy claimed in his latest statement that he had been involved in a fight at a house in Westmoreland Road with a person whose name he did not wish to disclose. 'I was then attacked by several individuals, and three of my friends came to my aid. They were Paddy Conroy, Scott Waters and David Glover,' he said. 'Things did calm down, and Conroy drove me home in his car. I subsequently learned that Conroy had been arrested. I immediately attended the police station where Conroy was being held and told the officers involved in the case that he had not been involved. The following day, I was threatened with violence by the family of the man that I had fought. Threats to kill were made against both me and members of my family. The family that threatened me are notorious throughout Newcastle, and I am in no doubt that they are both capable and willing to carry out their threat. I was in absolute fear of my life. I was told that I had to go back to the police station and give a different statement, in which I was to state that I had been kidnapped from a shop and then assaulted by Conroy, Glover and Waters. I did make that statement, but it is untrue and was made under duress. I have chosen to make this statement now because most of the family members who had threatened me are currently in prison and I intend to leave the country before they are released.'

Paddy was fighting extradition from Spain at the time Billy made his statement, and he thought that this new evidence would help him to prove to a Spanish judge that he was actually innocent of the charge he faced. If a judge accepted that Paddy had played no part in Billy's torture, he could rule that it would be wrong to send him back to the UK, where he would likely be imprisoned.

At the next hearing, the judge listened intently to Paddy's argument and adjourned the proceedings for 28 days while they sought clarification from the British authorities about all that Billy had said. Paddy knew that Northumbria Police would claim that he had threatened or somehow pressurised Billy into changing his evidence, and so he asked the Bull if he would speak to Billy about travelling to Spain to give evidence in person. Without hesitation, Billy agreed. He even told the Bull that he would obtain a false passport for the journey, as he feared the police might prevent him leaving the country if he was stopped and checked at one of the ports.

Billy successfully applied for a passport in the name of Paul Hunter using a stolen birth certificate and utility bill in the same name. On the day they were due to depart, Billy rang the Bull and asked him to pick him up from the flat of the girl he had previously stayed with in Wallsend rather than the safe house in Peterborough. 'I need to go to my house to collect some clothing,' Billy said when the Bull arrived. 'But please don't mention to my girlfriend that I have been staying at that flat in Wallsend.' When they arrived in Peterborough, the Bull parked in a street adjacent to where Billy lived, because he feared the police might have the property under surveillance and he didn't want to subject himself to being interrogated by them or by Billy's girlfriend. After 15 minutes, Billy re-emerged from his home and the pair set off on their long drive to the ferry port in Plymouth.

After purchasing their tickets, the Bull drove his car onto the ferry and Billy boarded as a foot passenger. If Billy thought for one moment that Paddy intended to harm him, then he had ample time and opportunity to make good his escape or at least to alert the authorities at the ferry port. Billy did neither. When both men were safely on board, they met up in the bar. Billy wanted to spend the night drinking, but the

Bull said that he needed his sleep as it was a 24-hour crossing at the end of which he had a 500- or 600-mile drive.

The following day, after the ferry had docked in Santander, the Bull and Billy drove to Cordova, where they stayed overnight in a hotel before heading on to Malaga. On the very morning that they arrived in Malaga, the Spanish authorities decided to move Paddy to a prison in Madrid. Paddy, the Bull and Collier were absolutely devastated, but there was nothing that they could do.

The Bull and Billy booked into a hotel in Malaga and decided to drown their sorrows in a local bar. The following day, they purchased a map and sat in their hotel room nursing hangovers and planning their route to Madrid. Suddenly, there was a loud, insistent knock at their door, and when the Bull opened it an Englishman who had been staying in the room next door warned him that he should be careful. 'I don't know what, if anything, you guys are up to, but a security guard was here last night asking what colour eyes you have, what accents you have and what car you drive. I didn't tell him anything, but you are definitely being watched,' the man said. The Bull thanked his hotel neighbour and closed the door.

Unsure what to do, the Bull told Billy to remain out of sight while he went downstairs to check on the car. Everything seemed in order, and so he returned to the hotel room to tell Billy to get his things together as they were leaving. Because the Bull had not been paying much attention to Billy's movements throughout their long journey, he was unaware that Billy had been telephoning home at every opportunity to talk to his girlfriend. She had obviously been taken in by the police's ridiculous stories about Paddy wanting her partner dead and had got it into her head that he was being taken to Spain to be murdered. Panic-stricken, she had contacted the police, and they had urged her to remain calm throughout the calls so that they could trace them and launch a full-scale operation to 'rescue' her partner.

When the Bull re-entered the hotel room, Billy was in the bath, and so he sat on a bed studying the map in preparation for their journey. Moments later, there was a knock at the door, and when the Bull answered it a security guard said, 'Do you own a Ford Granada, sir?'

'Yes,' replied the Bull.

The security guard explained that somebody had broken the window of his vehicle and stolen the radio and so it would need to be secured. Billy had got out of the bath by this time, and he told the Bull that he would accompany him downstairs just in case there was a problem. As they stepped out of the hotel and onto the car park, a large van pulled up directly in front of them and two cars skidded to a halt on either side. The vehicles' doors flew open simultaneously, and a group of armed men disembarked, shouting, 'Hands on the fucking car! Hands on the car, or we fucking shoot!' Within seconds, the Bull and Billy were in handcuffs and being led away to separate cars. At the police station, they were locked in the same cell and told that they would remain in custody until police officers from the UK arrived to interview them.

That night, as the Bull slept, Billy tried to take his own life by hanging himself from the cell bars. The sound of the chair falling to the floor saved him. The clatter as it hit the stone tiles awoke the Bull, and he leapt from his bed, shouting, 'No, Billy, no! Think of your lassie! Think of your bairns!' The Bull managed to free Billy from his noose and sat up with him for the rest of the night to ensure he did not try to harm himself again.

The following day, Billy received a visit from Northumbria Police and was immediately moved to another cell. The Bull was told that he was going to be deported to face a charge of kidnap. He naturally pleaded not guilty to such a ridiculous allegation and was remanded in custody to await an extradition hearing. After two months, the Bull was bailed, but the Spanish authorities retained his passport to prevent him from fleeing the country. Short of money and missing his family, the Bull pleaded with his Spanish solicitor to have his passport returned. Despite the best efforts of his solicitor, the judge refused every one of the numerous applications that were made, and so the Bull went to the British Embassy and successfully applied for a three-day temporary passport. When he arrived at Manchester airport later that night, the Bull was arrested and the passport was seized, but, to his astonishment, he was released without charge.

After arriving back in Newcastle, the Bull went to see a solicitor, who advised him that Northumbria Police had wanted to arrest him at the airport and charge him with kidnap but that for reasons known only to themselves they had mistakenly released him. The Bull decided that he would avoid the police until all matters concerning Paddy, Collier and himself became clearer.

To make matters worse, David Glover and another man were then arrested in Middlesbrough after a member of the public telephoned the police to report two men who were trying to break into a car. When Glover was identified as the man who had escaped with Paddy from the prison van, he was taken to court and remanded in custody at HMP Armley, in Leeds, to await trial.

Confinement, or the threat of it, did not agree with David Glover, and he was prepared to do anything or betray anybody to avoid it. Not long after he was incarcerated, he and his cellmate, Kevin Lowe, went on hunger strike. Lowe was awaiting trial for smuggling gun parts to an extremely dangerous prisoner named Simon Bowman, who had been locked up at the time in HMP Durham. Lowe and his estranged wife, Denise, had been arrested at HMP Durham after they had been searched prior to a visit and eight rounds of .22 ammunition had been found. Later the same day, part of a revolver was found on the security wing in the cell of one of Bowman's friends. Another gun part was found being 'intimately' secreted by another prisoner.

In 1990, Bowman had been sentenced to ten years' imprisonment for threatening to kill his girlfriend and conspiracy to rob. He and an associate had rented a lock-up garage, where a sawn-off shotgun, a pump-action shotgun and stolen security-guard uniforms were later found.

In March 1992, Bowman escaped from HMP Durham, but he was arrested two months later after terrifying a couple in Kent while attempting to break into their home armed with a shotgun. He received a further two years' imprisonment for making threats to kill and escaping. In March 1995, a further two and a half years were added for another escape bid, during which he threatened a female prison officer with a razor, which he pressed against her neck. In October 1996, another seven years were added to his sentence for the plot to smuggle a gun into HMP Durham with Glover's cellmate, Kevin Lowe.

One imagines that Bowman would have considered a change of profession after so many costly mishaps, but just six months after his eventual release, in October 2001, he was arrested for armed robbery.

After walking into a post office in Washington, Tyne and Wear, Bowman tricked the postmistress into opening the security screen by handing in a large parcel for posting. Armed with a nine-inch knife, Bowman had then jumped through the hatch and warned that he would stick it in her neck if she did not open the safe. He made off with £28,500 but was arrested after information about him was given to the police. Branded 'an extremely dangerous man' by the judge, Bowman was imprisoned for 16 years. Some people clearly do not feel deterred by the threat of prison. They consider it to be little more than an occupational hazard. Others, like Glover, would literally cut their throats rather than face years behind bars.

Lowe and Glover claimed that they were on hunger strike because they were being locked in their cell for 23 hours per day and having to share their exercise period with sex offenders. The protest lasted a week, with the pair surviving on water alone, but when prison staff took little or no notice of them Glover's resolve waned and he reached for not only the prison menu but also the phone to his masters in Northumbria Police.

The Bull had never got over the death of Neil Conroy. Deep down, he thought that Paddy somehow held him responsible for what had happened, and so he carried the awful burden of guilt. The Bull's mental health had deteriorated rapidly after he witnessed Neil die. He drank too much, embraced the use of illegal substances and would fight any man without regard for his own safety. It was as if the Bull had a death wish. His GP became so concerned about his mental health that he sent him to see a psychiatrist. The Bull told the consultant that he feared he was going to harm somebody, because he was embroiled in a feud with a rival Newcastle gang, he had access to legally held firearms, he was on medication and he felt extremely angry over the unnecessary death of Neil. 'I am not safe to be on the streets. I need help,' the Bull had said. Unfortunately, nobody appeared to be listening. The psychiatrist gave the Bull a prescription for antidepressants and sent him on his way.

One night, a fight broke out in the Grainger pub between a few of Paddy's associates and men loyal to the family of the pub's landlord, Billy Thompson. Bad blood had surfaced between the opposing sides, because Thompson was David Glover junior's father-in-law and it had become common knowledge on Tyneside that Glover was giving information to the police from his prison cell about the Conroys and others. The Bull, who had been drinking heavily all day, arrived at the Grainger in a taxi with three females just as the situation began to get heated. After paying his fare, the Bull and his friends walked straight into the bar. The ladies went to order a drink, and the Bull went to the toilet. When he walked out a minute or two later, two men were fighting in the pool room, and, unbeknown to the Bull, two other men were fighting in the bar. One of these men was Billy Thompson's son. As the Bull paused to watch the fight in the pool room, Billy Thompson walked up to him and punched him in the face. The Bull immediately tore his jacket off and said to Thompson, 'What did you hit me for? I'm going to do you.'

Thompson told the Bull to get out of the pub and, rather foolishly, added, 'Or I will have you shot.'

The Bull turned, glared at Thompson and then began to laugh. 'You will have me fucking shot? Wait there, you fucking idiot. I will be back.'

The Bull strode out of the pub and returned ten minutes later cradling a powerful Lee–Enfield .303 rifle. As the Bull aimed the deadly weapon at the landlord, Thompson pleaded for his life and begged him to put down the gun. Others in the crowded bar shouted, 'No, Bull, no!' For a split second, the Bull snapped out of his murderous trance, realised what he had been about to do and lowered the weapon. Foolishly, Thompson thought the Bull had lost his nerve and sneered at him. Before the smile had left Thompson's face, the Bull had raised the rifle and said, 'You don't think I will do it, do you? You daft cunt.' A deafening explosion filled the bar, and Thompson fell as if he had been cut in half. Blood began to pump out over the bar floor from Thompson's wounds, and people began to scream and run for safety. The Bull stood firm, glaring at Thompson as he writhed on the floor. He then calmly reloaded the rifle and pointed it once more at his target. Before the Bull could shoot Thompson a second time, a man named Kevin Best grabbed the rifle and ran out of the pub. Without saying another word, the Bull turned and walked away from the carnage that he had caused.

Out in the street, the Bull met a friend who happened to be in possession of a large hunting knife. 'Give me that blade,' the Bull said.

'I'm going to go back in the Grainger and finish Thompson off'. His friend could see that the Bull was in some sort of deep, emotionless trance and refused to hand over the weapon. Rather than argue with the man, the Bull simply turned away and walked home.

Early the following morning, the police raided Kevin Best's home and arrested him and his brother Craig. Both were charged with causing an affray. They were later convicted and each sentenced to serve 20 months' imprisonment. Both have always maintained their innocence. The Bull remained at large, but he knew that it would be only a matter of time before he was apprehended. The high-powered .303 bullet had hit Billy Thompson in the hip, which it obliterated, before exiting the other side of his body. He lost both his legs that night and owes his life to Kevin Best, but it's unlikely, in light of Best's conviction, that he will ever thank him.

For 11 months, the Bull moved from one address to another in his efforts to evade capture. He would use public telephones in faraway towns to speak to family and friends just in case calls to his home back in Newcastle were being monitored. But, as time went on, the Bull became less security conscious, and he began making calls from the bed-and-breakfast accommodation he was staying in. The police traced the calls, and in an early-morning raid armed police arrested the Bull and charged him with attempted murder. At his trial, he was sentenced to 12 years' imprisonment. The judge told the Bull that if it had not been for the fact that he had warned a psychiatrist of his mental state prior to the shooting he would have sentenced him to life imprisonment.

It didn't take the Spanish authorities long to rubber-stamp Paddy Conroy's deportation papers after officers from Interpol spoke to the judge presiding over his case. Two officers attached to Newcastle's Serious Crime Squad flew out to Spain to ensure that Britain's most wanted man was being placed on the correct plane home. Three club-class seats had been reserved for the prisoner and his two escorts. Paddy knew that he was going to be sitting in a prison cell later that night, and so he decided to make the most of his complimentary, lavish surroundings. The police are not allowed to leave prisoners handcuffed on an aeroplane just in case there is an accident or an emergency. So, once the doors had closed in preparation for take-off and Paddy's handcuffs had been removed, he raised his hand and summoned the pretty young trolley dolly. 'I'll have a beer please, and keep them coming throughout the flight,' Paddy said.

As Paddy took his first mouthful, the policemen looked at each other and then back at their prisoner. 'Sorry, Paddy, you can't drink. You're our responsibility,' they said.

Paddy laughed so much that he nearly spat his beer all over the back of the head of the man sitting in front. 'Get to fuck, you pair of clowns,' he said. 'Either get me another drink now or I am going to kick off.'

Without hesitating, one of the officers raised his hand and called out to the stewardess, 'One large Bacardi and Coke over here, please.'

Taking the drink, Paddy emptied the glass in one and said to the policemen, 'Now just sit there and shut the fuck up, and we will all get along just fine.'

By the time the plane had touched down at Gatwick, Paddy was mortal drunk. Barely able to stand up, he was helped off the plane by his two embarrassed escorts. 'How the fuck are we going to explain this to the Governor?' one of them said. On the flight from Gatwick to Newcastle, the police officers did their best to sober Paddy up with cup after cup of black coffee, but he was still intoxicated when the plane touched down. However, as the aeroplane taxied towards the terminal, Paddy glanced out of the window and sobered up immediately. Land Rovers with armed men standing in the back were racing across the runway towards the aircraft. A bank of police vehicles with their blue lights flashing appeared to be blocking the aeroplane's way. As the plane ground to a halt, the Land Rovers surrounded it and 30 or more policemen ran towards the steps, which the airport staff were trying to put in place. Turning to his escorts in astonishment, Paddy said, 'The fucking Army? You're joking, aren't you? A taxi would have done, lads.' Paddy was informed that an emergency hearing had been arranged for him at Newcastle Law Courts so that he could be remanded in custody to a top-security prison to await trial.

Driving away from the airport, all Paddy could see were armed men in a convoy of vehicles behind and in front of him. A helicopter hovered above the vehicle he was in, and when the cavalcade reached the courthouse, which faces the River Tyne, Paddy noticed a rigid police boat and several inflatables bobbing about on the waves. Within the hour, Paddy had been remanded in custody and was on his way to HMP Liverpool. Upon Paddy's arrival, the prison governor explained to him that the prison was not equipped to house double Category A prisoners, and so he had to spend the first four months of his incarceration in solitary confinement. Double Category A prisoners make up a very small minority of Britain's huge prison population. They are deemed to be so dangerous that they are not only kept in a prison within a prison but they cannot even visit the toilet without being given an escort.

One morning, Paddy's cell door opened and he was told to gather his belongings as he was being moved to the Special Secure Unit (SSU) at HMP Durham, which is only 18 miles from Newcastle. Paddy was pleased with the move, because he would be nearer his family, and many of the Geordie faces he knew were also imprisoned there. When Paddy arrived at HMP Durham, he was put in a cell next to a Londoner named John Kendall. Kendall was a well-respected villain whose escape from custody several years earlier had been far more dramatic than Paddy's and Glover's flight from the prison van.

At 3.16 p.m. on 10 December 1987, John Kendall and another man, Sydney Draper, had been airlifted from the sports field at HMP Gartree, in Leicestershire, by a helicopter that had earlier been hijacked. Kendall was serving eight years for breaking into cash-and-carry warehouses, and Draper was serving life for murder. It was the first successful escape by Category-A prisoners from a dispersal prison and the only escape in the UK using a helicopter. The helicopter had been hijacked by an associate of Kendall named Andy Russell. After boarding the helicopter, Kendall and Draper disembarked just a short distance from the prison and made good their escape by road.

A month after the escape, Kendall and Russell committed a £25,000 robbery in the Archway area of north London. During the heist, a security guard was shot and wounded. Kendall and Russell were arrested shortly afterwards. Draper was recaptured after 18 months.

Paddy's other neighbour in prison was a fellow Geordie named Bob Stokoe, who was awaiting trial for shooting John Sayers senior in the mouth on the Quayside in Newcastle. Sayers survived the shooting. A Newcastle-based tycoon, whose identity is protected, had been blackmailed by Michael and Stephen Sayers and a man named Nigel Abadom. (It was Abadom's brother Philip whom Glover and others had beaten unconscious outside the Oz nightclub in South Shields several years earlier.)

During a terrifying ordeal, the businessman had been told that he would be shot if he did not pay £50,000 in used £20 notes. Nigel Abadom had been recruited by the Sayers brothers to carry out the extortion as part of a widespread protection racket. He made a series of chilling phone calls to the man claiming that the Sayers firm had been responsible for fifteen shootings and three murders, one of which was the execution of Viv Graham. In an effort to convince the businessman that the threats were serious, shots were fired through the windows of his home. However, the intended victim refused to give in to their demands and contacted the police. When Abadom and Stephen Sayers arrived to collect the cash that they had demanded, armed police were lying in wait and arrested them.

The eventual trial of the Sayers brothers and Abadom was moved five times in a bid to find a jury that was not familiar with their reputation. It finally took place at Doncaster Crown Court, and all three were found guilty. Michael was sentenced to twelve years' imprisonment, Stephen to ten years and Abadom to four. Prior to the trial, John Sayers senior had arranged to meet Bob Stokoe in the hope that he could assist his sons. Nobody knows for sure how Stokoe could have helped or how the discussion deteriorated, but John Sayers senior was shot and drove himself to hospital. He survived the attack and was called to give evidence at Stokoe's old-style committal hearing, which is in effect a dry run of a Crown Court trial before a magistrate.

The hearing was held behind closed doors, because the prosecution and the police did not want 'sensitive material' becoming known to the public. John Sayers senior had been the victim of a shooting, and so nobody could understand what possible sensitive material there could be. It wasn't long before totally unfounded rumours began to circulate on Tyneside that the hearing had taken place in private because John Sayers had been assisting the police for a number of years. Paddy Conroy was far from fond of the Sayers family, and so he added fuel to the fire by repeating the allegations about John Sayers senior to anybody who cared to listen. According to Paddy Conroy, the mighty Sayers firm, whose members told all and sundry that they adhered to the criminal code, was not quite what it said on the tin.

Chapter Eight

JUDAS

ON 4 SEPTEMBER 1994, as dawn broke over Falmouth Harbour, the 25 waiting customs officers were visibly excited. After months of surveillance and investigations, their drug-laden target had arrived: the *Melanie*, a 42-ft schooner, was ending its voyage from Senegal in an inlet known as Smugglers Creek. Phil Berriman and two crew members were arrested as soon as they stepped ashore. On board the *Melanie*, customs officers soon discovered 3.5 tonnes of Afghan cannabis with an estimated value of £15 million. 'If ever a case looked bang to rights,' said one customs investigator, 'this one was it.'

Following his arrest, Berriman was interviewed by a customs officer and Crime Squad Detective Constable William McDougall. Berriman claims that halfway through this interview he was asked if Paddy Conroy was behind the importation of the cannabis, to which Berriman says he replied, 'Look, you know who it is, but I won't tell you.' Berriman was then charged and remanded in custody under maximum-security conditions at Horfield Prison, Bristol.

When Berriman's legal team went to visit him, he asked them how far could he go in court concerning 'dropping Paddy Conroy in it'. Berriman claims that his barrister explained that anything he used in his defence could not be used against any other person. Believing this to be true, when actually it's not, Berriman applied for all the case papers concerning Collier's kidnap and torture. As part of the application process, Berriman had to explain in some detail why he wanted the documents. He said that Paddy Conroy had forced him to import the cannabis and he needed the case papers to show why not only he but

149

anybody would be in fear if they were being threatened by such a man. The documents were disclosed to Berriman, but soon afterwards he received a visit from Northumbria Police, who said that they were considering charging him with helping Conroy to flee the country. According to Berriman, he was offered a deal: six years' imprisonment if he pleaded guilty to all offences. He declined.

By this time, Berriman had heard that David Glover was in custody and giving information to the police about people, and so he altered his story slightly. Berriman told detectives, 'Glover threatened to shoot me if I did not take Paddy on my boat. Nobody else in my crew knew who Paddy was. I helped him escape, but I did so under duress.' Berriman still maintained that Paddy had forced him to import the cannabis on his boat, but again he said he had done so only under duress. 'When Paddy escaped from the prison van, the next thing I knew he was demanding my boat,' Berriman said. 'That is my motorboat, the 46-ft *Michelle Louise*.' Berriman explained that the vessel was not seaworthy and Paddy had 'got shitty' when he had told him this.

Berriman claims that he travelled to Hartlepool and told his father to get the boat sorted out, as he wanted to go to Majorca. He said that he had recently sold his salvage business and was sick of crime and 'all the shit that went with it', and so he just wanted to get away. At that stage, customs officers already had Berriman under surveillance and were photographing everybody that he met. The boat was made seaworthy within two days, and the crew sailed immediately from Hartlepool. Berriman says that Paddy arrived in his yard at 3 a.m. that morning and demanded to know where the boat was. It's unclear what was said, but it is not in dispute that Berriman and Conroy drove to Torquay to meet the boat the following day. When they arrived, customs officers photographed Paddy and Berriman boarding the *Michelle Louise*. Later, when the photographs were developed and produced as evidence, the title underneath the photograph of Britain's most wanted man surprisingly read, 'Unidentified'.

Berriman is adamant that customs officers knew throughout their operation that Paddy Conroy was involved with him. Paddy, according to Berriman, had been involved with a gang who were importing huge amounts of cannabis into the UK, but Paddy felt that they were trying to oust him, and so he had ordered Berriman to go to Spain, as he wanted him to use his boat to import the drugs. Berriman said, 'I had a boat organised that was harboured in Gibraltar, the *Melanie*. I put my own boat up as security for it. Patrick, the guy Paddy had chosen to skipper the *Melanie*, was a fisherman from Alnwick, in Northumberland. Patrick was really game when I spoke to him, but when he arrived in Gibraltar he was a different bloke. He was late, extremely quiet and looked gutted. I formed the opinion that his bottle had gone.

'I spoke to Paddy in Spain, and he explained that a deal he had arranged in Morocco had now fallen through. A boat laden with cannabis, which he had agreed to meet to transfer the load onto my vessel, was being watched off the coast of Dakar by customs officers, and so nobody would go near it. Paddy told me to tell Patrick to sail to Tenerife instead, where he would receive further instructions. I did pass on Paddy's instructions, but Patrick left for home the same day, leaving me to sail the *Melanie*. Because of delays and a never-ending stream of misinformation, it was agreed that I should sail to Casablanca to pick up a man who was going to show me where the boat was moored in Tenerife.

'After the man had boarded and we were in the open sea, he said that we were no longer heading for Tenerife. I was to sail to Dakar instead. I had no charts to go to Dakar, and the *Melanie* wasn't fit to sail there in any event. What I did was call in at Morro Jable, a port in the south of Fuerteventura, in the Canaries, and I told the Spanish authorities there that I had engine trouble. I telephoned Paddy and asked him what was going on. Why was I being told that I had to go to Dakar? Paddy said that I should just go there and not ask questions. He would have a crew waiting there to take over from me when I arrived. So, I sailed to Dakar, but on the way we had gearbox failures, engine failure. You name it, we endured it. The *Melanie* was not up to making such a long voyage. She could have sailed to Tenerife and back, but that was her limit.

'When we arrived in Dakar, the people that met us wouldn't even pay for a new GPS aerial, which is vital for navigation. Whilst they sped around in Mercedes sports cars, snorted cocaine and hired groups of prostitutes, the crew and me were botching the boat up with soldering irons and second-hand parts. Without a GPS aerial, which would have cost £400, the *Melanie* would not be able to locate and rendezvous with the boat loaded with drugs. I tried to explain that sailing without one was pointless, and when my protests fell on deaf ears I said that the *Melanie* was not going anywhere. This resulted in the men promising me that I could have as much diesel as I needed, fresh water and a new GPS aerial. The diesel wasn't readily available, and so I was told to store as many empty drums as possible on the deck so that the boat the *Melanie* was meeting could fill them up.

'When I was happy that the *Melanie* was seaworthy, I told the men that the other crew that Paddy had promised could now take over. I shouldn't have been surprised when I was told that there was no replacement crew and I had to skipper the *Melanie* with my crew. Almost as an afterthought, the men said that I would be paid £1 million when the drugs had been landed in the UK. I tried to refuse their offer, but my crew and I were beaten and threatened until we agreed.

'We sailed from Dakar with a Cuban man aboard. It was his job to liaise with the crew of the boat that we were sailing to meet. On the second day, their vessel appeared, and as it approached I threw a crew member a line. I shouted out, "This is an aluminium yacht. I will never be able to go alongside you with the yacht fenders." The next thing, rifles were pointing at me and they were all shouting, "You will!" I had no choice other than to comply. The moment I pulled alongside the boat, the fenders just splintered, and it smashed all the side of the *Melanie*, and so I just cut the line. I spent the rest of the day doing makeshift repairs. As I did so, the crew from the other boat began loading a hundred bags of cannabis onto the *Melanie*. They said that they had very few supplies on their boat, and so they helped themselves to most of our supplies. When I asked for the 600 gallons of diesel that I would need to make the journey back to England, I was given just 140 gallons of sludge. It destroyed the *Melanie*'s engine within two days, and we were left listing in open sea. We had a hell of a job on the return journey, running electrics on a petrol generator with only five gallons of fuel, and eventually that ran out.

'When I left England, I told my girlfriend that I would only be three days, and here I was into my ninth week at sea. We were so hungry we stopped two ships for food and water that we had happened upon in the middle of the ocean. I had been told that when I was 20 miles from England we would be met by another boat, which would load the drugs and take them inland. However, when we reached the agreed spot, there was nobody there apart from a trawler, which I later learned was manned by customs officers.

'I waited until the next night, and when nobody showed I thought, "Bollocks to this. We have got no food, no water and no fuel. If I dump the drugs they will kill me, and so I may as well try and land them myself." So I got the pilot book out and had a look at this place called the Helford River, where about 50 people live in a village. I thought that was the perfect place to land, but as soon as the *Melanie* entered the Helford River boats laden with armed police and customs officers descended on me. For some reason, the police thought that the cannabis had been wired to explosives to prevent another gang from stealing it, but that was absolute nonsense.'

Two months after his arrest, Berriman received a visit at Horfield Prison from Detective Constable William McDougall and another officer, Detective Sergeant Hans Kitching. Unbeknown to the detectives, Berriman had met Brinks-MAT robber Tony White on the maximum-security wing, and he had advised Berriman to covertly record all interviews that he had with the police. White had explained that in 1984 a bank robbery trial had been abandoned after the accused had recorded officers during a prison visit. What the officers said to the defendant in private did not quite tally up with their evidence in court, and so the judge dismissed the case. Berriman felt that he had nothing to lose and everything to gain, and so he hollowed out an A4 lever arch file full of case papers and hid a small tape recorder in the middle.

Berriman was usually strip-searched before and after visits, but as he was being visited by the police on this occasion the prison officers refrained from being so rigorous. As Berriman walked into the prison visiting room, he turned the tape recorder on. He knew that the tape would last for only 45 minutes, and so he had to act fast. Rather cheekily, Berriman told the officers that he would not talk to them unless they agreed to be searched by him for hidden tape recorders. Both complied.

Berriman had been informed by his solicitor that the officers wished to speak to him about a CS gas gun that they had found at his home, but he suspected that wasn't true. So, when Berriman asked the officers what they wanted to know about the gun, he wasn't surprised when they said that they had just used that as an excuse to get to see him in prison. The officers did give Berriman a chargesheet with two matters relating to firearms on it, but he never appeared in court for any such offence. For the next 40 minutes, Berriman played along with the police, making light of his situation and appearing to sound keen when they suggested ways in which his situation could be improved.

At the end of the visit, Berriman returned to his cell and retrieved the tape recording. He passed it to his solicitor at the earliest opportunity. Nearly a year later, when DC McDougall gave evidence at the trial, Berriman's counsel asked him a series of questions about the prison meeting. Was it true that the officers had told Berriman about two police colleagues' supposed lesbian affair? Had they urged him to supply information about drugs to them exclusively, promising they could get the judge to cut his sentence? Had they buried their customs colleagues in a torrent of foul-mouthed abuse, even claiming they were 'conspiring against Berriman'? To each and every allegation, red-faced DC McDougall offered an emphatic denial. But, unknown to the police, Berriman's tape recorder in the prison visiting room had captured their every word. Now, accompanied by a transcript of the meeting, it was played in court to devastating effect.

On the tape, DC McDougall spoke at length about two female detectives who were 'half and half', adding that, despite their relationship, he had found that bisexual officers were 'usually a bloody good shag'. DC McDougall had also made an offer to Berriman to encourage him to turn informer. He had said, 'We can put a letter in to the judge saying you have been very helpful, and he lessens your sentence . . . If you can give us a nice tasty job, that's something that's going to help you.' No one, the officer had said, 'need ever know, not even customs. Come through me; don't go through them, because you can't fucking trust them.' DS Kitching added, 'Who would you rather deal with? Billy McDougall or the customs . . . the people who were bloody having a conspiracy around you?' The officers also suggested they might be able to get Berriman transferred to less burdensome security conditions.

The prison interview was not the only element that led to the case collapsing and Berriman being acquitted of all charges. He gave powerful evidence of how he had become indebted to Paddy Conroy and had undertaken the voyage only after months of threats and violence, which had left him in fear of his life. On the prison interview tape, the officers appeared to be aware of the intimidation Berriman claimed he endured. Judge Taylor asked the Devon and Cornwall Police to launch an inquiry into the conduct of DC McDougall and DS Kitching, but it was found that there was 'insufficient evidence' to bring any charges. Neither officer was disciplined by the police.

Berriman refused to become a police informant, but in January 1996, while Paddy Conroy was safely locked behind bars, three men decided to make sure that he wasn't about to change his mind. They lured Berriman to a scrapyard on the pretext of him assisting them with Paddy's appeal papers. When Berriman arrived, he was greeted by masked men wearing forensic-type suits and surgical gloves. They beat Berriman with a claw hammer and baseball bats for more than two hours, leaving him with broken ribs, a crushed elbow, broken fingers and twenty-three staples in his skull.

Paddy was never questioned by police about Berriman's claims concerning the importation of cannabis or the assault that Berriman suffered. He was, however, asked by a journalist if he was involved in the attempted importation of cannabis, to which he replied, 'Fucking hell. I couldn't find my way to Canary Wharf never mind the Canary Islands.'

When Berriman recovered from the terrible injuries that he had sustained, he retired from crime and opened a pub, an annex of which he named Smugglers Creek. However, Berriman could never give up his love of the sea and the excitement he derived from his 'naughty-cal' voyages. In 2007, the media dubbed Berriman 'the Booze Pirate' after he set up a floating off-licence in international waters, 13 miles off the coast of Hartlepool. Berriman claimed that he was getting even with Customs and Excise by exploiting a loophole in the law that allowed him to sell EU bottles of spirits for just £7 and cartons of cigarettes for £15. His first mission to sell cut-price beer, wine, spirits and cigarettes had been thwarted when customs seized £120,000 of cargo on suspicion that duty needed to be paid. After a legal battle, Berriman's goods were returned, and he once more put to sea, telling reporters from the *Hartlepool Mail*, 'I am not fully confident that I won't be in jail next week, but I believe that I am on the right side of the law. I am not afraid of customs.'

Shortly after Glover had been recaptured in Middlesbrough after escaping from the prison van, he indicated to a Detective Chief Inspector

Dudley that he wished to give Queen's evidence against Paddy Conroy concerning the kidnap and torture of Billy Collier. In documents that were later disclosed to Paddy's legal team, he learned that Glover had been informing on him, his family and his friends for years. It was Glover who had told his police handler that guns used to shoot members of the Harrison family had been hidden in the loft of the Happy House. Unfortunately for the police, after they retrieved the guns, they were unable to prove who had put them there, because the property had numerous tenants, none of whom was going to confess to anything. It was, in fact, extremely unfortunate that the police could not find the culprit, because the person who told them about the guns was the very same man who owned them and who had hidden them there.

Glover wasn't being public-spirited, nor had he found God. The sole reason he had for giving up his own cache of weapons was that he wanted to do a deal with the police regarding the charges that he faced. This is not an entirely new approach for a criminal trying to save his own skin and evade justice. John Haase and Paul Bennett, from Liverpool, were jailed for 18 years in 1995 for smuggling heroin, but they were freed early for the help they gave in locating firearms that had been hidden around the UK. Their 'unique' cooperation – tipping off the authorities about the whereabouts of more than 150 guns – resulted in them being granted royal pardons. The pair were released in 1996 after the then home secretary, Michael Howard, signed a Royal Prerogative of Mercy.

However, some detectives began to doubt the authenticity of the information, and a subsequent investigation revealed that Haase and Bennett had in fact purchased the weapons and arranged for them to be hidden. Once the guns had been planted, the pair pretended to turn informer and told the authorities where the guns could be found. When the truth had been unearthed, the two men were charged and later convicted of conspiracy to pervert the course of justice. Haase was sentenced to 22 years' imprisonment, and Bennett to 20.

In the hope of bolstering his bargaining power, Glover had not only told the police about the torture of Collier but had also said that he was willing to give them the names of the men who had driven the getaway cars on the day he escaped from the prison van. Other crimes Glover dangled in front of his police handler were the theft of a Greenpeace dinghy and diving suits, allegedly by Paddy Conroy, and an armed robbery at a club called the Excessor, which had been committed by two men Glover said he could not only name but also incriminate, because he knew where they had hidden the money they had robbed, some of which had been contaminated by red anti-theft dye. Glover also identified by name two men who were allegedly involved in robbing a post office van.

Saving the best until last, Glover said that Michael Conroy had offered to pay him to murder Viv Graham. Glover told the police that he had considered Michael's offer but alleged that when he had asked Paddy for his advice he had been told that he was not to get involved, the implication being that Paddy already had everything in hand. An internal police memo written at the time Glover made these wild allegations stated:

> The inmate who provided this information is seeking assistance from the police in the hope that they can move him to another prison to facilitate easier family visits and he is also seeking credit from the judge at his trial for any assistance he can give to the police by way of information. There is obviously no way at this stage of determining whether or not this information has any substance, but he has in the past provided accurate information to the police.

On 10 November 1994, Glover received a visit at HMP Armley, in Leeds, from a Detective Inspector Stoker of Northumbria Police. Glover had invited him to the prison, as he wanted to know if the authorities were prepared to take him up on his offer. Glover told DI Stoker that he missed his family and that Paddy Conroy had let him down badly so he was more than willing to repeat his allegations in a statement or in person in court. DI Stoker was not in a position to make promises to Glover, and so he said that he would speak to the Crown Prosecution Service on his behalf.

When he returned to Newcastle, DI Stoker visited special caseworker Mr D. Hyland at the Crown Prosecution Service offices and explained what Glover had proposed. After careful consideration, Mr Hyland advised DI Stoker that no deal could be made with Glover but that if he was willing to assist the police with the matters that he had mentioned, then facts could be made known to Glover's trial judge, meaning any sentence imposed might be reduced based on the quality of the information he had provided.

On Wednesday, 23 November 1994, Glover was being held at Market Street Police Station, in Newcastle, while awaiting a court hearing that was due to take place later that day. DI Stoker visited him in the cells, told him what Mr Hyland had said and reiterated the fact that if he did decide to furnish the police with information about himself or others it could earn him a reduced sentence. Glover was devastated. His allegations of theft, robbery, possession of firearms and conspiracy to murder had all been ignored. What, he must have thought, was it going to take to make the police sit up and listen to him?

When Glover and his cellmate, Kevin Lowe, ended their half-hearted hunger strike at HMP Armley, Glover befriended Ronnie Priestley, an inmate on the same landing as him, who allegedly told him that he was plotting to have a judge 'done in'. Priestley, from Leeds, was serving four years for offences involving counterfeit perfume. His wife had also been found guilty of committing crimes linked to his not so sweet-smelling business, and she was awaiting sentence.

His Honour Judge Hoffman, who had imprisoned Priestley, had indicated that he personally wished to sentence Priestley's wife. According to Glover, Priestley felt that the judge was being vindictive, and so he had decided to have him murdered. Glover agreed to assist with the conspiracy, and a note was smuggled out of the prison during a visit. This note allegedly offered John Chisholm, who was described by Glover as a Sunderland-based hit man, £50,000 to kill the judge. According to Glover, Priestley is said to have agreed to pay the money only if the judge went on to jail his wife. Unfortunately for Ronnie Priestley and John Chisholm, before sentence was passed on Mrs Priestley, David Glover was moved to HMP Winson Green, in Birmingham. I say it was unfortunate because the move that took Glover further away from his family in the north-east was the only reason he had made his ridiculous allegation against these two totally innocent men.

On Monday, 6 February 1995, Glover was processed without incident by the reception staff at Winson Green and allocated to cell number D3.

When officers escorted Glover to his new home, he refused to exchange the clothes he was wearing for prison-issue items. The officers feared that the situation could escalate into violence, and so Glover was taken to cell A1, in the segregation unit. Once there, he was spoken to by a senior officer, after which he agreed that he would wear prison garb and return to his cell peacefully. Glover adhered to his promise, but later that evening he smashed up his cell and fought with the officers who tried to restrain him. Glover is a powerful man, and so it took some time and effort to get him under control, but he was eventually handcuffed, and three officers physically carried him back down to the segregation unit.

Glover remained in solitary confinement until 14 February, when he once more agreed to wear prison clothing and behave. At lunchtime that day, Glover spoke to Senior Officer Underwood and informed him that he knew the whereabouts of a firearm that had been smuggled into HMP Holme House, in Stockton, on Teesside. The officer listened to Glover's story for an hour and a half, and at the end of it he concluded that the information appeared to be 'unfounded'. Two nights later, the same officer once more spoke to Glover, whom he described as being in a distressed state. Glover explained that he was missing his family in the north-east and was willing to write a letter detailing his involvement in numerous crimes if the authorities would move him nearer home. SO Underwood explained to Glover that he was not in a position to do deals and that if he felt like unburdening himself of his previous criminal activities then the police could be notified if he so wished. The officer then continued on his rounds.

Glover did write a letter, in which he claimed that Paddy Conroy and others had been involved in the attack on Brian 'the Taxman' Cockerill. He also claimed that members of the Conroy family had shot members of the Harrison family and that Paddy was guilty of the kidnap and torture of Collier. Glover, of course, played down his role in any wrongdoing. He said that he had been present on the day Collier was attacked only because his mother is Paddy's sister-in-law and he had wanted to back Paddy up. Rather bizarrely, Glover alleged that Cockerill had been attacked because of trouble the Conroys were having with the Sayers family at that time. According to Glover, Cockerill was a 'Sayers man'.

A few days after writing this fictitious nonsense, Glover, like his predecessor Judas Iscariot, decided to take his own life. Glover attempted to cut his throat and wrists, but prison officers managed to intervene before he caused himself any serious harm. In order to protect Glover from himself, prison officers placed him in a body belt, which is a thick leather device that fits around the waist and has handcuff attachments at either side. The person wearing the belt can stand upright and walk, but his hands are effectively fixed to his waist, and so any attempt to harm himself or others is futile. Because Glover had attempted to commit suicide, he was transferred to the prison's hospital wing for observation. Staff were clearly concerned about his mental health, but they were not the only ones.

Glover's state of mind was of great concern to many beyond the prison walls. He was clearly getting desperate, and whenever he got desperate he was prone to inventing stories about those closest to him in order to improve his own situation. HMP Winson Green is just a four-hour drive from Newcastle, but for Glover and his family he might as well have been incarcerated in Birmingham, Alabama. With the family breadwinner in jail and young children to care for, Glover's partner was unable to afford to visit him. This caused Glover untold distress, and his broken heart brought out the worst in him.

Glover informed Northumbria Police that the Conroys were using the Happy House to cultivate cannabis and that he knew the house that the gunmen had fled to after murdering Viv Graham. According to Glover, this was a safe house that had once been owned by the father of a man named Stephen Craven. The property, a bungalow, had been empty and put on the market following a campaign of hostility towards the family after Stephen Craven was convicted of the murder of a girl named Penny Laing.

On Christmas Eve 1989, 28-year-old Craven had been at the Studio nightclub in Newcastle. Nineteen-year-old Penny had been walking across the dance floor when Craven had made a remark that she considered to be inappropriate. Penny had slapped Craven across the face, and he had responded by smashing a glass on her neck, which severed her jugular vein. Penny's boyfriend attacked Craven, and in the chaos that ensued Craven made good his escape. The following day, Craven attended hospital for treatment to a cut on his finger and then flew to New York, where he remained for three days. Upon his return, he was arrested, charged and eventually convicted of Penny's murder. Craven was sentenced to life imprisonment but released after just seven years.

Glover claimed that Viv's killers or their co-conspirators were aware that Craven's family had vacated the bungalow and so they had obtained the keys from an estate agent on the pretext of viewing the property. They had then had a spare set of keys cut before returning the originals. Having secured a base from which to work, the men then set about putting their grisly plan into action.

In exchange for detailed information about the Conroys' alleged cannabis farm and Viv Graham's killers, Glover asked the authorities if he could be moved to Strangeways Prison, in Manchester, which would make visiting easier for his wife.

The police knew that Glover's allegation concerning the Happy House cannabis farm was false and based on spite rather than fact, because they had almost taken the property apart in their search for guns following the shooting of the Harrisons. However, the unsolved murder of Viv Graham has posed more questions on Tyneside than who shot JFK, and so Glover's information was not something that the police were prepared to ignore.

At 11 a.m. on Wednesday, 22 February 1995, a DC Trotter and a colleague named DC Bower travelled to Birmingham in order to speak to Glover. With them, the officers had brought a video recording of houses in Sackville Road, Heaton. Glover was going to be shown the video, and he was then to be asked to point out which house Viv's killers had gone to after the shooting. After arriving at the prison for the visit, the police officers were told that they would not be able to see Glover, because he had been disruptive that morning. Because they had travelled so far, it was suggested that they return after lunch, when, it was hoped, he would have calmed down.

At 1.30 p.m., the officers were taken to a room within the prison complex, and Glover entered shortly afterwards, surrounded by a number of officers, the wing governor and the security chief. Glover was wearing a body belt and was ushered to sit down at a table. After introducing themselves to Glover, the police officers explained the purpose of their visit, and Glover agreed to view the video. Appearing to stare intently at the screen, Glover said that he recognised the row of bungalows but couldn't say for sure which one the killers had sought refuge in. The police officers asked Glover how he knew for sure that those responsible for murdering Viv Graham had gone into one of the bungalows. Glover's reply shocked everybody in the room. 'I drove the getaway car,' he said in a matter-of-fact way.

Barely able to contain his excitement, one of the officers said, 'What exactly do you mean by that?'

Glover replied, 'I drove the getaway car after the shooting.'

At this point, the wing governor asked the police officers if all his staff needed to be present, and it was agreed that the only persons to remain would be the police and the chief security officer. Glover was then cautioned and asked who had shot Viv Graham. 'Michael Sayers,' he replied. 'Michael Sayers shot Viv Graham.' Glover claimed that on the morning of the murder he and Sayers had travelled to Birtley, near Chester-le-Street, and stolen an old blue Ford Escort from a car park near the swimming baths. Glover said that he had managed to get into the car by 'jiggling the locks'. From Birtley, they had driven approximately eight miles to Heaton, where they parked 'somewhere in Sackville Road'. According to Glover, they had then parted company until later that day, when he picked up Sayers after retrieving the stolen vehicle. Glover said that they then scoured the streets looking for Viv's distinctive Ford Cosworth.

Sayers, according to Glover, had told him that he was going to shoot Viv in the legs in retaliation for some ongoing dispute during which Sayers had been assaulted. Unable to locate their intended target, Glover and Sayers had driven to Viv's home, but his car was nowhere to be seen. It was common knowledge that Viv frequented the bars in Wallsend High Street, and so they decided to search for him there. The duo soon discovered Viv's blue Cosworth parked in a side street near the Queen's Head Hotel. Glover told the police that he parked the stolen Escort he was driving in a back lane that had a view of the rear of Viv's car. Sayers is then said to have walked over to the vehicle and smashed the driver's window. The hazard lights came on, and Glover said that he assumed that the alarm had been activated.

Glover told the officers that shortly afterwards he heard three loud shots and as he looked across the street he saw Viv on all fours next to his vehicle. 'Sayers ran back to the car and ordered me to drive,' Glover said. 'I was directed to a quiet lane in Heaton, and the vehicle was torched.' According to Glover, both he and Sayers were then picked up by two other men in a burgundy Shogun vehicle. Glover told the officers that Sayers had used a .357 Magnum that was grey in colour. 'He kept it in a shoulder holster, which he always wore,' Glover said. He added that Sayers had been high on cocaine when he had shot Viv and that afterwards they both believed that he had only been wounded, because they had seen him trying to get to his feet.

The stunned detectives realised that Glover's evidence could not be ignored, because he was not only naming Viv Graham's killer but was also implicating himself as an accomplice. Deciding to test the authenticity of what he had told them, the officers put it to Glover that he could have gleaned all the information in his account from newspaper articles. 'Tell us something only people involved in Viv's murder would know,' they asked. Glover thought for a moment and then said that as he had sped away after the shooting the vehicle had hit something and damaged the bumper. He added that he knew the stolen vehicle had belonged to a female because there had been a box of tissues in the glove compartment and some furry toys on the dashboard. If that was not proof enough of his involvement in Viv's murder, Glover then claimed that he had a tape recording of Michael Sayers boasting about the killing. This had allegedly been recorded without Sayers' knowledge at a karaoke night in a Newcastle pub. When the detectives asked Glover the whereabouts of the tape recording, he would only say that he had it in safe keeping.

For reasons known only to Northumbria Police, David Glover was not charged with any offence in relation to Viv Graham's murder, nor was Michael Sayers, the man Glover had blamed. Perhaps Northumbria Police know that Glover, like Berriman, is prone to inventing stories in order to save himself.

Chapter Nine

TRIAL AND RETRIBUTION

PADDY CONROY'S TRIAL, or 'the torture trial', as it became known, began on 6 October 1995. Paddy's legal team had applied to have it moved away from Newcastle, because his reputation in the city was such that they did not think he would get a fair trial. Rightly or wrongly, the application was turned down. Rather than risk another embarrassing escape by Paddy and Glover, police chiefs put in place security measures unlike anything the city of Newcastle has seen before or since. A cavalcade of motorcycle outriders surrounded the prison van, a helicopter and a fixed-wing aeroplane patrolled the skies and police marine launches bobbed up and down on the River Tyne.

Every man is entitled to be tried by a jury of his peers, and Paddy, Glover, Peachy and Waters all decided to exercise that right by pleading not guilty to the charges they faced. Paddy, Glover and Waters were accused of kidnap, false imprisonment and grievous bodily harm with intent, and Peachy was charged with false imprisonment and attempting to pervert the course of justice.

There was a real sense of drama prevalent throughout the proceedings. The media used lurid phrases in banner headlines such as 'the battle-torn streets of the West End', 'gangsters who terrorised a community' and 'gun law having gripped the city'. The prosecution undoubtedly earned its fee throughout the trial. They made Paddy Conroy sound like the devil incarnate. In fact, one female juror became so upset by the nature of the evidence that she suffered a panic attack. The judge acted promptly and discharged her from continuing with the trial. When evidence of Collier's torture was given, a second female juror indicated

164

to the jury bailiff that she was unable to continue. Her doctor delivered a medical report to the court the following morning:

> This person is a very anxious lady. Since the trial began she has developed symptoms of an anxiety state – loss of appetite, nausea, insomnia – and she feels she cannot continue with jury service. I do not believe that she is medically fit to serve.

This lady was also discharged, and so it was thought that the judge would have to order a retrial with a new jury, but, despite protestations from the defence barristers, the judge ruled that the trial should be allowed to continue.

The most damning evidence given against Paddy didn't come from the police or Billy Collier; it came from none other than his co-defendant David Glover. While assisting the police with solving every crime that he had ever invented, Glover had written a 'confession' in HMP Winson Green, in which he said that he had been enlisted by Paddy as 'backup' for the attack on Collier. However, when he gave evidence at the trial, he claimed that his confession was in fact false, because he had been 'psychotic' at the time that he had written it. Glover told the jury that he had heard voices in his head while in prison. These voices were telling him that he was going to end up in a body bag. He shaved off all his hair and became convinced that the police were trying to kill him and fit him up for a murder. Despite there being plenty of evidence available to support Glover's claim that he had been suffering from mental illness, the judge ruled that the statements he had written *could* be given in evidence against Paddy.

More than a decade later, in December 2007, Glover was interviewed by the *Evening Chronicle*. He told a reporter that he had never signed any statements against Paddy, written any confession or been a police informant. In a bizarre effort to add weight to his denials, Glover told the reporter that he had tried cutting his own hands off in prison by 'smacking them against the edge of a broken toilet seat', to ensure that he would be physically incapable of signing anything.

Paddy has always held the view that when the trial judge ruled that Glover's confession about the attack on Collier was admissible as evidence, rather than rubbishing it as lies, the authorities should also have accepted Glover's confession concerning his involvement in the murder of Viv Graham as true. There was evidence to suggest that Glover was being honest: he had told the police things that only those involved in the killing could have known. He knew about a box of tissues being in the getaway car, and he knew a female had owned it. When the police forensically tested the thing Glover had collided with while speeding away, which turned out to be a low wall, it had traces of blue paint that matched samples taken from the stolen getaway vehicle. It was bizarre that Glover's confession had been ignored. Only Glover knows if he was telling the truth, but if he was he has escaped prosecution for the most notorious murder ever committed in the north-east.

While cross-examining Paddy in the torture trial, Mr Batty for the prosecution asked, 'Have you ever heard of the Green Man pub?'

'No, but I have heard of the Green Tree pub,' Paddy replied with a degree of sarcasm.

'Is it right that your brother had his brains blown out in there?' Mr Batty asked.

Rather than give Mr Batty the satisfaction of an answer to such an unnecessarily disrespectful and hurtful question, Paddy picked up a jug of water that had been left in the witness box for refreshment and drenched him with it. The prison officers sitting either side of Paddy attempted to restrain him, but he tossed them aside, and for a few moments it looked as if the judge was going to order the court to be cleared. As Paddy struggled with the prison officers, the judge was shouting, 'Order! Order!' and Paddy's family and friends were shouting obscenities at Mr Batty. When Paddy felt that he had made his point, he sat down. His barrister pleaded with him to apologise, but Paddy refused, and so his barrister asked if he could do so on his behalf. It was a meaningless apology, but Mr Batty accepted the barrister's sincere regret regarding the incident. Everybody present thought that the judge would have Paddy removed from the court, but when he did comment on the incident all he said was, 'You are lucky, Mr Batty. It could have been the microphone that he had thrown.'

After seven long weeks of evidence, Conroy and Glover were convicted of kidnap, false imprisonment and grievous bodily harm, and Waters and Peachy were both found not guilty of all charges. Before sentencing Paddy, Judge Carr said that the nature of the offences he had been convicted of called for a long term of imprisonment: 'I am satisfied that you were the organising force that day and that you were the one who controlled, by and large, what went on. I say by and large because, insofar as Glover is concerned, I am perfectly satisfied that he is a dangerous young man on his own account, but you were the organising force that day and therefore you must bear the responsibility.' Paddy was sentenced to serve eleven and a half years' imprisonment, and Glover was given ten and a half years.

The Northumbria Police witness support scheme financed protection for nine different people during the trial. Some, such as Collier and his girlfriend, were relocated and given new identities. A senior CID officer who worked on the case was quoted in the *Newcastle Evening Chronicle* as saying:

> In the past, people have been too scared to give evidence for fear of reprisals. The witness protection scheme has been able to give support to people who were prepared to stand up for justice. They have had the courage to give statements and now some of the witnesses have been re-housed away from friends and family – but it was a price that they were willing to pay.

Law-abiding members of the community were outraged that somebody such as David Glover had been permitted to follow a life of criminal brutality while acting as a registered police informant. Although there is a strong element of truth in the old adage of setting a thief to catch a thief, the fact that Northumbria Police had knowingly recruited a man capable of such violence as David Glover should have given rise to concern.

In recent years, there has been increasing anecdotal evidence and rumour about the striking of deals in which a blind eye is turned to some crimes in order to gather information on so-called major criminals and their activities. On 6 June 2007, DC Alan Jones of Northumbria Police was arrested by his colleagues. At a gym that he frequented, he had forged a friendship with a man named Allan Foster, who had just been released from an 11-year prison sentence for violence, drug dealing and possession of a sawn-off shotgun and ammunition. Before long, Jones had recruited Foster as an informant, and he dutifully gave the policeman information about his criminal associates.

But Foster was soon demanding sensitive material from the police national computer in return, and the crooked policeman complied. In order to exploit his relationship with Jones further, Foster treated him to a weekend in London. The pair were chauffeur driven from bar to bar before returning to Foster's 'weekend apartment', where three £250-a-time escort girls were hired. The quality of information that Foster was giving to Jones about his fellow criminals soon saw him promoted from a source of local interest to what the police these days call 'a covert human intelligence source'.

Foster began working directly with the Serious and Organised Crime Agency. His status was not known by the average bobby on the beat, and so when they raided his home looking for an £80,000 ring that he had stolen from the MetroCentre, in Gateshead, he was outraged and told his masters in Northumbria Police that he no longer wished to work for them. A week later, he lured a friend and father of seven named Noddy Rice to the car park of a South Shields beauty spot and shot him nine times. Foster immediately fled the country after the murder and is currently listed as one of the top ten most wanted men in Britain. For passing on information to Foster, DC Jones was convicted of misconduct in a public office and sentenced to five years' imprisonment.

It cannot be disputed that informants are useful if they can maintain credibility amongst their criminal associates. This, of necessity, often involves them being closely involved in the whole business of crime. But it is a very dangerous path to tread, because, as in Glover's case, there is a risk that criminal informants will attempt to take advantage of their position and step up their criminal activities while promising a result to their police handlers. Glover has admitted that while he was supposedly helping the police to combat crime he was responsible for beating, torturing and shooting people. It is not known, however, if his admission concerning the murder of Viv Graham is true.

Paddy Conroy found it hard being away from Maureen and their children. The very thought of spending so many years of his life in jail ate away at Paddy, and so he tried to distance himself from life outside the wall. Life inside the wall was best described as extremely dangerous, chaotic and brutal.

Lifers and other prisoners considered to be a security risk are accommodated in what is known as the dispersal system, which was created following the deliberations of a committee chaired by Sir Leon Radzinowicz. Lord Mountbatten had previously recommended housing high-risk prisoners in a single institution, which was to be known as HMP Vectis. This prison was going to be situated on the Isle of Wight, but Sir Radzinowicz opposed this in favour of several maximum-security prisons between which Category A prisoners could be dispersed. This, he believed, would dilute their influence in the system and make it easier to transfer them in the event of trouble.

It can be argued that Sir Radzinowicz was responsible for introducing every major criminal from every major city to his counterparts in cities throughout the UK, which has led to an explosion in organised crime. For instance, if Mr A from Manchester had not been forced to serve his sentence in an exclusive prison for criminals of his own calibre, he would never have met Mr B who operated in London, Birmingham, Bristol or Leeds. Friendships are forged in the dispersal system, because the inmates are all there long term, and those friends become business partners when they are released. From the point of view of the authorities, it would have been much wiser to keep criminals in local prisons, as they did years ago. There are currently eight dispersal prisons in England: HMPs Belmarsh, Frankland, Full Sutton, Long Lartin, Manchester, Wakefield, Whitemoor and Woodhill. Paddy Conroy ended up spending time in them all.

During his time in the dispersal system, Paddy witnessed at first hand one of the worst prison disturbances this country has ever known. HMP Full Sutton, near York, was renamed 'Half Sutton' because of the damage caused by rioting inmates. The unrest had started after the prison staff union, the Prison Officers' Association (POA), threatened to strike for better working conditions. A tidal wave of tension rippled throughout the penal system after a work-to-rule by the officers resulted in delayed mail, cancelled visits and inmates being locked in their cells for 23 hours a day.

Paddy had sensed what was going to happen, and so he said to one of the officers, 'There is going to be a major riot in here if this work-to-rule nonsense continues. This is no ordinary jail. A lot of men in here are serving life sentences and have nothing to lose. If it does kick off, it will be a bloodbath.' The officer paused to think for a moment before smiling at Paddy and saying that if there was a riot then maybe the government would sit up and listen to the POA. For three weeks, Paddy pleaded with his fellow inmates on the wing not to create any kind of disorder. 'It's what the screws want,' he said. 'If you do riot, then you will be playing right into their hands.' Paddy's advice fell on deaf ears. A large number of men on the wing had given up hope the day that they were sentenced. They no longer had families, friends, freedom or expectation, and rioting would almost be a welcome change to their day-to-day mundane existence.

When the inmates' cells were opened on the morning of 20 January 1997, Paddy went to the communal kitchen and put several pieces of prime steak in the oven, setting the timer so that they would be slowly cooked and ready for lunchtime. Paddy was then locked up again until around the time he had calculated that his steaks would be done to perfection. As soon as Paddy was unlocked, he went directly downstairs to the kitchen area to ensure that his meal had not been burned. As Paddy did so, he saw that an inmate named Dessie Cunningham was in the process of being dragged to the segregation unit for committing some sort of misdemeanour. Several bystanders had gone to his aid, and this had resulted in a tense stand-off with the prison staff. Cunningham began to shout, swear and struggle, and those inmates who had been facing up to the officers began fighting with them and throwing furniture. As more and more inmates became involved, the prison officers conceded defeat and beat a hasty retreat from the wing. As they did so, they locked every door they passed through in order to contain the inmates and prevent others joining in with the melee.

Paddy had no intention of getting involved, and so he found himself locked in the kitchen with his perfectly cooked steak lunch. His only complaint was that he had to make do without the pepper sauce that he had made and left in his cell. At the rear of the kitchen was a stairway that led up to one of the landings. At the top of the stairs, there was a security gate, which had been locked. Paddy could see out onto the landing, but there was no way that he could reach his pepper sauce. As Paddy settled down to tuck into his lunch, the sounds of men screaming and shouting and the destruction of property reverberated throughout the wing. Years of built-up tension was being unleashed in an orgy of hysterical violence.

Expecting a counter-attack from the riot squad, the inmates began to erect barricades using tables, chairs and doors that they had torn from their hinges. When the riot squad failed to materialise, the prisoners decided to render the wing unfit for human habitation. Water pipes were ripped from the walls, and electrical switches and fuse boxes were smashed. Fires were started, heavy steel cell doors were removed and anything that could be damaged or destroyed was. Access to the exercise yard was gained by battering down a steel gate with a cell door. An impromptu barbecue party was staged by the marauding mob, using files, documents, inmates' records and furniture to feed the flames. An attempt by the fire brigade to extinguish the fire was met with a salvo of missiles. The firemen, fearing for their lives, soon abandoned their equipment and ran for the safety of the main gate, where police had set up a cordon to prevent inmates escaping.

After finishing his meal, Paddy looked out of the barred window and saw that smoke was billowing out of several cells and missiles were raining down on the exercise yard. There was nothing he could do to either deter or incite the other inmates, and so he made himself a cup of tea and settled down into a chair to watch the chaos unfold all around him. Above the sound of the rioting inmates, Paddy could hear somebody shouting from a window that an informant had been murdered. The inmates took a break from their destructive spree and began to cheer and stamp their feet in celebration. Paddy later learned that the victim had not in fact been murdered but had been stabbed and slashed and received a total of 49 stitches to his wounds.

As Paddy sat sipping his tea, he saw one young lad from Newcastle run and push over a pool table. 'Stop what you're doing now, and come over here, you soft bastard,' Paddy shouted at him.

'What's wrong with you, Paddy?' he replied. 'I'm only doing what everybody else is doing.'

Paddy advised the lad to look over to his left and explained that the inmate who was watching him was the wing grass. 'Go and pick up the pool table, walk slowly back to your cell and slam the door behind you,' Paddy advised.

Thankfully, Paddy's words of wisdom were absorbed, and the lad was spared the ordeal of facing the serious charge of rioting, for which several inmates were later sentenced to an additional five years' imprisonment.

A small fire that had been started in the TV room on the landing above Paddy's location was by now raging out of control. Several foam-filled chairs were ablaze, and thick black smoke had begun to gather like a toxic cloud on the wing ceiling. Adjacent to the TV room, a 60-year-old Dutchman who was serving a lengthy sentence for importing drugs into the UK was locked in his cell. Twelve months earlier he had undergone open-heart surgery, and he was still suffering from poor health. Frail and weak, he had shut himself in his cell as soon as the riot had started. The black cloud from the burning foam seats had begun to descend from the ceiling, and the open windows in people's cells were creating a chimney-like effect, drawing the acrid smoke under their cell doors. Fearing for his life, the Dutchman had lain on the floor and covered his face with a wet cloth in an effort to minimise smoke inhalation.

Paddy began shouting to a group of prison officers who had gathered on the other side of the security gate that the old Dutch guy who was locked in his cell was going to die if they didn't get him out. Paddy believed that the officers thought he was trying to lure them into a trap, because for the first ten or fifteen minutes they refused to acknowledge him. As Paddy's concern for this elderly man grew, he became increasingly irate and vocal. Eventually, the officers began shouting, 'Stand back, Conroy. Stand away from the gate. We are coming in.' Paddy did as they asked, and moments later several apprehensive-looking officers came running onto the wing. As the officers dragged the semi-conscious Dutchman from his smoke-filled cell, the wing governor switched the powerful extractor fans on and within minutes all the deadly smoke had been blown outside.

Some time after midnight, the prisoners ran out of property to burn or wreck and so decided to retire to their beds. Fearing repercussions from the prison officers, they decided to share cells rather than face the possibility of retribution alone. The following morning, the cell doors remained closed as a mass of RoboCop-lookalike officers carrying riot shields advanced across the landings chanting, 'One, two, advance, one, two, advance.' Later in the afternoon, inmates identified as key members of the rioting faction were moved to other prisons, and several others, including Paddy Conroy, were escorted to the segregation unit.

Dessie Cunningham, whose initial confrontation with the officers had sparked the riot, was also being held in solitary confinement, and he was told by another inmate that Paddy had assisted and encouraged the prison officers to come onto the wing. This was, of course, true, but Cunningham interpreted it as if Paddy had asked the screws to come onto the wing to quell the riot rather than to save the Dutchman's life. Rather foolishly, Cunningham began referring to Paddy as a lackey and a grass. When Paddy was told what Cunningham had been calling him, he sent word that he wished to speak to him urgently. Cunningham was a violent career criminal serving 20 years for committing armed robberies, and so he was certainly no mug, but, then again, neither is Paddy Conroy.

Before Paddy was released from the segregation unit and was able to confront Cunningham, Cunningham had been shipped out to HMP Whitemoor, in Cambridgeshire, where he became friends with John Henry Sayers.

Sayers had recently been moved to HMP Whitemoor following a government decision to abolish SSUs. This downgrading, which was seen by many as a means of securing an IRA ceasefire in Northern Ireland, led to the reclassification of 13 IRA prisoners from exceptional-risk Category A to high-risk Category A. The only other prisoner in the UK with the same status at that time had been Sayers. He had been held at the SSU in HMP Full Sutton, but when that was mothballed he and others had been transferred.

On one occasion, Sayers was transferred to HMP Frankland, in Durham, for his accumulated visits, but instead of being placed in a normal location he was allocated a cell in the segregation unit, next door to David Glover, who had recently arrived from HMP Winson Green. The week Sayers arrived in HMP Frankland, the visiting room that is used by high-risk prisoners was being decorated. It was decided by the powers that be that visits should therefore be held in the rooms normally allocated to solicitors for legal visits with their clients. It is standard practice for all high-risk prisoners to be accompanied by at least one prison officer whenever they are outside their cells. This includes visiting times, when officers sit at the same table as prisoners and their visitors.

It has since been alleged that, for reasons known only to the prison staff, John Henry Sayers and Glover were permitted to have totally unsupervised visits with their partners in the solicitors' offices. A few months later, the *Sunday Sun* newspaper published a story on its front page with the headline 'Our Jail Baby Joy'. It was claimed that 'one of the North's toughest gangsters' was set to become a dad again after he fathered a child behind bars at a top-security jail. In an exclusive interview, John Henry's wife, Yvonne, told a reporter that she had spent the last six years travelling Britain to visit her man and always looked forward to Christmas, when he was allowed to spend a month at HMP Frankland for family visits. 'I didn't go there that day expecting to have sex with my husband,' she said. 'It just happened. To be honest I think that prison officers turn a blind eye to this sort of thing.'

Hazel Banks, the deputy governor at HMP Frankland, told the newspaper that she did not believe the baby had been conceived behind bars. She added that she was not aware of the 'incident' and that all visits were strictly monitored: 'And when it comes to Category A prisoners, there are always several officers around at any time. It would be very difficult – if not impossible – for this to take place.' Yvonne Sayers responded to these comments by saying that she knew people would think she had been having an affair and that it was not John Henry's baby but that she would never do such a thing.

When John Henry Sayers became acquainted with Dessie Cunningham at HMP Whitemoor, fuel was poured onto an already volatile situation. John Henry repeated the story that his brother Michael had told him concerning the time DC Perky had allegedly claimed that Paddy was a grass. Initially, Paddy was unsure what motive John Henry had for trying to incite trouble, but word soon reached him via the prison grapevine that the Sayers family were upset because he had been repeating the allegation that their father had enjoyed an unhealthy relationship with the police. When Paddy was told a few months later that he was being transferred to HMP Whitemoor, he just knew that his arrival would spark trouble. Paddy assumed that the trouble would be with John Henry, but, unbeknown to him, Dessie Cunningham had pre-paid an inmate nicknamed 'Jesus' to murder him.

Shortly after arriving at Whitemoor, Paddy was sitting at a table in his cell writing a letter when the door burst open. Before Paddy had a chance to react, the inappropriately nicknamed Jesus had plunged a long metal spike into the top of his head. The spade-shaped weapon tore through Paddy's flesh and partially penetrated his skull, but instead of piercing it and killing him instantly it deflected and chipped a fragment of bone. As Paddy tried to turn to face his attacker, Jesus pulled the spike out of his head and attempted to stab him in the face, but Paddy managed to throw himself forward. The spike glanced off the back of Paddy's head and tore a long, deep furrow down his back. With blood pouring from his wounds, Paddy knew that he had to get to his feet and fight Jesus off or die at his hands in that cell. Mustering all his diminishing strength, Paddy hit Jesus as hard as he could, and when he fell back Paddy pounded his face and body until he collapsed at his feet.

The sound of the fracas had attracted the attention of the prison staff, who raced en masse to the cell. When they burst through the door, Paddy was still hammering Jesus, and so it was Paddy who was dragged off to the security block. When the seriousness of Paddy's injuries became apparent, he was rushed to a local hospital, where a doctor described his survival as miraculous. Back at the prison, Jesus was treated as the victim of a vicious assault and Paddy was charged with being the perpetrator. Paddy knew that the prison staff were not that naive. He had two gaping holes in him that would indicate to the most sceptical of men that he was in fact the victim.

Paddy was repeatedly asked to make a formal complaint against Jesus, but he was no Judas. Paddy believed that a decision had been made to charge him simply because the prison officers thought that he might save himself from punishment by telling them the truth. Jesus could have quite rightly faced an attempted murder charge, but, fortunately for him, Paddy is not an informant, and so it was Paddy who faced being punished for a crime that he did not commit.

On the morning of Paddy's trial, he was frogmarched into the governor's office, and after the charge of assault had been read out he was asked to plead guilty or not guilty. Staring straight at the governor, Paddy smiled and said, 'Guilty.'

'Get out of this room, Conroy! Get out!' the governor bellowed.

Out in the corridor, the escorting officers stood glaring at Paddy and shaking their heads. A few minutes passed, and then the governor's door flew open. 'Take Conroy down the segregation unit, and get the other person involved in this matter up here now!' a voice screamed. When Jesus appeared in front of the governor, he too refused to cooperate, and so he too was sent to the segregation unit, where he ended up in a cell next to a man from Liverpool named Frankie Mullen. When Mullen asked Jesus why he had been put in solitary confinement, Jesus said that he had stabbed a man named Paddy Conroy. Mullen had been a very good friend of Paddy's long before he had been sent to prison, and so he turned on Jesus immediately. 'If you have stabbed Paddy, you will soon be fucking dead,' Mullen warned him.

Before Paddy had been imprisoned, Mullen had stayed at his home in Newcastle after falling out with a Liverpool-based drug-dealing firm who were claiming that he was responsible for the disappearance of 30,000 of their Ecstasy pills.

The Bull and Paddy would occasionally go shooting game and rabbits at a place known as Tam's Camp, which is approximately 40 miles north of Newcastle. They were not particularly interested in blasting bunnies. It was considered to be more of a lads' night out with shooting practice thrown in for good measure. As any Geordie will tell you, when residing in the West End of Newcastle, it is important that one maintains a degree of regular firearms practice. The Bull and Paddy would take a tent and a few beers, go shooting during daylight and then sit around a campfire talking at night.

One time, Mullen asked the Bull and Paddy if he could accompany them, and they readily agreed. As they made their way to Tam's Camp, the Bull spotted what appeared to be a freshly killed rabbit at the roadside. Paddy asked Mullen to get out of the vehicle and pick up the creature so that they could cook and eat it later. After arriving at their destination, making a fire and inspecting the rabbit, the trio decided not to eat it after all, as the corpse was stiff and the rabbit had therefore been dead much longer than they had first thought. The Bull threw the rabbit on the blazing fire, and within a very short time it was engulfed by the flames. Mullen sat staring at the animal's body as it was devoured by the fire. It appeared as though he was in some sort of deep trance.

When the Bull and Paddy got into their sleeping bags that night,

Mullen, who had hardly spoken a word all evening, remained sitting staring at the fire. A week later, Mullen murdered two of his adversaries, chopped up their bodies and burned them. He was serving a double life sentence for those murders when he encountered Jesus in the segregation unit.

Fearing for his safety, Jesus blurted out the truth to Mullen about the attack on Paddy. He told him that it was Dessie Cunningham who had paid him to carry out the stabbing. 'I have no personal grievance with Paddy,' Jesus said. 'It was Cunningham who wanted him done.' Four weeks later, Cunningham was found dead in his cell. His lifeless body hung from the bars at the end of a bed sheet. It is not known if Cunningham took his own life or if somebody with a grievance had murdered him.

One morning, a notorious south-London villain named Dennis Arif arrived at Paddy's cell door. 'I have a message for you, Paddy,' he said. 'John Henry wants to see you out on the yard this afternoon.'

'Right you are,' Paddy replied. 'I will be out there.'

Later that day, Paddy walked out onto the exercise yard with Dennis. The wing Paddy was housed in had its own yard, and the wing in which John Henry was housed had a yard that adjoined it. Only a wire mesh fence separated the two, and so it was possible to converse with inmates from the other wing.

Paddy strolled around the yard chatting to Dennis until John Henry and Dennis's brother Mehmet appeared on the other side of the fence. Dennis then asked Paddy to go over and speak to John Henry. Paddy approached the fence with a broad grin on his face and asked John Henry what he wanted. 'What have you been saying about my father?' John Henry asked.

'I think that he is a grass. In fact, I know that he is a grass,' Paddy said as he stared straight back at John Henry. Paddy then went into some detail to explain why he had reached that conclusion. The Arif brothers stood open-mouthed as they absorbed what Paddy was saying and looked in disgust as John Henry slouched off with his head bowed. 'Come back, man,' Paddy shouted. 'I haven't finished yet.' Paddy's words fell on deaf ears as John Henry continued to walk away from him. That incident was the catalyst for a lot of the bad blood that flowed between the Conroy and Sayers families thereafter.

Later that day, Paddy was approached by a cockney who alleged that John Henry had put a contract out on Paddy's life. Thrusting a long-bladed knife into Paddy's hand, the cockney said, 'Take this, Paddy. I think you're going to need it. When they come for you, strike first, ask questions later.'

As word spread throughout the prison about the simmering feud between Paddy and John Henry, inmates began to swear allegiance to one side or the other. The next time Paddy and John Henry crossed paths, it was in the visiting room. John Kendall, who in 1987 had escaped from prison in a helicopter, was sitting at a table adjacent to Paddy's, and Mad Frankie Fraser, who was visiting another prisoner, Eddie Richardson, was sitting at another. John Henry and his visitors were also sitting around a table that was in view of Paddy and his visitors. Paddy wanted to confront John Henry about him allegedly having a contract out on him, but he decided to bide his time and have his say when they were alone.

Five minutes before the visit was due to end, Paddy saw John Henry get up and walk out of the room. Paddy immediately told his friends and family that he had to leave, and set off in pursuit of his target, who by this time had left the main visiting hall. When prisoners have had a visit, they are searched for contraband and then kept in a holding area before being returned in groups to their respective wings. Paddy knew, therefore, that John Henry could not have got very far. After being searched, Paddy went into the holding area, but John Henry was nowhere to be seen. When Paddy entered the toilet block, John Henry was standing at the urinal with his back to him. 'Perfect,' Paddy thought as he approached him. 'He won't even know what has hit him.'

As Paddy was revelling in his good fortune, John Henry spun around and caught him under the chin with a right hook, which sent him flying across the room and into a wall. 'Fucking hell,' Paddy thought. 'What sort of a punch was that?' Momentarily dazed, Paddy struggled to stay on his feet. John Henry, realising that he might have won by delivering a single sucker-punch, leapt on top of Paddy and began pummelling his head and face. Regaining his composure and fearing defeat, Paddy summoned every ounce of rage and strength that he had in him and began to hit back. Blow after blow found its target until John Henry fell and curled up into a defensive ball.

Standing back, Paddy allowed John Henry to get to his feet, but as soon as he was upright Paddy sent him sprawling back across the room and crashing into a radiator with a right hook. As John Henry now struggled to remain on his feet, Paddy kicked him as hard as he could in the reproductive organs and grabbed him by the head. Plunging his thumb into the back of John Henry's eye socket, Paddy threatened to gouge it out. 'It's over right, fucking over. I want no more bollocks from you,' Paddy said. Standing John Henry upright, Paddy punched him as hard as he could in the face, and he flew backwards into a toilet cubicle, where he slumped down onto the seat. At that moment, a group of prison officers stormed into the toilets and grabbed the two men. Paddy was put into solitary confinement, and John Henry was returned to his wing.

The *Sunday Sun* reported this brawl on its front page with the headline 'Gangster Families Go to War'. The police, the newspaper claimed, had issued secret warnings about a 'turf war' between two notorious gangland families, one headed by bank robber John Henry Sayers and the other by violent blackmailer Paddy Conroy. It's untrue that John Henry had been convicted of robbing a bank and Paddy of blackmail. The story had clearly been sensationalised to enrage law-abiding suburban husbands and excite their bored housewives. The newspaper went on to report that a 'chilling top-level dossier' had spelt out the police's fears about this so-called turf war. John Henry, according to this dossier, 'continued to run his crime empire from inside Britain's most secure jail, tried to interfere with witnesses in a trial concerning his brothers and attempted to set up a partnership to smuggle cocaine into jail'. In an attempt to add weight to this drivel, extracts from the police intelligence report were published alongside in diary form:

17 February 1996: Ongoing feud between Newcastle gangsters John Sayers and Paddy Conroy for the position of top family.
May 1996: Alliance is formed to get cocaine into Whitemoor Prison between Sayers and a fellow prisoner called Gomez.
23 July 1996: Police warnings state that another criminal faction,

headed by Conroy [called 'a very violent leader'] is opposing the Sayers family gang.

December 1996: Sayers apparently gives the impression that he expects the duty governor to be at his beck and call, hinting that 'staff will have to change their ways' when certain other prisoners arrive at the jail.

11 December 1996: Police regard Sayers as a top echelon criminal in the north-east. They believe he has close links with 'much of the organised' crime in the rest of the North. The police also believe he has accumulated substantial wealth. He is recognised as a sophisticated leader of a criminal organisation based in Newcastle, and it is said he has considerable influence among other prisoners. He is polite to staff but should be kept separate from Paddy Conroy. Northumbria detectives believe Sayers may be conducting criminal enterprises from inside prison both by telephone and instructions through visitors. His two brothers Michael and Stephen Sayers face blackmail charges, and intelligence suggests there may be an attempt to interfere with witnesses. These witnesses now have a police guard 24 hours per day. Senior police officers believe 'Sayers presents a serious threat to human safety and should be held in exceptional-risk conditions'.

Shortly after this 'secret dossier' was published in the newspaper, Paddy was transferred back to HMP Full Sutton, in York.

The prisoners whose arrival would result in 'officers having to change their ways', according to John Henry, were his brothers Michael and Stephen. When the Sayers brothers were reunited at HMP Whitemoor, a story appeared in the *Sunday Sun* under the banner headline 'Crime Brothers Reunited in Jail.' It's not known if the good people of the north-east were interested in reading that it had been almost seven years since the brothers had all met, but the story appeared in the paper in any event. The Sayers may well have been in the same prison, but reunited they most certainly were not. The authorities ensured that they were kept on different wings within HMP Whitemoor, and so, apart from an occasional fleeting glimpse of one another, contact was minimal.

Paddy wasn't in HMP Full Sutton long before a fight broke out between him and one of the top Yardie gangsters named Cokie. Paddy had watched in horror as Cokie and several of his henchmen threatened a prisoner named Price in the shower block with a knife. Price apparently owed the Yardies £10 for cannabis, and they were intent on slashing his throat if he failed to pay. Causing serious harm or killing somebody over such a trivial debt may sound excessive, but every day in the dispersal system people are cut and stabbed – or worse – for less. The gangs that control the drugs and contraband within the system believe that if they let anybody get away with anything, however trivial, their reputation will be ruined and their illicit business will collapse or be taken from them.

At the time, Paddy was not aware that Price was being threatened as a result of a drug debt and shouted out, 'Back off, you goat-molesting mongrels, and leave the man alone.' Glaring at Paddy, Cokie and his associates stepped back but assured him that he would pay for involving himself in their business.

Three days later, as Paddy walked along the landing, Cokie smashed a large glass bottle of cooking oil over the back of his head. Momentarily stunned, Paddy held on to a safety rail and a wall, as he was convinced that if he hit the ground he would die. Regaining his composure, Paddy grabbed Cokie by his dreadlocks and smashed his head against every hard surface he could find. *Bash, bash, bash.* The sound of Cokie's head and body being bounced against the doors and walls brought half a dozen prison officers racing towards the fight from across the wing. Before they could reach Paddy, he had held Cokie by the throat with his left hand and punched his face with his right until his adversary collapsed at his feet in a bloody heap. 'Step back. Step back from him, Paddy!' the prison officers shouted. There was no need, as far as Paddy was concerned. He had done all that he had set out to do: the bully had lost all the credibility that his illicit business had thrived on.

Some time later, Paddy was in the Special Secure Unit. A young man from Manchester who was serving 20 years for shooting a rival drug dealer called Paddy over to look at something in his cell. 'What do you think of those, Paddy?' he asked, pointing to three long dreadlocks pinned to a board on his cell wall.

'Nothing really,' Paddy replied. 'Why do you ask?'

The Mancunian began laughing and said that the day Paddy had bashed Cokie he had followed him down the landing, picking up the dreadlocks he had torn from his opponent's head during the struggle. 'I was trying to get rid of the evidence, because I thought you were going to kill him, and when I heard he was OK I kept them as souvenirs,' the man explained.

For assaulting Cokie, Paddy was put in solitary confinement for four months. When Paddy was due to be returned to his normal location, he was escorted to the governor's office and asked to shake hands with Cokie, which he did without hesitation. Why wouldn't he? As far as Paddy was concerned, the chew they had between them had been resolved when they fought on the landing, Conroy 1 Cokie 0 being the full-time score.

Chapter Ten

HOMEWARD BOUND

WITH THE CITY'S two most powerful families in prison, control of the Newcastle underworld was up for grabs, and there proved to be no shortage of potential takers. The rise in gang-related violence created by the power struggle resulted in Northumbria Police launching a two-year investigation, code named Operation Domino. Three of the investigation's main targets were Gateshead men Robert Webber, Paul Ashton and Ashton's close associate Paul 'Monkey' Lyons. (Ashton is the man who took on Viv Graham for 20 gruelling minutes in a fight that failed to produce a clear winner. Following that encounter, Billy Robinson hired Graham as a doorman.)

On Thursday, 11 January 1996, Ashton and Webber were driving around Gateshead in a Mercedes. Ashton was in the passenger seat, and Webber was at the wheel. As they made their way down Bensham Bank, they encountered Stuart Watson and several of his friends. Watson was in a blue jeep being driven by a man named Terry Mitchell. (Watson is the man Viv Graham, Stephen Sayers and others were sent to prison for assaulting at Hobo's nightclub in 1989.) When Mitchell saw Ashton and Webber, he immediately turned the jeep around and gave chase. He managed to overtake the Mercedes and block the road ahead before coming to an abrupt halt. A gun was then fired. The bullet went through one of the windows of the Mercedes and struck Paul Ashton in the chest. Personal safety equipment was high on everybody's shopping list during those troubled years in the north-east, and the bulletproof vest that Ashton happened to be wearing that day undoubtedly saved his life.

After the bullet had struck the vest, it fell to the floor, where it was retrieved by Ashton. Fearing he would be the gunman's next target, Webber reversed the Mercedes at speed before doing a U-turn and heading towards Newcastle across the Redheugh Bridge. The jeep gave chase, and five or six more shots were fired, but none hit the occupants of the fleeing Mercedes.

The following morning, Ashton and Webber lay in wait for Watson to return to his home in Bensham. When Watson and Terry Mitchell pulled up in a van outside, several shots were fired from a Jaguar parked across the street. Watson and Mitchell returned fire and raced towards their attackers. Ashton tried to flee the scene on foot, but it is alleged that Mitchell struck him across the back with a sword. Rather wisely, Ashton then ran into a nearby police station seeking refuge. Meanwhile, Watson dragged Webber from the Jaguar and peppered the vehicle with shotgun pellets.

The seeds of this gang-related feud had been sown when Ashton had clashed with a friend of Watson named Stevie 'the Hammer' Eastland at a club called After Dark. Witnesses told the police that the men had chased one another around the premises with knives. A straightener was arranged for the following day so that the men could settle their differences, but for reasons unknown Ashton failed to attend. The next time that Ashton and Eastland had met, they had both pulled out knives and Eastland had run away from Ashton, but not in fear. He had drugs in his possession, which he later claimed were steroids, and he was concerned that if the police were called he would be found with them, although, it has to be said, it is not illegal in the UK to be in possession of steroids for one's personal use. After hiding the drugs under a brick in nearby bushes, Eastland returned to Ashton and the pair began to fight. A member of the public called the police, and Eastland was arrested, but not before he had managed to throw away his knife.

Fearing that other gang members might get involved and that violence could escalate, the police refused Eastland bail, and he was kept in custody until the following Monday, when he appeared in court. When Eastland had convinced the magistrates that this was an isolated incident, he was granted bail and picked up from the court by Stuart Watson. They immediately returned to the scene of the fight, as

Eastland wanted to retrieve the drugs he had hidden. However, as he was doing so, the police arrived. Unbeknown to Eastland, the police had already retrieved the stash following a tip-off. However, the drugs the police had recovered were not steroids; they were in fact Ecstasy pills.

Eastland has since claimed that Ashton set him up by switching the steroids for Ecstasy pills before telephoning the police, but no evidence exists to support his allegation. At Eastland's trial, the jury did not accept that Ashton was responsible for planting the Ecstasy pills, and Eastland was sentenced to five years' imprisonment for possessing drugs with intent to supply and a further six months for affray concerning the knife fight.

Shortly before Eastland's trial, Ashton had been sentenced to four years' imprisonment for a commercial burglary. One day, when Watson went to visit Eastland in prison, he found Ashton glaring at him from across the prison visiting room. The man visiting Ashton also began to stare at Watson. After the pair had mouthed obscenities and threats at one another, Watson approached Ashton's table and they began to fight. Watson, who was getting the better of his opponent, was dragged away by prison officers and held until the visiting room had been cleared.

When Ashton was released from prison, a gunman attempted to murder Watson's friend Terry Mitchell. Fortunately, Mitchell had dived for cover as the shotgun blast had rung out, and he escaped injury. From that day forth, Watson, Mitchell and their opponents all armed themselves whenever they ventured out. One morning, as he left his home, Mitchell was surprised to see Ashton's friend Paul 'Monkey' Lyons hiding nearby in bushes. Mitchell confronted Lyons, who denied that he was up to anything before fleeing down the street. Somewhat puzzled, Mitchell walked to his garage and reversed his car out, as he had to take his daughter to school. As he turned out of his road, Mitchell saw Ashton and Robert Webber driving towards him. When they passed Mitchell, they appeared to be pretending not to have noticed him.

After dropping his daughter off at school, Mitchell went to the gym. After two hours, he then drove home and parked his car in the garage. As he leant over to the passenger side of the vehicle in order to activate the immobiliser, Paul 'Monkey' Lyons opened the driver's door and plunged a bayonet deep into his shoulder. Mitchell shouted out, 'When I get out of this car, I am going to fucking kill you!' but Lyons replied by stabbing him repeatedly with the bayonet. Convinced that he was going to die if he did not get out of the car, Mitchell began kicking at Lyons' legs. He then raised his hand to try to push Lyons away from him, but the bayonet was thrust straight into his wrist and exited via his forearm.

Bleeding profusely and in excruciating pain, Mitchell managed to exit the vehicle and grip Lyons by the throat. As the two men struggled, Mitchell was being repeatedly stabbed. One thrust of the bayonet went straight through his ear into his mouth and exited through his cheek. Unable to extract the blade, Lyons tugged left and right in an effort to free the weapon, which caused the wound in Mitchell's face to tear and split even wider. With one last surge of energy, Mitchell shoved Lyons backwards over a wall and started beating him with his fists. Mitchell's injuries and massive loss of blood meant that he soon tired, and Lyons was able to make good his escape.

Mitchell chased after Lyons and saw him run to a car in which Ashton and Webber were waiting. 'You've fucking killed him. You've killed him. You've killed him,' Ashton was shouting as he bounced up and down in his seat. But his apparent joy was short-lived, because he soon learned that Mitchell had not only survived the attack but was also seeking revenge.

Before Mitchell was able to confront his attackers, both he and Watson were arrested, charged with conspiracy to murder and remanded in custody to HMP Durham to await trial. While in prison, Watson was approached by Nigel Abadom, a major player in the Newcastle underworld. Abadom, acting as peacemaker between the warring factions, said that Ashton was prepared to get his wife to withdraw a statement that she had made and dispose of the incriminating bullet that had struck him if Mitchell and Watson would pay him £50,000. Abadom had recently been sentenced for the blackmailing of a Tyneside businessman with Stephen and Michael Sayers, and so he was considered a man to be respected amongst the criminal fraternity. Watson told Abadom that he was insulted by such a proposal and that he should never have agreed to pass such a message on. If Ashton was genuinely asking him to pay to prevent him from informing, then he needed to think again. 'Tell him to keep his big, fat mouth shut,' Watson added. 'He is not out of the woods yet.'

When the charge against Mitchell and Watson of conspiracy to murder was dropped to one of possessing firearms, Ashton agreed to hand over his Mercedes to the police. Nine months had passed since the shooting incident had occurred, but the vehicle, which had been stored in a garage, still had the bullet hole in the windscreen. Watson and Mitchell saw this move as a deliberate attempt to get them charged with a more serious offence, and so they sat down and, after much hand-wringing, agreed to do the previously unthinkable. They both made statements to the police against Ashton, Webber and Lyons. They were not offered any deal by the police for doing so, nor were they shown any leniency by the judge at their trial. Both Mitchell and Watson were sentenced to seven years' imprisonment for firearms offences.

In March 1998, Ashton and Webber appeared at Newcastle Crown Court to face charges of conspiracy to murder and possessing firearms with intent to endanger life. They were both sentenced to 18 years' imprisonment for conspiracy to murder and 11 years for firearm offences. The year before, Ashton had additionally been sentenced to eight years' imprisonment for conspiracy to supply drugs. In December 1999, Ashton was back in the dock facing charges of violent disorder and attempting to pervert the course of justice. The judge sentenced him to a further five years' imprisonment, making a total of forty-one years to serve. Paul 'Monkey' Lyons received fourteen years' imprisonment for the attempted murder of Terry Mitchell and a further four and a half years for 'other' offences, making a total of eighteen and a half years to serve.

The message from Northumbria Police was loud and clear; nobody was untouchable on Tyneside, and anyone with aspirations to take over the city would find himself facing a lengthy term of imprisonment. But, as everybody knows, nobody, not even the police, can stop the hands of time, which is all villains have to serve before they are once more back on the streets to wreak mayhem and murder.

Paddy Conroy was nearing the end of his sentence and so was beginning to take an interest in the outside world once more. During idle chat on one visit, he was allegedly told about a man from the West End of Newcastle who appeared to be getting involved with Tony Leach, John Henry Sayers' right-hand man. Leachy, as he was known, would not normally have given such a person the time of day unless it was beneficial to him.

Freddie Knights was a family man who had committed little more than petty crimes. His mother, Ella, owned the flower shop where Paddy had ordered the wreath for DC Perky, and it had been Freddie who delivered it. Paddy claims to have known the Knights family, but he admits that they were not close friends. Members of the Sayers gang allege that the Conroys were in fact a threat to Freddie Knights and that they had put a gun to his head following a dispute. The Conroys vehemently deny this. Paddy believed that there was no way that the Sayers firm would embrace a man like Freddie, unless, of course, the embrace was going to turn into a baited lure.

The rumour mill in the West End of Newcastle was awash with theories. Some people were claiming that Freddie was selling cocaine on behalf of the Sayers gang, and others were alleging that he was entertaining one of their wives. Whatever Freddie was up to, Leachy had taken an interest in him. Paddy rang Ella Knights from prison and pleaded with her to tell her son to have nothing to do with his new friend. 'They are befriending him so that they can learn his habits, his day-to-day movements,' Paddy said. 'And when they know him inside out, Ella, they will make their move.' Ella was naturally distressed by Paddy's call and said that she would talk to her son. It's not known if Ella did speak to Freddie, but if she did take Paddy's advice then Freddie most certainly did not.

On 5 November 1999, John Henry Sayers completed his sentence and was released from HMP Full Sutton after serving almost 11 years. He returned to Newcastle outwardly bristling with bravado, but deep down something was troubling him. John Henry claims that while he had been in prison his father, a freemason, had visited him to tell him grave news. According to John Henry, his father had been warned by a fellow freemason, who happened to be a serving police superintendent, that senior police officers in Northumbria Police wanted John Henry taken off the streets for good. As a result of this information, John

Henry's solicitor wrote to Chief Constable Crispian Strachan. In that letter he stated:

> Our client has had information that certain informants and police officers working at senior levels within Northumbria Police are conspiring against him. The conspiracy will take one of the following forms:
>
> (a) That he will be arrested in a motor vehicle and that cocaine, heroin or some other drug will be placed in the vehicle and he will be arrested and placed on remand immediately because of the unexpired portion of his sentence.
> (b) A criminal will approach him and lure him into a fight, and then he will be charged with Section 18, and remanded.
> (c) That there will be a report by an informant, which the police will confirm, that he is carrying a weapon in a vehicle, the armed response unit will attend and he will be executed by the police.
>
> You may feel that scenarios (a), (b) and (c) are far-fetched, but our client feels that he has been victimised whilst in prison by the police and that he has information which has been given to him that police officers and informants are conspiring against him. We simply have been advised by our client to place this on record so that internal investigations may take place. We can confirm that our client does not wish to speak directly to the police about this or any other matter, and therefore there is no point in sending any officer to see him. We are copying this letter to the Director of Public Prosecutions.

John Henry claims that he was not only given the name of at least one superintendent allegedly involved in this conspiracy but that he was also given the name S. Watson as one of the alleged informants. John Henry says that he racked his brain trying to think who S. Watson might be but could think of only one, and that was Stuart Watson. While in prison, John Henry had met Paul Ashton and Robert Webber, who had informed him that Watson had given evidence against them. John Henry was also aware that his brother Stephen had been imprisoned with Viv Graham and others for assaulting Watson, and so he began to wonder if he was the S. Watson that he had been warned about.

The solicitor's letter was ignored by the police, but John Henry was most certainly not. From the day he was released, he was placed under almost constant covert surveillance. Officers shadowed him and his family on holiday in Spain, and he found a tracker device on his Land Rover Discovery.

In an effort to go (almost) straight, John Henry set up a taxi firm called Newcastle Taxis. The office was in an area of the city frequented by gays and known as the Pink Triangle. Prior to John Henry's arrival in the area, macho beer-swilling Geordies would push gays to the back of taxi queues when clubs closed, and some had even been assaulted. John Henry began issuing numbered tickets to circumvent the usual problems caused by drunks trying to queue in an orderly fashion and warned potential troublemakers to behave. Within weeks, Newcastle Taxis was employing approximately 50 drivers and business was booming.

Northumbria Police were not happy with the fact that John Henry was involved in ferrying citizens around Newcastle, and so they opposed his application for an operator's licence. Detective Inspector Max Black of Newcastle West CID told magistrates, 'The running of taxis can have significant benefits. My experience is that career criminals use taxis to transport drugs, guns and prostitutes. It's been a common practice for a number of years, and if you have taxi firms you can get away with all sorts of criminal activities. Taxis virtually never get stopped, and if they do and there are drugs in the back they say they must have been left there by a customer.' Detective Inspector Black added that he believed Sayers was not a fit and proper person to operate or drive taxis because of his reputation for violence and the fact he was allegedly already involved in the taxi industry in Newcastle without owning a licence. John Henry's application was refused, but he appealed the decision immediately, which allowed Newcastle Taxis to continue operating until the next hearing.

Fearing he would lose his thriving business, John Henry signed it over to an associate named Alan Maughan, who in turn leased it to a man named Younes Mohammed. When he applied to renew the taxi operator's licence, the council objected on the grounds that Mohammed was not a fit and proper person. They claimed he was not in control of the business but operated it on behalf of John Henry and Maughan.

Mohammed told magistrates he owned the business and denied any business dealings with John Henry or Maughan, but he did admit that Maughan did some work as a self-employed driver and had done some computer training for the firm and that John Henry did visit the business. The court also heard from the council of their concerns that Mohammed did not appear to be in control of the business as he knew only the first names of his employees and had failed to submit 18 out of 22 monthly reports, a condition of his licence. Mohammed's application was denied, and John Henry lost an almost legitimate business. So much for encouraging ex-offenders to rehabilitate.

Since his release, John Henry had become acquainted with a former soldier named Alan Coe. After a successful career in the Army, Coe had worked hard in the licensing trade and won promotion to become an area manager for Scottish & Newcastle Breweries. Coe and John Henry had a mutual friend, Robert Orange, who ran a pub in Jesmond called the Brandling. It was here that John Henry would often meet Coe and question him in detail about his role in and knowledge of the pub trade. At John Henry's suggestion, Coe resigned from his job and accepted a £15,000 loan from him to take over two pubs in Newcastle, the John Gilpin and the Hillheads, which Coe then ran in his own name.

After these premises were established, Coe became the director of a firm called Neptune Inns, which one by one took on the tenancies of a succession of run-down pubs in 'challenging locations' across the north-east. John Henry kept his name away from the business, but he was always lurking in the background, taking a lion's share of the profits and instructing Coe as to which premises to target. If an honest publican had been running these pubs, there wouldn't have been much profit for John Henry to take. However, there was very little that was honest about Neptune Inns. The company failed to pay any of the 17.5 per cent VAT that was due, and it failed to pay business rates and council tax. It was a lucrative crime that Coe and John Henry were committing, but it was one that somebody somewhere would inevitably have to take responsibility for. John Henry thought that somebody would be Alan Coe, because it was his name alone that was associated with the business. Unfortunately for John Henry, an incident was about to occur that would expose just about everything the Sayers firm had ever been involved in.

At 3.30 p.m. on 19 September 2000, two thieves, Paul Hunter and Terrence Mann, met Michael Dixon, a friend of the Sayers family, to go and steal a car. Less than an hour later, Hunter and Mann had stolen a silver Volkswagen Golf from Fowler Street, in South Shields. Dixon was captured on CCTV cameras shortly afterwards returning to Newcastle via the Tyne Tunnel.

At seven that evening, two men, Eddie Stewart and Dale Miller, made their way to the Longbenton area of Newcastle in the stolen Volkswagen. Stewart's intention was to bang on the windows of Ella Knights' home so as to frighten her into calling her son Freddie for assistance. Depending on whom you believe, Freddie had either upset a notorious Geordie villain by sleeping with his wife or set up a lucrative cocaine business in Longbenton that others wanted to take over. Regardless of the reason, somebody had hired a team to shoot Freddie on his mother's doorstep. Stewart and Miller were unable to locate Ella Knights' home that night, and so the hit was temporarily aborted.

On 20 September 2000, Sir Bobby Robson had picked his strongest side for Newcastle United's Worthington Cup home tie against third-division minnows Leyton Orient. Success in the competition would guarantee the club European Cup football, something their supporters, the Toon Army, had longed for. Thirty-eight-year-old Freddie Knights, an ardent Newcastle United fan, had the game, and the birthday of his fourteen-year-old son, on his mind as he and his wife, Grace, drove towards his mother's home that night. He certainly wasn't aware of what others had planned for him.

At 7 p.m., driver Eddie Stewart and gunman Dale Miller had arrived at Ella Knights' home in the Volkswagen Golf. Michael Dixon and Lee Watson had followed them in a burgundy Renault. (Watson is the man who had been arrested with Michael Sayers for the killing of Viv Graham.) For the next hour, a flurry of mobile phone calls between Dixon, Stewart and Watson were made. At 8.10 p.m., Dixon had telephoned Stewart to ensure that he and Miller were in position at Ella Knights' home. Twelve minutes later, Freddie had telephoned a friend who was watching the Newcastle United game at St James' Park to enquire about the score. 'Nil–nil,' Freddie was told, 'but we should be slaughtering them.' Disappointed, Freddie decided to forget about the match and concentrate on his son Alan's birthday celebrations.

Alan was a promising footballer who played for the county and had been selected for trials with Newcastle United. On this particular evening, Alan had left his school satchel at his grandmother's house and had wanted to return with Freddie to collect it. Fortunately for Alan, his mother had insisted that he stay in and have a bath while she and Freddie went to Ella's to pick it up. Grace and Freddie were a close couple. They had met and fallen in love at the age of 14 when they both attended John Marley School, in the West End of Newcastle. Their first son, John, had been born in 1977, but tragedy had struck when he was just nine years old. John had run into the road to retrieve a football and had been hit by a bus. Grace has said that Freddie never really got over the loss of their son. Freddie, Alan and his other son, Mark, used to go to the crematorium every Saturday to pay their respects to John. The loss of his son at such a tender age had certainly made Freddie extremely protective of his other children, who everybody agreed he adored.

Two minutes after Freddie made the call to his friend at St James' Park, he and Grace arrived outside Ella's home in Lutterworth Road. Freddie parked his van and began the short walk to his mother's front door. As Grace followed her husband up the path, she saw a hooded man emerge from bushes just a few yards away. Without saying a word, Dale Miller pointed a shotgun at Freddie and fired. Grace could not believe what was happening; she was numb with fear and unable to move. The shot had fortunately missed Freddie, and so he had tried to make himself a more difficult target by crouching down on his mother's doorstep in case the gunman fired again. Freddie's attempt to save himself was in vain, because the gunman was determined to carry out his cowardly attack.

Rather than risk missing his target again, the gunman walked up to Freddie and from point-blank range shot him in the face. Eight balls of steel from the shotgun cartridge penetrated Freddie's skull and destroyed his brain. He was dying before his wife's eyes, and nobody was going to be able to save him. The gunman's initial shot had slammed into Ella's front door. The noise brought her and her neighbours rushing outside. When Ella saw Freddie lying on her doorstep, she knew that he was beyond help. All she could do was rub her son's leg and plead with him to hang on to life until help arrived. Grace cradled him in her arms while neighbours brought towels to try to stem the flow of blood from his head.

By the time the ambulance had arrived, Freddie was already dead. After Miller had shot Freddie, he had run back to the Volkswagen, and Stewart had driven away at speed. Seconds later, Dixon had telephoned the man who had ordered the hit to tell him that Freddie Knights was no more. At 9 p.m., the gang arrived at a flat owned by a friend named Steven Carlton. Miller and Stewart washed and changed their clothing in the hope of destroying any forensic evidence. At 12.05 a.m., the clothes they had worn during the murder were put in the Volkswagen, which was then driven to a street in the West End of Newcastle and set on fire. The shotgun was later buried.

Paddy Conroy spent the last six and a half months of his imprisonment in solitary confinement. He had decided from the outset that he would complete the end of his sentence alone. The dispersal system is an environment few can begin to understand, unless, of course, they have had the misfortune to live through it. Violence is part and parcel of everyday life. Intimidation, stabbings and rape are commonplace. Inmates live in a constant state of alert. It is simply wrong to release a man back into a 'normal' environment after spending years in such conditions.

Paddy elected to be alone simply because he felt that he needed to adjust back to having some form of relaxed state of mind. In order to be put in solitary confinement, inmates have to have committed an offence. Rather than risk doing something serious that could have affected his release, Paddy simply refused to take part in an anger-management course. Initially, Paddy was told that he would be kept in the segregation unit for 14 days, but when he said that he was refusing to leave his cell until he had completed his sentence nobody argued.

Tommy Adams, the north-London crime boss, was in one of the cells next to Paddy. Paddy, however, refused to speak to him, because he had heard that a member of the A Team, as the Adams firm is known, had shot Mad Frankie Fraser in the head outside Turnmills nightclub in London. Paddy's father had been friends with Mad Frank and had always spoken very highly of him, and so there was no way Paddy could bring himself to even acknowledge Tommy Adams.

Robert 'the Cannibal' Maudsley was Paddy's other neighbour. He was considered to be so dangerous that the authorities had built a Hannibal Lecter-type box in which to house him. Within his cell, a solid-steel door opened into a small cage, which was encased in thick Perspex. A small slot at the base of this barbaric contraption was used to pass Maudsley food and other items. The only furniture he had was a table and chair, which were made of compressed cardboard. The toilet and sink were bolted to the floor, and his bed was a 4-in.-thick concrete slab. It is a sad indictment of our so-called civilised society to think that a fellow human being is incarcerated in such unnecessarily barbaric conditions.

Robert Maudsley was born in June 1953. One of twelve children, he spent most of his early years in Nazareth House, an orphanage run by nuns in Crosby, Liverpool. Maudsley, two of his brothers and his eldest sister had been removed from the family home because they were said to be suffering from 'parental neglect'. Aged eight, Maudsley was placed in the care of Liverpool City Council. Occasionally, however, he and the other children were allowed to go back to their parents for 'trial periods'. It was during these stays that Maudsley suffered mental and physical abuse at the hands of his father. His pleas for help fell on deaf ears.

During the late 1960s, Maudsley found himself in London working as a rent boy to feed his heroin addiction. Following several suicide attempts, he was referred to a psychiatrist, who he told he could hear voices telling him to kill his parents. In 1974, Maudsley was picked up by a paedophile named John Farrell, who paid him for sex. During their seedy encounter, Farrell showed him photographs of children he claimed he had sexually abused, and so Maudsley strangled him. After being assessed by psychiatrists, Maudsley was declared mentally unfit to stand trial and was sent to Broadmoor Hospital for the Criminally Insane.

Three years later, Maudsley and another inmate killed a paedophile. They grabbed the man, locked themselves into a room and tortured their victim before slaying him. A prison officer later gave a statement in which he said that Maudsley 'fractured the man's skull like an egg and then ate part of his brain with a spoon'. Maudsley was convicted of manslaughter for this crime and, having been found mentally fit to stand trial, was moved to the 'normal' prison dispersal system.

In 1978, Maudsley killed two convicts. The first was a convicted sex offender named Salney Darwood. Maudsley lured him into his cell, where he strangled and stabbed him before hiding the body under his bed. He then went on the prowl around the prison, eventually grabbing and stabbing to death an inmate named Bill Roberts. Maudsley then calmly walked into the office of the prison governor and told him that the next roll call would be two people short. Because of the prison killings, Maudsley was placed in the segregation unit. He has spent longer in solitary confinement than any other prisoner in British history. Maudsley has described his living conditions as like being buried alive in a concrete coffin. According to the authorities, he is 'untreatable' and will never be released.

Directly above Paddy's cell was housed a prisoner named Ferdinand Lavelle, a black South American who is without doubt one of the most dangerous prisoners ever to have been held in a British jail. Forget Charles Bronson or John McVicar; this guy really did not give a fuck about who or how many people he had to fight in order to get his own way. 'Absolutely fearless' is the best way to describe him. Ferdinand would stab somebody, get dragged down to the segregation unit, emerge two months later and stab the same person again. The occasional inmate might have got lucky and put Ferdinand down, but their luck wouldn't last, because Ferdinand would not stay down. He is largely unheard of outside the prison system, but within it Ferdinand Lavelle is without doubt legendary.

While at HMP Whitemoor, Lavelle was alleged to have thrown into the face of a prison officer a substance that inmates call 'gee'. One or two pans of margarine are boiled until the ingredients separate. The pure oil rises to the top of the pan, and this is skimmed off and mixed with sugar. When the boiling oil is thrown at somebody, the sugar sticks to the victim's skin, which maximises the damage caused. It is an evil weapon to use on a human being. It is said that the injured officer at HMP Whitemoor collapsed with his head literally smoking after the attack. Ferdinand stood trial on two separate occasions for the offence but was eventually found not guilty.

People loyal to the Sayers firm had been circulating an article in prison that had been published in the *Newcastle Evening Chronicle*. An MP was allegedly outraged that David Glover 'and others' had been paid as police informants while continuing to commit crime. Inevitably, the article reported the gory details of the kidnap and assault on Collier. Unfortunately for Paddy, the newspaper published a photograph of him to accompany the story. When people read the headline and then saw Paddy's photograph, some assumed that he was being exposed as a police informant.

Enraged, Paddy sent what is best described as a 'stern letter' to the editor of the newspaper, complaining bitterly about the article. When the letter arrived on the editor's desk, he promptly contacted the police, claiming that Paddy had threatened him. Two officers were immediately dispatched to the prison to interview Paddy, but he refused to answer their questions, and so they merely advised him to stop writing to the editor and to stay away from him when he was released.

Three months before Paddy was due to be released, two detectives from the Northumbria Police intelligence unit went to visit him to ask about the murder of a man named Peter Gowling. Paddy considered Gowling to be little more than an 'inbred mongrel'. Gowling had owed Paddy a sum of money, and it's fair to say that he had sent him what can only be described as 'urgent reminders' that he should pay or risk having the matter handed over to the Conroy debt-recovery department. Gowling was in prison at the time Paddy had been in contact with him, but he was due to be released within days and so Paddy had guessed that he would flee.

On Valentine's Day 2001, before he could flee anywhere, Peter Gowling was gunned down at his flat in Osborne Road, Newcastle. He died after suffering multiple gunshot wounds to the head, chest and back from a small calibre handgun. In 1996, Gowling had been arrested while travelling to Ireland with two suitcases stuffed with £540,000, which was going to be used to fund a drug shipment. He was sentenced to 11 years' imprisonment, and £1 million worth of his assets were seized. As soon as he was released from prison, he made a point of telling a reporter, 'I believe that my debts to society have now been paid in full.' Paddy did not believe that Gowling was making such a statement for the benefit of the wider community. He believed that it was also a message to all those he owed money. Gowling believed that because he had served his time his debts should be wiped clean.

The police wanted to know every detail of Paddy's relationship and business affairs with Gowling and repeatedly asked why he had been sending him demands for money. The answer was elementary: he owed it to Paddy, and the rest was none of their business. Paddy did not wish to appear rude or callous, but he did tell the detectives that he was pleased Gowling was no more and that if they had any decency they would not bother looking for those who had killed him. In Paddy's opinion, the killer had done the world a favour. The officers were not impressed with Paddy's outburst and threatened to have him arrested on the morning of his release so that they could talk to him in more detail about the murder.

Two months before Paddy's release, he had a Category A status review. Nobody should be released from prison while they are still deemed to be Category A or, in layman's terms, extremely high risk and a threat to society, and so Paddy was absolutely positive that he would be downgraded. However, for reasons never explained, Paddy was deemed to still be a Category A prisoner and was told that he would remain so until he walked out of the prison gates. The only people who are usually released as Category A prisoners are terrorists. What possible threat to society or humanity did the powers that be honestly think that Paddy Conroy posed? It was ridiculous, absolutely ridiculous, the only thing Conroy wanted to do was to go home to his family and sort out the editor of the *Newcastle Evening Chronicle*.

On the morning of his release, Paddy completed all the relevant paperwork, got changed into his own clothing and stood waiting for his escort to take him to freedom. Four prison officers led him out of the building and were then joined by two officers with dogs. 'What the fuck is going on?' Paddy asked. 'I'm going home. I'm hardly going to want to escape in the next five minutes.'

'You are Category A, Conroy,' a smug-looking officer replied. 'And you will be treated as such until you cross from HMP property into the outside world.'

And so it was. Paddy was handcuffed to an officer and surrounded by his colleagues as they walked to the gate flanked by the dog handlers. 'Raise your hands,' an officer said as he fumbled for the handcuff keys. Seconds later, a door was opened and Paddy stepped through it to freedom. Paddy headed for the car park, looking all around him as he did so. He didn't know why, but he was convinced that police officers were lying in wait to arrest him for ordering Gowling's murder. Paddy had made his mind up that the first one to approach him was going to be knocked out.

'Paddy! Paddy!' shouted somebody with a Geordie accent. Paddy turned to see Dave Garside waving manically and gesturing him to his car. Three hours later, Paddy was reliving an experience of his youth, crossing the Tyne Bridge and gazing up at the two huge arches that seemed like arms embracing him. They had welcomed many a Geordie lad home to his beloved Newcastle. Crossing that bridge and looking down on the River Tyne after years in prison must have felt magical. For the umpteenth time in his life, Paddy did his best to settle down and live a straight life. He did visit the offices of the *Evening Chronicle*, but the editor who had enraged him had moved on.

Within a week of Paddy's release, the police visited his home and warned him that his life was in danger. They said that an attack on him was imminent and that he should leave Newcastle immediately, but Paddy told them that he was not leaving his town or any other town for any man or gang. 'Tell your informant to tell whoever is behind this that they should ensure that they get me first time around or it will be them leaving town, in a box,' he said. Threats were an everyday reality of the life that Paddy had chosen to live, and he knew that only a fool becomes complacent and ignores them.

Paddy put certain security measures into place and armed himself every time he left his home. The police were informed about one or two of the measures that Paddy had implemented, and he was subsequently arrested after taking his children to school. A futile search of his home for firearms took place, but police did find a kitchen knife with an 8-in. blade wrapped in foil inside his jeans pocket. A further search of his car unearthed two more daggers, one in the glove compartment and another in the driver's door.

Initially, Paddy tried to claim that officers had planted a knife on him, but he did eventually concede that the weapons were his. When Paddy appeared in court, his solicitor told the magistrates, 'Mr Conroy told the police very frankly that he believed his life was under threat. He has a genuine belief that people in high authority are out to get him. You might think it's paranoia, but he has a genuine belief that his life is threatened by people. This is not a case where he's out in the street using the knives. The knife he had in his pocket was wrapped up. It was, as he said, for his own protection, not to cause harm to anyone, unless they were going to harm him. He has held, and he still holds, the belief that people are after him, and that's why he has knives. Perhaps in extraordinary circumstances they might be used.' The magistrates accepted Paddy's explanation for possessing the knives and ordered him to carry out 80 hours of community service and pay £55 in court costs.

The warnings that the police had given Paddy about people wishing to execute him proved to be anything but just cautionary. One evening, he was invited to a secluded house by a man he believed to be a friend. It was only when Paddy entered the house that he began to feel all was not well. His host kept glancing nervously towards the door, and when there was a tap on the window he appeared to turn white. The man tried to tell Paddy that he was going to see who was outside, but all he could do was stutter and mumble instead.

Now convinced that foul play was afoot, Paddy followed the man out of the room and saw that he was opening the door to a well-known figure from the West End who had gone to live in Spain several years earlier. As Paddy stepped into the hallway, he came face to face with the man, who immediately thrust his right hand into the inside pocket of his jacket. Instinctively, Paddy pulled out a knife and lunged at the man, who stumbled backwards out of the door before turning and running away. Paddy slammed the front door shut and telephoned his friends, who arrived amidst the sound of screeching brakes and skidding tyres.

Turning his attention to his host, Paddy politely asked the trembling man at knifepoint who had wanted to have him murdered. 'It's a policeman, Paddy. That's all I know. It's a policeman,' he whined. Paddy had no way of telling if the man was telling the truth or if he was simply trying to protect the guilty. Paddy explained to the jabbering wreck now curled up on the settee and weeping that he would be requiring a full explanation about the incident at some stage. He then walked out of the door, climbed into his friend's car and was driven away.

Chapter Eleven

KNIGHTMARE ON ELLA'S STREET

FOUR DAYS AFTER Freddie Knights had been executed on his mother's doorstep, henchman Michael Dixon was arrested for non-payment of £120 in fines. Before Dixon had time to settle in his cell at Byker Police Station, John Henry Sayers had arrived and paid the outstanding cash, and Dixon had been released. John Henry, who knew Dixon through his taxi business, is adamant that he had no ulterior motive for assisting Dixon. He was merely doing him a favour, and he was repaid the money upon Dixon's release.

Forty-eight hours later, two detectives called at John Henry's home, but he wasn't in. The officers informed his wife, Yvonne, that they did not intend to arrest John Henry but that they did wish to speak to him about the murder of Freddie Knights. At 6.35 p.m. that evening, John Henry and his solicitor presented themselves at Market Street Police Station. John Henry refused to speak to the police, and so his solicitor elected to talk on his behalf. Two detectives led them into an interview room, where they said that they wished to be given an account of John Henry's whereabouts between Tuesday, 19 September and Wednesday, 20 September, the day Freddie Knights had met his death.

Ignoring the essence of the question, John Henry's solicitor replied, 'The purpose for us coming here tonight is to set things straight so you realise what is going on. Mr Sayers has had a number of unfortunate experiences in the past with previous cases in which there has been a lot of skulduggery going on by the police. We are not aiming it at you two, because I don't think it should be. I don't know you as individuals. He is concerned that police informants are trying to place him in a position where he could be connected with this offence. We have already sent a letter to the chief constable some months ago, outlining the fears that we have for his safety. I can tell you that he does have an alibi for last Wednesday evening, which was communicated to myself, and it involves your own officers.

'He has got nothing whatsoever to do with the murder that you are investigating or any of the circumstances, and anybody that has put his name forward has done so for their own purposes. He is very concerned that his family have been contacted again. You weren't to know this, but his wife is very ill because of the constant fear of him being arrested for things he hasn't done. Finally, I wish to put on record that he will not say anything whatsoever without a legal representative – whether it is at his home, in his car, in a police station – because of these fears, and that's why we are here. We are not here to waste your time; we are here to set this down for you so you understand, and we felt the only way we could do that was to come into a police station and speak to you, or at least I will on his behalf. He doesn't wish to answer any of your questions whatsoever or communicate any more information tonight.'

The officers emphasised that John Henry was not under arrest and urged him to put forward his alibi so that they could research it and possibly eliminate him from their inquiries, but he refused. Within 30 minutes of arriving at the police station, John Henry and his solicitor were walking out the front door.

On 13 October 2000, less than a month after Knights' murder, his killer, Dale Miller, and Miller's accomplice, Lee Watson, were arrested by traffic officers after failing to stop at a red light. Following a high-speed chase, the pair abandoned their vehicle and fled on foot, but they were apprehended shortly afterwards. Watson had been seen to drop a package, which was later found to contain 9 oz of heroin. When cornered by the officers, Watson pulled out a butterfly knife and screamed, 'Come on then, come on!' Once Watson had been overpowered by the use of CS gas spray, he was conveyed to the police station, where he was charged with possession of heroin with intent to supply. He pleaded guilty and was later imprisoned for three years. Miller, who denied all knowledge of the heroin being in the car, was remanded in custody to await trial.

In December of that year, John Henry sent a £200 cheque to both

Watson and Miller. He claims he did so because Watson was a good friend of his brothers, Michael and Stephen. According to John Henry, in the summer of 2000, Watson had sent his mother £1,000 for his brothers, who were then in prison themselves. John Henry maintains that he was simply repaying that favour. He is adamant that he did not know Miller but that Watson had told him that Miller didn't have a penny. It was Christmas, Miller was Watson's co-accused, they were sharing the same cell and Miller had recently been diagnosed with cancer. How could John Henry possibly refuse?

When Watson had shouted out at Gateshead Magistrates' Court that he was responsible for the murder of Viv Graham, he had not done himself any favours. Rightly or wrongly, his name was now on everybody's lips whenever there was a shooting in the north-east. It was hardly surprising, therefore, when the police began receiving information that Watson might have had something to do with Knights' murder, and so they decided to visit him in prison. Initially, Watson refused to answer their questions, because he thought there was no evidence to link him to the crime. However, when the officers returned to the prison just a week later, Watson was left in little doubt that they had enough circumstantial evidence to charge and possibly convict him of involvement in the shooting.

Mobile phones are made up of small radio transmitters and receivers. They operate by sending and receiving signals to and from the masts that are dotted all around the country. The phones are designed to automatically make contact or link up with the mast with the strongest signal. This is invariably the mast that is closest to the mobile phone. Some of these masts contain antennas that are positioned to face in different directions. The mobile phone companies are able to identify the antenna with which a phone has connected and therefore provide a rough location for that phone when it makes or receives calls. Using this method to track Watson's movements, the police were able to show that on the night of the murder he had been either present or near Ella Knights' home at the time Freddie was gunned down.

Realising the predicament that he was in, Watson agreed to talk to the officers, but only off the record. Watson told the police exactly what had happened in the days leading up to Freddie's death and who had done what on the night he died. There were no real surprises for the officers, as most of the participants had some form or another of drug addiction. That was until Watson claimed that John Henry Sayers and his right-hand man, Tony Leach, were the men who had recruited the hit team and planned the murder for them. Detectives involved in the murder inquiry were said to be 'overjoyed' by the breakthrough, but they knew there was a lot of work to be done before they could make any arrests.

On 28 January 2001, a heroin addict named Steven Carlton was arrested following a botched armed robbery at a post office in Chopwell, near Gateshead. After a few hours in the police cell without a fix for his addiction, Carlton pleaded with officers to be released. He claimed that if they were willing to help him then he could help them, as he had valuable information about the murder of Freddie Knights. Carlton, who has been described by friends as having 'three or four personalities', told officers that seven days before Freddie's death John Henry Sayers had been to his flat to collect shotgun cartridges and that the gunmen had also attended his home after the shooting.

The net appeared to be closing in on those responsible for executing Knights, but the police knew that the testimony of an assortment of heroin addicts would not carry much weight in court. They knew they had to bide their time and meticulously sift through every shred of information until they had enough hard evidence concerning what had happened and who had done what that night.

Unaware of Watson's treachery, John Henry paid him a visit at HMP Durham just a few days after he had spoken to the police. According to John Henry, Watson's girlfriend had contacted Watson and said that members of the Conroy family had put a gun to her head. Because of this alleged threat, Watson had wanted to speak to John Henry about protecting her. Watson appeared uncomfortable and evasive when John Henry met him in the visiting room; he certainly didn't discuss the alleged threat that the Conroys posed to his girlfriend. All he did was to make small talk and shift nervously in his seat.

Approximately six weeks later, Watson, who had since been transferred to HMP Acklington, in Northumberland, once more requested that John Henry visit him. Instead of being shown to a table alongside the other visitors in the visiting room, John Henry was taken to a small cubicle that had a glass partition separating him from Watson.

A prison officer stood on each side of the divide, and so their every word was monitored. Once again, Watson remained tight-lipped about the real reason for the visit. In fact, he hardly spoke.

Watson's motive for requesting these visits seemed to stem from one of two things. Either he was going to attempt to coax John Henry into confessing to taking part in Knights' murder or he was going to warn him that he had given an off-the-record account of the shooting to the police. The latter explanation seems more plausible, as no official statement had been made by Watson and so at that stage his confession had no evidential value. Forewarning John Henry of the blame that he had placed at his door would mean that Watson not only wanted to demonstrate that he regretted his actions but also wanted John Henry to be able to prepare for any allegations that might be made against him.

At HMP Durham, Watson may have been too frightened or ashamed to admit what he had done to John Henry. At HMP Acklington, the authorities had clearly guessed that he was about to confess what he had told police to John Henry, and so they had put officers in place to prevent him from doing so.

On 8 May 2001, John Henry was at home watching Arsenal defeat Manchester United 1–0 at Old Trafford, a decent night's entertainment for any Newcastle United fan. Glancing out of the window, he noticed that a large red van with mirrored windows was parked near a grassed area adjacent to his home. Instinctively, he knew that it was the police. When the football match ended, he began to prepare himself for bed, but the covert police surveillance van, which had not moved, was making him feel uneasy. At 11 p.m., John Henry's home phone rang and a voice said, 'It's the police. They are coming to fit you up.' According to John Henry, he knew exactly what the message meant: he had to leave, and do so quickly.

That night, he stayed at a friend's home in the north-east before travelling to Birmingham the following morning. His fears had not been unfounded. As John Henry was making his way down the A1, Northumbria Police were arresting gunman Dale Miller and his getaway driver, Eddie Stewart, for the murder of Freddie Knights. Officers who raided the homes of John Henry, Tony Leach and Michael Dixon found that they had already left the area.

Dixon had fled to Glasgow with a taxi-driver friend named Craig Shepherd. When they had been unable to secure a hotel, Shepherd had telephoned his friend ex-Scotland, Celtic and West Ham United football legend Frank McAvennie and asked for his help. McAvennie later told police, 'On the day in question, Craig rang my mobile while I was in Glasgow. He said he was finding it difficult to find a hotel because Celtic were playing at home. I said that I would see what I could do. Craig didn't say what he was doing in Glasgow – I didn't ask. I phoned two hotels in Paisley. One was the Glynhill Hotel. They told me they had no vacancies. I told them it was for a friend of mine. I played football for Scotland years ago, and I get deals at certain hotels. They put me on to the Brabloch Hotel, in Paisley, and I booked a twin room for Craig.' Five days later, Dixon was arrested sporting dyed blond hair in a photo booth at Glasgow passport office. He had intended fleeing the country using false documentation. Shepherd was also arrested and charged with assisting an offender.

On 2 June 2002, John Henry was arrested by armed officers in Essex following a car chase through the streets of Dagenham and Romford. When his blue Ford Mondeo was finally cornered in nearby Gants Hill, his first words to the arresting officers were, 'I am innocent of this crime.' The following day, John Henry was interviewed by murder squad detectives in the company of his solicitor. Rather than answer questions, John Henry elected to remain tight-lipped. His solicitor did read out the following prepared statement on his behalf:

> I was not involved in any way with the death of Frederick Knights; I did not conspire with anyone to kill him. I am not prepared to answer any questions put to me during interview. My reason for doing this is I have been advised that the drip-feed disclosure method of giving information to my legal advisors to pass on to me is unfair. I should be given any statement in full which the police intend to quote from. The reason for this is to allow me to take full legal advice before I can decide whether to answer questions put to me. I cannot be expected to deal with partial disclosure. I therefore await the service of the prosecution case in full, when I can take advice from my full legal team, solicitor, barrister and Queen's Counsel.

The interviewing officers did ask John Henry questions about the murder, but he would only reply, 'No comment.' When asked about his alibi for the night of Freddie's murder, John Henry said that he was frightened of the police and was therefore going to tell them 'fuck all'.

Elsewhere, Dixon and Miller were also refusing to answer questions. Eddie Stewart, on the other hand, had chosen to respond to all that he was asked. Initially, he admitted to being Miller's best friend but insisted that he was staying at his sister's home in Birmingham on the night Freddie was murdered. Three months after the initial police raids, Tony Leach was arrested in the Lake District, but he too refused to assist the police with their inquiries. All five men were charged with Freddie Knights' murder and remanded in custody to await trial.

While in prison, Eddie Stewart penned a letter to the police admitting that he had been the getaway driver for Dale Miller and named the others who, he alleged, had taken part in the murder plot. Because Watson had confessed to playing an active part in Freddie's execution, he too was charged with murder. When he appeared at Leeds Crown Court, Watson pleaded guilty, but sentencing was adjourned until after the trial of his co-accused. In the UK, there is only one sentence that a judge can hand down for murder, and that is one of life imprisonment. It is therefore difficult to understand not only why Watson would plead guilty but why he would choose to assist the police in the first place? They could not offer him any sort of deal, and he would have to spend many years in prison in fear of attack, as he would be known as an informant. That is unless, of course, Watson had been given some sort of off-the-record assurances of his own prior to pleading guilty.

The Freddie Knights murder trial opened at Leeds Crown Court on 26 June 2002 amid tight security. As an armed convoy ferried the defendants to the court building, a police helicopter hovered overhead. Leeds city centre was brought to a standstill as the 'Black Special alert' security operation unfolded. A squad of police marksmen armed with machine guns stood guard as a ring of steel was thrown around the court, which was subject to the sort of security usually reserved for terrorists. Inside, armed police were positioned in every corridor. Outside court number five, a dozen heavily armed officers stood sentinel while members of the public were searched with metal detectors before being allowed to enter.

Tension filled the room as the accused took their seats in the dock. The Honourable Mr Justice Douglas Brown ordered the jury to be sworn in before Mr Batty QC rose to his feet and began outlining the prosecution case. With the assistance of Carlton, Stewart, Watson and telephone cell site evidence, Mr Batty had little trouble in painting a very detailed picture of what the prosecution believed had happened and who had been involved prior to and following the shooting. Mr Batty told the jury that sometime on 13 September 2000 John Henry Sayers had attended the home of Steven Carlton to collect 'some shotgun cartridges'. Aided by the telephone cell site evidence and eyewitness accounts, Mr Batty then led the jury through events the prosecution said were relevant to Freddie Knights' murder in chronological order.

Tuesday, 19 September 2000

2.00 p.m.: John Henry Sayers calls the hit team together for a meeting in a lay-by (which is known locally as Peter Barrett's lay-by) near a garden centre in Gosforth to discuss the murder plot. This particular lay-by is just a six-minute drive from Ella Knights' home. The group is allegedly spotted by Detective Chief Inspector Pallas, who had pulled over into the same lay-by.

3.30 p.m.: John Hunter and Terrence Mann are recruited to steal a getaway vehicle to be used in the murder.

3.42 p.m.: Michael Dixon escorts the two car thieves to get the vehicle.

4.29 p.m.: A silver Volkswagen Golf is stolen from Fowler Street, South Shields. Minutes later, Dixon is captured on CCTV cameras driving back towards Newcastle through the Tyne Tunnel in a burgundy Renault 19.

5.30 p.m.: Car thief John Hunter telephones John Henry Sayers' mobile phone. The call lasts 40 seconds.

5.56 p.m.: John Hunter is captured on CCTV cameras on a garage forecourt in the stolen Volkswagen Golf. The Renault 19 containing Michael Dixon is parked directly behind. The prosecution allege that John Hunter was therefore in possession of the stolen Volkswagen Golf when he made the 5.30 p.m. call to John Henry Sayers' mobile phone.

6.04 p.m.: Eddie Stewart rings John Henry Sayers' mobile phone. The call lasts approximately four minutes.

6.11 p.m.: The Volkswagen Golf is parked at Four Lane Ends Metro station. It is exactly one mile from this station to Ella Knights' home.

7.00 p.m.: Getaway driver Eddie Stewart and gunman Dale Miller drive to Longbenton. Stewart is supposed to bang on the windows of the home of Freddie Knights' mother to frighten her into calling her son round. Stewart is unable to locate the correct address, and so the hit is aborted.

7.47 p.m.: John Henry Sayers' mobile phone calls Eddie Stewart's mobile phone. The call lasts 15 seconds.

7.56 p.m.: Eddie Stewart rings John Henry Sayers' mobile phone. The call lasts approximately 20 seconds. Site cell analysis indicates that John Henry's mobile phone was located in Peter Barrett's lay-by, where he had allegedly been seen by Detective Chief Inspector Pallas.

8.00 p.m.: Sergeant Mitsides of Northumbria Police claims he sees John Henry Sayers in a vehicle parked alongside a Renault in Peter Barrett's lay-by.

8.30 p.m.: John Henry Sayers arrives at the King Neptune restaurant in Newcastle's Chinatown district with Tony Leach. Mobile phone records show that a total of 27 calls were made around this time between Michael Dixon, who was in the Longbenton area, and Tony Leach.

9.30 p.m.: John Henry leaves the restaurant, but he is stopped by police and asked to produce his driving licence. When he can't, he is issued a ticket and told to present his documents within seven days. He then drives home.

Wednesday, 20 September 2000

Lee Watson claims that he received and made a number of calls on his mobile phone during the morning and early afternoon. These were to and from John Henry Sayers' mobile phone, allegedly concerning Watson's taking over the running of the hit. These calls were all confirmed by the relevant phone companies as having been made.

7.00 p.m.: Eddie Stewart drives Dale Miller to Longbenton in the Volkswagen Golf. Michael Dixon and Lee Watson follow in the Renault 19.

8.00 p.m.: A stream of mobile calls between Michael Dixon, Lee Watson and Eddie Stewart begins.

8.10 p.m.: Michael Dixon rings Eddie Stewart to make sure that he is in position at Ella Knights' home.

8.20 p.m.: John Henry Sayers' mobile phone rings Lee Watson's mobile phone. The call lasts 57 seconds.

8.22 p.m.: Freddie Knights, travelling into the Longbenton estate in his van, calls his friend at St James' Park on a mobile phone to ask what the score is between Newcastle United and Leyton Orient.

8.24 p.m.: Freddie Knights pulls up outside his mother's home in Lutterworth Road, Longbenton.

8.26 p.m.: Dale Miller guns down Knights. Within seconds, Michael Dixon allegedly telephones Tony Leach to tell him that the job is done.

8.31 p.m.: John Henry Sayers walks into Market Street Police Station to produce his vehicle documents.

9.00 p.m.: The hit team arrives back at a flat owned by gang member Steven Carlton.

9.01 p.m.: John Henry Sayers' mobile phone rings Lee Watson's mobile phone. The call lasts 60 seconds.

9.06 p.m.: Lee Watson telephones a taxi to take him to his home address.

10.07 p.m.: Landline at Lee Watson's home address calls John Henry Sayers' mobile phone. The call lasts 46 seconds.

12.05 a.m.: Miller and Stewart put their clothes in the Volkswagen Golf and set it on fire in a side street in the West End. The murder weapon was buried later.

Watson claimed that the day after the murder he and Dale Miller met John Henry outside Eldon Square, Newcastle's main shopping precinct. Watson alleged that he and Miller got into John Henry's car and that they were driven to an area on the banks of the River Tyne where the phone he had used during the murder was then thrown. Watson told police that he and Miller were then given part payment for murdering

Knights. On 24 September 2000, John Henry Sayers changed his mobile phone number.

Throughout the time the prosecution presented its case, John Henry Sayers listened intently, scribbling notes that he then passed to his legal team. Dale Miller, a dark-eyed, gaunt heroin addict with thinning hair, who was in remission from cancer, seemed doomed to his fate. Occasionally, he would laugh nervously at something before reverting back to his usual cold, emotionless expression.

Michael Dixon, who was known as 'Micky Muggins', because as a youth he had stolen a chicken from a van and missed a wallet stuffed with money that had been left on the floor, was portrayed as a brainless figure of fun for much of the trial. Dixon appeared impassive to the situation he found himself in and seemed happy to play on the fact that he could at best be described as dim. The court heard how Dixon had been arrested after dying his ginger hair peroxide blond before fleeing to Glasgow with £120. His plan had been to obtain a passport using a false name and then escape abroad. Laughing at the absurdity of such a plan, his own barrister asked the jury, 'Can you really imagine Micky Muggins sitting on a sun-drenched hacienda with his £120?'

Eddie Stewart sat behind his co-accused in the dock and, at just 5 ft 2 in. tall, remained barely visible to the jury. Stewart had refused to sit amongst his fellow defendants after he had admitted his part in the murder in a letter to the police. Throughout the trial, he was referred to by his former associates as 'the ginger munchkin'.

When gang member Steven Carlton took the stand to give evidence, Mr Goldberg QC for John Henry Sayers poured scorn on him. Carlton claimed that John Henry had collected shotgun cartridges from him and that his flat had been used as a safe house by the hit team following the shooting. Peering over his steel-rimmed glasses, Mr Goldberg told the jury, 'Carlton is all over the shop in an opium dream. He has admitted that he was like a zombie at the time of the murder and was out of his head all of the time. He said that he could hear people's thoughts when he took magic mushrooms. Perhaps we should give some to the jurors; it may well help them.'

When Lee Watson was brought to the court to give his evidence, he was surrounded by six armed officers. It was obvious to everybody present that Watson was doing everything he could to avoid the hate-filled glares from those in the dock. The scar-faced informant told the court that he had confessed to the police not only his account of Freddie Knights' murder but also of a catalogue of crimes he claimed to have knowledge of or involvement in. They included the murder of Viv Graham in 1993; the disappearance of Chris 'Kicker' Minniken, who vanished in 1986; the shooting of fitness centre manager and ex-policeman Bob Morton in 1996; the October 1995 shooting of three customers as they stood at the bar in the Star Inn, Newcastle; and the attempted letter bombing of Peter Donnelly in 1994.

Watson told the jury, 'I did not kill Freddie Knights, but I did help to organise the shooting. Once Freddie had been shot, the plan was for me to take over his drug-dealing business on the Longbenton Estate. It would have earned me around £100,000 a year.' Watson added that he was making approximately £175,000 a year from crimes that included armed robbery, protection, prostitution, debt collecting and drug dealing. When asked why he had become an informant, Watson replied, 'I realised that the prosecution had some powerful evidence against me, and so I pleaded guilty to murder because I was told that I could still be convicted of it even though I only wanted him shot in the legs. I am giving evidence because I agreed to shoot Freddie Knights in the legs, not murder him. I would not have agreed to have him shot in the head, so why should I take the blame?' His words didn't appear to make much sense at the time, but as was later proven they had been carefully chosen for future reference.

Claims of police corruption and conspiracies emerged following critical evidence given by Detective Chief Inspector Pallas. A senior officer with more than 20 years' experience, DCI Pallas claimed he had seen John Henry and other members of the alleged murder gang sitting in a black BMW in the Peter Barrett lay-by in Gosforth. The detective said he had stopped in the lay-by for a sandwich while on his way from Byker Police Station in the East End to an important meeting at Westerhope Police Station in the West End. He insisted that he had passed the lay-by because the circular route was quicker than going directly from the east to the west of the city. However, the defence claimed that the route he had used would have taken 27 minutes instead of just 11 minutes via the normal route. DCI Pallas also claimed to have seen a police dog van entering the gates of

Newcastle Racecourse close to the lay-by at the same time he saw John Henry and the gang. But the court heard that no police dog van had operated in that area at that time and that the gates DCI Pallas had described had been permanently locked for more than 20 years. Mr Goldberg QC told the jury, 'This gives his story away and shows that he is lying and proves there was a fit-up against Sayers. Some of the evidence is very fishy.'

When John Henry Sayers entered the witness box, he gave an account of his relationship with each of the relevant people allegedly involved in Knights' murder and of his movements at crucial times. He said that he had known Tony Leach all his life and that since his release from prison they had worked together as debt collectors. Leach, he said, was a technology freak who would sometimes change his mobile phone number three times in a day. He was also a cocaine user and a hopeless womaniser, often entertaining up to four different females per week.

John Henry said that he had met Micky 'Muggins' Dixon just a month before the murder. He said that he was a former taxi driver with a 'mechanical mind' and so was useful to have around because of the taxi business he ran. 'If we needed a new car or one needed a repair, I would say, "What's your advice on it?"' John Henry said.

John Henry said that he had met Eddie Stewart in May or June 2000 at a bar in Ryton, Gateshead. Stewart smuggled cigarettes from the continent and had contacts in Thailand who manufactured fake football shirts. John Henry said he had discussed purchasing contraband from Stewart but that after the initial meeting their paths had not crossed again.

Dale Miller had telephoned John Henry to ask him a favour long before the pair had met. It had been Lee Watson who had advised Miller to do this. Watson and Miller had shared a prison cell together, and John Henry had sent them money as a goodwill gesture at Christmas. According to John Henry, Miller said that his girlfriend had begun using heroin and he wanted to use the Sayers name to frighten her supplier away. John Henry had given Miller his permission, and the ploy had apparently worked. The drug dealer never approached Miller's girlfriend again.

John Henry said that he did not know John Hunter, the alleged car thief, but that he was aware that he occasionally used his taxis and would book vehicles in person at the office.

As for Steven Carlton, who had allegedly supplied him with shotgun cartridges, John Henry said that until the trial he had never set eyes on him in his life.

Lee Shaun Watson was a long-time associate of Stephen and Michael Sayers. He and Michael had both been arrested for the murder of Viv Graham. It was in December 1998 while at HMP Frankland, in Durham, that Watson had first met John Henry. At that time, John Henry had not yet been notified that an informant named S. Watson might try to set him up, and so he had no qualms about conversing with his brother's friend. Watson had been released from prison just four months prior to Knights' murder. He had contacted John Henry and asked him for assistance with setting up a sandwich bar-cum-café in Blaydon Shopping Centre, but the project had failed to materialise. Shortly after this failed venture, John Henry had been warned about an S. Watson trying to frame him, and so he decided to extend a gloved hand of friendship in order to keep an eye on his possible enemy rather than upset Watson by ignoring him.

John Henry said that Watson was never a part of any Sayers firm or gang, which he denied existed in any event. Watson, according to John Henry, was in fact an enforcer for the Conroys. 'He had already killed Viv Graham for breaking Michael Conroy's jaw years before. He admitted it to the police, and they still haven't nicked him for it,' John Henry told the jury. Not only had Watson allegedly murdered Graham for the Conroys, but he had also – John Henry claimed – gunned down Freddie Knights on their behalf.

John Henry alleged that when Stephen and Michael Sayers had been arrested for blackmailing a Tyneside businessman, his own cousin Peter Donnelly had been aware of a police surveillance operation being mounted but had failed to warn them. (Donnelly is the man who had been disarmed by Viv Graham when he turned up at Santino's restaurant with a knife and a shotgun.) For failing to warn Stephen and Michael Sayers of the police surveillance operation, Donnelly, according to John Henry, was awarded a £1,000,000 security contract with the help of Northumbria Police. John Henry was incensed by this perceived betrayal by a family member and went in search of Donnelly. Freddie

Knights, who John Henry said he had known since the 1980s, had shown him where Donnelly lived, where his office was and where his business partner lived. John Henry had then visited one of these locations and assaulted Donnelly. Denying that he had any reason to want Knights dead, John Henry said that the only people he knew who wanted to harm him were the Conroys. They had allegedly waged a campaign of harassment and violence against Knights, which led to him and his family fleeing from their Scotswood home and resettling in the Longbenton area of Newcastle.

John Henry said that the day before Freddie Knights was murdered he had been debt collecting with his friend Tony Leach. They had recovered a £30,000 debt on behalf of a self-employed builder named Pringle. For their services, John Henry and Leach had each been paid £5,000. To celebrate their success and John Henry's forthcoming birthday, in six days' time, they had decided to enjoy a meal at the King Neptune Chinese restaurant, in Newcastle. At 7 p.m., they had set off for the restaurant, but Leach had asked John Henry to stop en route at a particular pub, as he said he needed to see somebody there. That 'somebody', according to John Henry, was a married woman with whom Leach was having an affair. Leach had asked the woman to meet him at a well-known lover's lane, known as Peter Barrett's lay-by, within the next few minutes, and she had agreed. Romance in the north-east is apparently not dead.

John Henry had driven Leach to the lay-by for his liaison, but they had waited in vain for five or ten minutes, as she failed to appear. One imagines that she was elsewhere seeking some form of much-needed relationship guidance. John Henry claimed that it was while they were waiting for Leach's mistress that Sergeant Mitsides must have spotted them. He was adamant that no other vehicle was near his, and certainly no Renault 19, as stated by the police. The mysterious lady has never been identified, and Leach has refused to name her, because he has said that he did not wish to cause her problems by revealing their affair to her husband.

After leaving the lay-by, John Henry drove Leach to his home, which, coincidentally, is near where Freddie Knights was due to be murdered. The pair then drove to the King Neptune Restaurant, where a number of calls were made and received on John Henry's mobile phone. These included calls to and from the murder gang's getaway driver, Eddie Stewart. At this time, Stewart was searching in vain for Ella Knights' home with other members of the gang. It is not in dispute that, after being unable to find Ella's home that night, the hit team postponed their attack. After leaving the restaurant at approximately 9.30 p.m., John Henry was stopped by the police and asked to produce his driving licence. Because he didn't have the licence with him, he was given a producer and told that he must present his licence within seven days.

John Henry has always denied that he made or received any of the calls to or from Eddie Stewart. According to John Henry, Leach would purchase SIM cards in packs of fifty or one hundred and change his number up to three times per day. He did this because he was supposedly a 'technology freak'. Because Leach's associates would not know his latest number, they would call either his sister or John Henry, who was always with him. 'If those calls were made and received, nobody spoke to me,' John Henry said. 'If I was with Leachy, he would have spoken to Eddie Stewart.' However, John Henry was quick to add that he did not believe the phone records were accurate in any event. John Henry told the jury that he had complained to the prosecution that some of his phone records had disappeared and calls he disputed making had appeared. 'The whole thing stinks,' he said.

On the morning of Knights' death, John Henry had taken his son to school before attending his taxi office. John Henry had remained there for most of the day. At 3 p.m., he collected his son from school and took him home. The next undisputed sighting of John Henry was at 4.40 p.m., when a police officer saw him talking to Tony Leach and Michael Dixon in a street near his home. At 6.05 p.m., the three men were seen, again by a police officer, leaving John Henry's home. Ninety minutes later, John Henry was observed talking to a man outside his taxi office by the manageress of a strip club located next door. Another police officer saw John Henry and his son enter a fish and chip shop near the taxi office at 8.15 p.m. John Henry then dropped his son off at his mother's house before attending a nearby police station, where he produced his driving documents. When he left the police station, John Henry visited the strip club next door to his taxi office, where he was captured by CCTV cameras.

The prosecution alleged that, throughout the evening prior to Knights' murder, John Henry had ensured that he was being seen in places by people who would give credibility to his alibi. However, John Henry told the jury that Billy Shearer, the uncle of Newcastle legend Alan Shearer, was a good friend of his and that if he had wanted a cast-iron alibi for the time of the murder he could easily have gone to the Platinum Club at St James' Park, an exclusive area in the ground where executives and their guests watch matches.

After leaving the strip club, John Henry went home, where he remained until the following morning. John Henry claims that it was while taking his son to school that he first heard about Freddie Knights' murder, on a radio news bulletin. When asked outright if he had ordered the murder of Freddie Knights or played any part whatsoever in his death, John Henry had replied with an emphatic no. He was adamant that the police and others were conspiring against him in order to get him locked up for life. Regardless of whether they were to succeed or not, the pressure the police investigation had put on the Sayers family had resulted in John Henry and his wife, Yvonne, separating. In effect, the alleged conspirators had secured a partial victory, because they had managed to keep him off the streets while on remand for a year and had destroyed his marriage and home life.

In his closing speech, John Henry's barrister, Jonathan Goldberg QC, told the jury, 'There is an extraordinary relationship between Sayers and Northumbria Police. It's along the lines of the Wild West and Billy the Kid. Sayers says he has tried to go straight but that the police won't let him. We allege police corruption, not in the sense of police taking bribes but what we would call "noble cause corruption". The police think Sayers is guilty and assume he is guilty and so want him badly. They have given the system a nudge because they think they can't trust the system to get it right and they think that he is a menace to society. Fit-ups do happen, and this kind of corruption is hard to detect, because who is better at covering their tracks than the detectives? Sayers may be paranoid, but just because you're paranoid doesn't mean the bastards aren't out to get you.'

After the jury had been sent out to deliberate, the police were ordered by the judge to investigate a menacing phone call that had been made to a male juror's home. Each member of the jury was interviewed and asked if they felt they could carry on. All agreed to continue deliberating, including the male who had received the threat that had been made to himself and his family. The call was eventually traced to a public payphone in the north-east, but the caller was not identified. Earlier in the trial, the police had been called in to investigate a letter that had been sent to the clerk of the court and the offices of the *Yorkshire Post*. The letter suggested a member of the jury had been the subject of an 'improper' approach by someone, but it was not known at the time whether the letter was genuine or a crude attempt to abort the proceedings.

Mr Justice Douglas Brown adjourned matters for 40 minutes in order to interview each jury member. Then, in their absence, he told the defendants and their legal representatives, 'I have now seen each juror individually. Each juror denies writing any letter to the court or the newspaper, and they have no knowledge of any other juror doing so. I don't propose to take the matter any further. It is a serious matter so far as the court is concerned, and I hope it will be fully investigated by the police.' Despite a thorough investigation, which included the letters undergoing tests for DNA, no arrests were made.

After the jury had returned and given their verdicts concerning Freddie Knights' murder, members of his family gasped in shock and others in the public gallery cheered in celebration. To everybody who had heard the evidence, the jury's findings were surprising to say the least. Gunman Dale Miller, 38, was jailed for 16 years after the jury acquitted him of murder but found him guilty of manslaughter. Getaway driver Edward Stewart, 39, was also cleared of murder but found guilty of manslaughter and jailed for 13 years. Henchman Michael Dixon, 34, who helped organise the attack, was acquitted of murder and manslaughter but found guilty of conspiracy to cause grievous bodily harm with intent and jailed for nine years. Craig Shepherd, who had travelled to Glasgow with Dixon, was found guilty of assisting an offender and sentenced to 12 months' imprisonment. Both John Henry Sayers and Tony Leach were acquitted of murder, manslaughter and conspiracy to cause grievous bodily harm.

Despite having pleaded guilty to murder, an offence that carries a mandatory life sentence, Lee Watson was given permission to withdraw his plea and instead admit to manslaughter. A cynic might think that Watson had been given a deal after all. It's difficult to comprehend how anybody could accept that men who had attended an address armed with a shotgun, stood over a defenceless man and shot him in the face as he cowered on his mother's doorstep could possibly be described as people who were guilty of manslaughter rather than murder. The difference between the two offences is that the offender who commits manslaughter does not intend to kill. Blasting somebody in the head with a shotgun would, one imagines, generally be a determined effort to kill.

Sentencing Watson to just 11 years, Mr Justice Douglas Brown said, 'You are a ruthless and violent professional criminal. You arranged for Freddie Knights to be ambushed and shot. You chose the gunman and driver and took part in the planning of this offence. You knew a shotgun was going to be used. However, you are entitled to a substantial reduction for giving evidence.'

Speaking outside the court, Freddie Knights' 78-year-old mother, Ella, told reporters, 'I want to thank every single policeman involved in the investigation, and the liaison officers. They could not have done more to bring me justice for Freddie. The first shot had hit my door, and I couldn't get it open in time. When I got out, I saw Freddie lying there. I couldn't do anything for him. I was so shocked, I just rubbed his leg. He couldn't speak to me; his eyes were gone, closed. His sister, Shirley, came out and helped me. Neighbours brought towels, which we wrapped around his head to stem the blood. It was too late. I will never forget that sight. The ambulance came and took him away, and I couldn't go with him. I was driven to hospital after him, but he was pronounced dead.'

Fighting back tears, Freddie's wife, Grace, added, 'We sat and listened to all the court evidence. It was a shocking and vicious attack. I am surprised that, having listened to the evidence, they came to a manslaughter verdict. The only comfort I can get is that the judge gave them lengthy sentences. But for me, my life is over. Freddie meant everything to me, and he was devoted to the boys. He was a big, soft-hearted man who would go without himself rather than see his family and friends deprived. Whoever they jailed or didn't jail, it still won't bring back Freddie into our lives.'

Caught up in the emotion of the event, John Henry, who had been forced to consider the prospect of spending the rest of his life in prison, felt that he too had to have his say: 'My defence all along has been that I was not guilty and that I was a victim of a fit-up by the police. Now I just want to live my life and go straight. Every day I was in court, I was sure I was going to get sent down and that I might never get out. This whole thing has had a real effect on me. It has put my relationship with my wife, Yvonne, under real strain. In fact, I have split up with Yvonne, and she has had to sell our home. There were rumours going around about me having a motive for wanting Freddie shot, because they tried to say my son was in fact Freddie's son and he had had an affair with Yvonne. But we have had the laddie DNA tested, and that proved that I was his dad. Northumbria Police decided I was guilty a day or two after Freddie Knights was shot, so it must have been a fit-up for them to target me so early on.'

John Henry's claims of corruption within Northumbria Police were angrily denied by Chief Constable Crispian Strachan: 'We had over 200 separate witnesses, and I don't believe it is possible to manufacture a criminal case if it were manufactured to that size. Having worked for nearly 30 years in the police force, I don't believe there are officers in this force of such a frame of mind. There is a high standard of integrity within this force demonstrated by two facts. Firstly, we have an outstandingly good, successful record in tackling criminality in prosecuting offenders and taking them before the courts for the courts to deal with them as they see fit, as has happened in this case. Secondly, we have an independent measure in terms of the number of complaints that are made against this force, which is at an all-time low and is very low in terms of metropolitan forces, and in that respect there has been no complaint of corruption substantiated against any officer in this force for the last five years.'

Rather foolishly, John Henry had decided that the matter should not end on the steps of the court. He told reporters, 'I want a fully independent inquiry into the police handling of the case, and my solicitor will be writing to the Home Secretary, our local MP, Stephen Byers, and Amnesty International demanding there is a full investigation. I know things have happened in the past, but I just want to move forward if I am allowed to. I know they will be taping me and watching me, and while I hope they won't come back for me there's always a chance they will.'

'Be careful what you wish for' may have been appropriate advice for somebody to give John Henry at that point, but he was still on a high after being released and probably wouldn't have listened in any event. However, he should have listened to his own words about the police watching, waiting and possibly coming back for him.

Chapter Twelve

JUDGEMENT DAY

IT IS IMPOSSIBLE to say why they decided to meet. A man loyal to the Conroy family claims that Paddy was invited to act as an intermediary between the Sayers gang and 'another' Newcastle-based group of criminals. A man loyal to the Sayers family claims that the meeting took place to decide which parts of Newcastle the opposing families would control. One assumes that meant control of criminal enterprises in certain areas rather than relieving the city council of their street cleaning, refuse and maintenance duties. What isn't in dispute is that, one evening, bitter rivals the Conroys and the Sayers agreed to meet at a snooker club in Newcastle city centre.

Paddy and the Bull arrived early and entered the premises via a staircase at the rear. It didn't appear as if anybody else had arrived, and so they began to play pool. Moments later, a man ran out of the manager's office shouting, 'They've got guns. Run. They've got guns.' Paddy and the Bull glanced at each other before running into the office. A member of the Sayers gang was pointing a revolver at an associate of the Conroys, who was pointing a handgun back at the man threatening him. Paddy shouted, 'Woah, woah, you put the fucking gun down, and you put the fucking gun down.' One weapon was lowered, but the other remained firmly in line with the head of the Sayers man. Paddy stepped forward and, raising his voice a few decibels, roared, 'Put the gun down, and I mean now. You have come here to talk not shoot each other. Can we get on with this meeting?'

With the atmosphere now slightly more relaxed, negotiations got under way. A member of the Sayers gang said that they had put a lot of time and effort into 'enterprises' in the city centre and that they didn't want others getting involved. A member of the opposing gang said that they had the West End of the city 'sewn up' and that they too did not want others interfering in their business. It was agreed, therefore, that the Sayers gang's interests would not be competed against or disrupted in any way in the city centre and that the other gang would enjoy the same monopoly in the West End.

According to the Conroys, the following day, members of the Sayers gang were 'strutting around Newcastle' telling people that Paddy had 'shit himself' after having a gun pulled on him at the meeting. When Paddy heard what was being said, he quickly made his way to the hostel run by John Sayers senior. When he arrived, the premises looked deserted, but as Paddy went to pull away he saw their cousin Peter Donnelly. Paddy pointed ahead as if to say to Donnelly, 'Wait there. I want a word,' but as he did so a vehicle pulled up in front of his. John Sayers senior, his son Stephen and three other men got out and looked directly at Paddy. He leapt out of his car and began shouting, 'Who said I shit myself? Who pointed a gun at me? Who? Who?' Nobody replied. The men just stood staring at Paddy, in disbelief rather than fear.

John Sayers senior turned and walked away without saying a word. There seemed little point in asking the same questions, as no answers had been forthcoming at the first time of asking, and so Paddy walked back to his car. As he did so, one of the men mumbled something under his breath. Paddy didn't bother asking what had been said. He just sent the guilty party flying backwards into his friends with a powerful right hook. As the man struggled to regain his composure, Paddy struck him again. The man knew that there was only ever going to be one winner in this contest, and so he remained where he was on the floor. Paddy warned him about his future conduct, got back into his car and disappeared down the street.

The following day, Paddy was with Tommy Cowan, his former partner in the Hydraulic Crane pub. They had arranged to meet Paddy's brother Lenny at his home, but he was not in. Rather than wait for him in the street, Paddy suggested to Cowan that they drive into town for a sandwich and return in an hour. As they passed a church, they noticed that a funeral was in progress, and Paddy had recognised several of the mourners. With time on his hands, Paddy decided to park the vehicle and speak to his friends. They told Paddy that members of the Sayers family had been at the church service but that they had all since left. Paddy didn't appear to be interested in this news, and shortly afterwards he bade his friends farewell and headed towards the city centre with Cowan.

As they passed the top of the street where Yvonne Sayers, the mother of John Henry, Michael and Stephen, lived, Paddy and Cowan noticed a dozen or so members of the Sayers gang standing outside a café. A few of the men glared at Paddy as he drove past, but none of them said anything. As Paddy and Cowan reached the outskirts of the city, their vehicle was caught at a red traffic light. As they sat waiting for the lights to change, Paddy glanced in the rear-view mirror and saw a cavalcade of vehicles racing towards him. Their lights were flashing, and as they neared Paddy could hear their horns blaring. Paddy instinctively knew who it was: the Sayers gang.

Cowan, a non-violent individual who was known as 'two-stone Tommy' because of his slim build, looked terrified. As Paddy glanced across at his trembling friend, he realised that he was going to have to sort this particular problem out alone. If only it had been the Bull sitting opposite him instead of Cowan, the odds of victory would have been greatly improved. When the lights changed, Paddy pulled away and began to prepare himself mentally for the battle he knew would shortly take place. He knew that if he backed down or showed cowardice the baying mob would descend upon him. People who fight back in such situations rarely suffer life-threatening injuries. It is the ones who go to ground and curl up in a ball that the cowards in a mob kick and stamp on.

The cars containing the Sayers gang were by now tailgating Paddy's vehicle, and so he began looking for somewhere to pull over. Suddenly, a car driven by Tony Leach, John Henry's right-hand man, appeared in front of Paddy's vehicle. Leach had taken a different route from his associates and was approaching from the opposite direction. Paddy slammed on the brakes and jumped out of his vehicle. Throwing his coat to the floor, he shouted at John Henry, 'Come on you shit. Let's have it, just me and you.' John Henry's associates had not yet alighted from their vehicles, and so he quickly began to back away. However, as soon as the Sayers gang were all around Paddy, John Henry began to advance on him. Suddenly he stopped, gazed at the floor as if trying to compose himself and then landed a right-hand punch on Paddy's chin. Paddy staggered back a pace but remained on his feet. Instead of brawling, John Henry kept his distance from his opponent, jabbing and punching him with his fists before stepping back out of range.

Rather than be picked off where he stood, Paddy launched himself at John Henry, gripping him in a headlock. He punched him two or three times and then took him to the floor. As Paddy grappled with John Henry, members of the Sayers gang began kicking him in the head and body. Unable to get to his feet, Paddy let go of John Henry and covered his head in order to protect himself. It was a drastic mistake; the mob became frenzied, kicking and stamping on him until he was barely conscious. It was only when Paddy lay motionless that the onslaught stopped.

One of the gang stepped forward out of the crowd from Paddy's left side. He bent down and stabbed Paddy in the face with a craft knife. Instinctively, Paddy grabbed his assailant's hand with both of his own, but it was snatched away in a downward motion, tearing the skin and flesh wide open. As the knifeman got back to his feet, the Sayers gang attacked Paddy again. Like a pack of hyenas, they savaged their defenceless victim until he slipped into unconsciousness.

That night, members of the Sayers gang trawled the city's bars and nightclubs informing everybody that Paddy Conroy was a spent force and that they alone now ruled Newcastle. Shortly after being attacked, Paddy had made his way to Newcastle General Hospital, but the staff in A & E began talking about notifying the police, and so he left before being treated. Twenty minutes later, he arrived at an out-of-town hospital and explained that he had been injured while replacing a pane of glass at his home. After having his face stitched, Paddy began to make his way home, but the police arrested him en route.

When he was interviewed, Paddy was asked if he wanted legal representation, but he declined, as he felt that he had done no wrong. To Paddy's surprise, the police had already obtained CCTV footage of the incident, which they played to him and asked him to explain. 'That's not me on the video. You have the wrong man,' Paddy said.

'Explain why the man who isn't you looks like you and why he is getting out of the car of your business partner, Tommy Cowan,' an officer replied. Paddy's liberty was still subject to the terms and conditions of his parole licence, and he knew that if the police so wished they could have him returned to prison for this incident. 'How did you get that wound on your face, Paddy?' an officer asked.

'A pane of glass I was fixing in the bathroom fell out and cut me,' Paddy lied.

Realising their questions were not going to be answered, the detectives terminated the interview and seized Paddy's blood-stained clothing as evidence. The officers said that they were going to obtain a DNA sample from the blood on Paddy's clothing and compare it with blood found at the scene. Several eyewitnesses to the incident had come forward, and so Paddy was photographed. His image was going to be used in a photo identity parade. Only after this evidence-gathering exercise was complete was he granted bail and allowed home to nurse his wounds and bruised pride. A month later, Paddy returned to the police station, where a beaming detective informed him that the blood at the scene was his and that a nun had picked him out on the photo identity parade. 'Please tell me the jury aren't going to believe her,' the officer had said, laughing. Paddy refused to answer any more questions from the police or to make a complaint about his attackers, and so both he and the Sayers gang escaped prosecution.

The Conroy and the Sayers families were not the only ones making their presence known on the streets of Newcastle at the time. As two men, Joseph Wood and Robert Dunwiddie, stood looking at clothing on a stall at the city's famous Green Market one day, the Conroys' old adversary Geoffrey Harrison walked up to them and carved their faces open with a large knife before stabbing them. Fearing for their lives, the men fought back, stabbed Harrison and beat him senseless. Witnesses described how terrified women and children who had been shopping in the market fled the scene in tears as blood literally ran down the street.

The initial attack by Harrison and the counter-attack against him were caught on CCTV cameras, but the images were not clear enough to distinguish who dealt which knife blows. However, a female stallholder who witnessed the attack by Harrison said that he had walked up behind Wood and carved open his face with a knife before repeatedly stabbing both Wood and Dunwiddie. The stallholder told police that the incident had then turned into a grotesque stabbing frenzy as the tables were turned on Harrison. 'The man being attacked looked to have been cut from ear to ear and across the chest. He was totally covered in blood. It was horrible,' she said.

Using CCTV cameras, the police were able to follow those involved in the violence as they made their escape, and they were arrested shortly afterwards. Speculation was rife on an underworld motive for the attack, including a long-standing vendetta between Harrison and Wood. The previous year, Wood had appeared at Newcastle Crown Court accused of shooting Harrison's friend David Francis, who had been blasted in the chest and leg as he walked his dog. The hit man had fired several shots from a car that was then driven away before being found burned out in Gateshead six hours later. However, the case was dropped by the Crown Prosecution Service through lack of evidence.

The shooting had sparked a spate of tit-for-tat gun attacks over several weeks. Among those incidents, two windows were blasted out at a terraced house where three people were sleeping, including a nine year old and a twelve-month-old baby. Then a gunman shot twice at the door of a terraced house in Rye Hill, in Newcastle's West End. Twenty-seven-year-old Cheryl Carter was peppered with approximately thirty shotgun pellets when hooded gunmen turned up on her doorstep and opened fire. On the same day, shots were fired at a house in Kirkdale Green while a woman and her 19-year-old pregnant daughter were inside and a white Nissan Sunny was blasted with a shotgun near Newcastle College. Nobody was ever convicted of any of these offences. However, police believe that they were definitely linked to the bloodbath in Green Market involving Geoffrey Harrison. At his trial, Harrison denied cutting and stabbing Wood and Dunwiddie, but he was convicted and sentenced to seven years' imprisonment. Following his release, Geoffrey Harrison was found dead at his home. He had suffered horrific head injuries after being repeatedly struck with a hammer. As one Tyneside villain faded into oblivion, another was unwittingly emerging back into the spotlight.

John Henry Sayers had been cleared of any involvement in the attack on Conroy and the Knights murder, but some police officers, rightly or wrongly, believed that John Henry was not the reformed criminal struggling to make a living that he had portrayed himself to be. Rather than let John Henry go about his business, they decided to monitor him extremely closely. After losing his taxi business, John Henry had thrown himself into building up the chain of pubs that Alan Coe was running for him. According to Coe, Neptune Inns, the original company that he had fronted for John Henry, had run up massive tax debts, and so a decision had been made to fold it and launch an identical business using the name Pubs 4 Us. Coe was again registered as the company director.

Coe has since alleged that, approximately 12 weeks after Freddie Knights' murder, John Henry marched into the John Gilpin pub, where Coe was working, and ordered him into the cellar. 'He demanded the Christmas takings and threatened to kill me if I even told my wife that the Sayers were involved in any of the pubs,' Coe said. Pubs 4 Us expanded rapidly, taking over more than 30 premises in the north-east, but the company's unpaid debts and taxes were also mounting rapidly, and Coe alone was the man who was responsible for them.

Each week, Coe would deliver brown envelopes containing the pub's takings to a member of the Sayers family. Coe claims that John Henry would 'froth at the mouth' at the very thought of having to pay taxes to the government, a policy he apparently adopted as payback for the trouble he and his family had suffered over his arrest for the murder of Freddie Knights. It was inevitable, therefore, that HM Revenue and Customs (HMRC) eventually invited Coe to a meeting to explain the company's unpaid tax. Coe lied to the HMRC officers, claiming that Pubs 4 Us Ltd was in fact a relatively new company. The HMRC appeared to accept Coe's explanation, and he left the meeting on a high. When he got into his vehicle and telephoned John Henry's mother, Yvonne, to tell her the good news, he was unaware that his vehicle had been fitted with a covert listening device. 'I have done every one of them. Fucking unbelievable. There is nothing they can do now; we are protected. I tricked them all,' Coe boasted.

Yvonne replied, 'Aye, thank you very much.' Yvonne was then heard telling a third party in the room that Alan had 'sorted the VAT thing out'.

Coe and Yvonne Sayers may be forgiven for talking so openly on the telephone, as their world bore no resemblance whatsoever to that of

John Henry. His criminal lifestyle had ensured that he was painfully aware of the lengths that the police would go to in order to gather evidence. It's surprising, therefore, that John Henry does not appear to have learned valuable lessons from his experiences with Northumbria Police. Following his acquittal for Knights' murder, John Henry had predicted that they would record his conversations. It seems, therefore, that John Henry had thrown caution to the wind and wrongly assumed that Northumbria Police were no longer interested in his activities, because his car had been bugged too. Although Coe thought that he had tricked the HMRC officers, he knew that, because John Henry was still refusing to set aside money for taxes, it was only a matter of time before they would return and ask awkward questions about the company. Coe knew that he would be the fall guy, and so he made a decision to refuse to sign any more important company documents and asked John Henry if he would hire an assistant to speak to officials and creditors on his behalf. Yvonne Sayers began to think that Coe was becoming secretive and trying to distance himself from the business, and this led to several angry exchanges between her and John Henry. In one row, which was recorded while John Henry was on the phone in his car, he had said to his mother, 'What are you on about with Alan?'

Yvonne Sayers replied, 'Just what he's on about. He wants a secretary and all this, and we can't afford one anyway, and he doesn't need one anyway. It's bullshit.'

John Henry was then heard saying, 'Mother, you see for the sake of just asking that you're making mountains out of molehills.'

Yvonne Sayers replied, 'Oh, shut up.'

The conversation captured on the bug continued with Yvonne Sayers saying, 'He hasn't written one letter in the last four years. Now he's wanting somebody, but he doesn't want a little lassie. He wants somebody who can talk to the breweries. I can talk to the breweries.'

John Henry replied, 'OK then, so you're finance director, personal assistant, any other titles?'

Yvonne Sayers replied, 'Fucking chief fucking bottle-washer. Bye bye.'

John Henry then signed off by saying, 'I love ya.'

Mothers, as most men know but rarely care to admit, are always right. In March 2005, Alan Coe was declared bankrupt because of the huge debts Pubs 4 Us had run up. After effectively washing his hands of the business, he unwittingly became a liability to John Henry, because he no longer had a purpose and had enough information to send his former boss back to jail. The police, who were monitoring the conversations between the parties, contacted Coe and issued him with what is known as an Osman Warning. These are given to people when the police have credible evidence that others are planning to take someone's life. A series of James Bond-style bugs and cameras was immediately installed in Coe's home. One camera and recording device was disguised as a washing machine and another as a spade in the garden. An immobilised car was parked on Coe's drive, which was to prevent others driving up to his door. This too was fitted with covert cameras. Coe and his family were also given personal panic alarms to wear around their necks.

Shortly after Coe had received his Osman Warning, police officers carried out a series of raids and arrested Coe, John Henry and Yvonne Sayers for tax evasion. The police found £50,000 in cash at John Henry's home, and £49,000 stashed in two plastic bags was recovered from a bathroom cabinet at Yvonne Sayers' address. Initially, Yvonne Sayers claimed that the money was part of her life savings. 'My father was a builder and demolition contractor,' she said. 'There was always money in the house. He used to keep it in baby-food tins. I don't think there is anything odd or unsafe about having money in the house.'

Coe, on the other hand, told police a very different story about the origins of the money. He admitted his role in the fraud but said he had only been carrying out John Henry's orders because he had been threatened by him. There did appear to be an element of truth about Coe's version of events, because shortly after his arrest a Volvo owned by his wife was torched. Days earlier, a Nissan belonging to her parents had had its windows smashed and tyres slashed. Unfortunately for Coe, although the police accepted relations between him and the Sayers had now soured, they refused to believe that he had not been a willing participant in the fraud from the outset.

John Henry and Alan Coe were both charged with a variety of offences relating to tax evasion and money laundering. Yvonne Sayers faced a single charge of money laundering. John Henry pleaded guilty and was sentenced to four years' imprisonment. Yvonne Sayers also pleaded guilty and was given a nine-month suspended sentence. Alan Coe pleaded not guilty after offering a defence of duress, but after a four-week trial at Newcastle Crown Court he was convicted of all charges. Judge Michael Cartlidge sentenced him to two years and nine months for each offence, all to run concurrently. He told Coe, 'You assisted John Henry Sayers and his criminal organisation to evade taxes and rates. You were a willing subordinate of Sayers. After becoming bankrupt, you became of little use to Sayers or his organisation, and so you were effectively discarded. The Sayers organisation became convinced, probably wrongly in my view, that you were taking money away from them. As a result of all this, you were informed that you were at risk of being killed. You have lost your family life, you have lost your home, you have lost everything. There has been no benefit from the fraud to you apart from the wages you received from the Sayers organisation. The man described as the evil genius behind this operation, John Henry Sayers, pleaded guilty and was sentenced to four years. It is apparent that John Henry Sayers is a ruthless and dangerous criminal.'

When John Henry was led to the cells to begin his sentence, officers from Northumbria Police congratulated one another, but they were not quite finished with the 'evil genius' or his 'organisation' just yet.

In May 2003, career criminal Errol Hay pistol-whipped a 26-year-old man named John Scott as he slept on a settee at his home in the East End of Newcastle. The prolonged attack left Scott fighting for his life. He did survive but suffered a fractured skull, deep lacerations to his face and permanent brain damage. In the days leading up to the attack, Hay had boasted that he wanted to fight Scott 'man to man' after hearing rumours that he had bullied a teenager. However, when Hay eventually tracked Scott down, he wasn't confident that he could defeat him in an orthodox encounter. Instead, cowardly Hay repeatedly smashed the butt of a replica gun into the sleeping man's head. After leaving his victim for dead, Hay threw the gun into the River Tyne and paid an associate £800 to wash the blood out of Scott's carpet.

When he learned that Scott had survived the attack, Hay convinced his friends to lend him £2,000 in an effort to buy his victim's silence. When this failed, Hay fled Tyneside and washed up in Pattaya, one of Thailand's seediest resorts. After marrying a local prostitute, Hay worked as a barman before immersing himself in the local drug trade. Pattaya is awash with ex-pat villains, and those who met Hay firmly believed that he was beyond reproach, a 'proper man' who would never grass on his associates. In reality, Hay was a devious, deceitful individual, one of the least trustworthy people anybody would wish to have around them. Hay had been a registered informant for almost 20 years, pocketing thousands of pounds from Northumbria Police in exchange for shopping his drug-dealing accomplices.

When travelling Tyneside villains learned that Hay was working at a bar in Pattaya, they made their local counterparts aware of his treachery. People began to shun Hay, and it wasn't long before he lost his bar job and his drug-dealing business dried up. Solely reliant upon his wife's poorly paid horizontal performances, Hay turned to alcohol for solace. As there is no benefits system in Thailand, Hay knew that he would have to get additional income from somewhere to survive, and so, three years after fleeing Newcastle, he decided to make a late-night call to 'Phil', his former police handler. It had been almost a decade since Phil had heard from Hay, and so he scribbled notes of their conversation:

> Sounded extremely drunk. Hay claimed that he had consumed a few gins, but he knew exactly what he was doing. Hay is claiming that he left Newcastle because he feared that John Henry Sayers was going to put a bullet in his head. He stated: 'I have evidence that could send Sayers and others to prison for a very long time.'

When asked by Phil about the crime that John Henry had supposedly committed, Hay said that Sayers had 'nobbled the jury' at his trial for the murder of Freddie Knights. Phil was aware that a member of the jury named Robert Black had received a chilling phone call at his home on the night before the not-guilty verdict was reached, and so he suggested that officers from Northumbria Police fly out to Thailand to meet Hay. In a series of extraordinary interviews, Hay told detectives, 'I had attended the Freddie Knights murder trial in Leeds in support of my associate John Henry. During the hearing, the name of juror Robert Black was mistakenly read out by the court clerk, despite the fact he was supposed to have complete anonymity. On 9 September 2002, the jury returned guilty verdicts on Dale Miller, Michael Dixon and Eddie

Stewart. The jury had not yet concluded their deliberations concerning John Henry and Tony Leach, and so the court adjourned until the following morning. As people began to leave, John Henry leaned across the protective glass that surrounds the dock and told me to make a threatening phone call to Robert Black, the jury member. "Make sure my brother Stephen helps you sort this; it's very important," John Henry said.'

According to Hay, after relaying the message to Stephen Sayers, he, Stephen and another man, named Mark Rowe, drove to Hetton-le-Hole, a small town on the outskirts of Sunderland. Upon their arrival, Hay was given a list of telephone numbers to ring and a script to read. At approximately 11 p.m. that night, Robert Black's wife answered their home phone. 'Is Robert there?' a man with a Geordie accent asked.

'Hello?' Robert Black said as he took the handset from his wife.

'Do you realise you have a big decision to make tomorrow? Ten thousand pounds and your family are safe,' the caller said before hanging up.

Hay's story had more than the ring of truth about it, because Robert Black had immediately contacted the police, who traced the call to a phone box in Hetton-le-Hole. The morning after the call was made, the jury, which included Robert Black, found John Henry Sayers and Tony Leach not guilty of Freddie Knights' murder. Hay told detectives that, following John Henry's acquittal, Sayers had held an impromptu party at a Newcastle pub to celebrate his freedom. Hay claimed that during the party he was approached by John Henry, who simply said, 'Thank you.' Approximately two weeks later, Hay was allegedly taken out for a meal by John Henry, who asked questions about the call to Robert Black.

The detectives listening to Hay's story could hardly contain their excitement. If found guilty of nobbling a jury member during a murder trial, the Sayers brothers and Rowe would go to prison for a very long time, if not for life.

At the time Hay was briefing detectives about the alleged jury-nobbling plot, John Henry was still languishing in prison for tax evasion offences. He had no idea what was going on until police officers attended the prison on his birthday, 24 September 2009. John Henry may well have doubted that Northumbria Police had attended to wish him a happy birthday, but he was left in no doubt about the allegations that

Errol Hay had made, because he was charged with perverting the course of justice, an offence that carries a maximum sentence of life imprisonment. Therefore, if 46-year-old John Henry were to be found guilty, it was likely that he would be spending every birthday thereafter in custody.

Back in Newcastle, John Henry's brother Stephen and family friend Mark Rowe were also arrested and charged with perverting the course of justice. It's fair to say that many on Tyneside believed that this was the bitter end for the Sayers firm. Paddy Conroy wrote on a social-networking website that a conviction for the Sayers would lead to further charges and further trials regarding other serious unsolved matters. He did not elaborate, but others added fuel to the fire by claiming that, now John Henry and Stephen were off the streets, fresh charges concerning the murders of Freddie Knights and Viv Graham would follow. What these people didn't know was that Northumbria Police had built their entire case around the wholly uncorroborated evidence of Errol Hay. He had told detectives that he was racked with guilt over his part in the jury-nobbling plot and was desperate to cleanse his soul and give justice to Freddie Knights' family. The evidence suggested otherwise. Down on his luck in a foreign land, Hay demanded assurance that, if he were to return to the UK to give evidence, he would not be imprisoned for any length of time for outstanding offences that he had committed, such as the attack on John Scott. He also wanted Northumbria Police to pay his Thai prostitute wife's air fares to visit him in the UK, weekly benefits, his rent and school fees for his two children. The law, some may think surprisingly, allows for such deals to take place, and so Northumbria Police agreed.

In October 2010, Errol Hay appeared in court for pistol-whipping John Scott, the young man who nearly died as a result of his injuries. Judge David Hodson told Hay, 'You would normally be looking at a nine-year term for such an attack, but the agreement made with the Serious Organised Crime Agency entitles you to a two-thirds discount.' Hay was then sentenced to three years' imprisonment, but this was suspended for one year, meaning Hay was a free man. Sadly, John Scott will never be free from Hay's attack; he suffered memory loss and insomnia and has been told that he can never return to work.

In November 2010, the Sayers brothers and Rowe stood trial at

Woolwich Crown Court, in London. Sitting in the dock, they looked remarkably confident for men who were potentially facing life behind bars. Only three people were sitting in the public gallery, and each one commented on the almost cavalier attitudes of the defendants. An announcement was then made that seemed to explain their confidence. A week before the trial opened, Hay had stumbled and fallen. When somebody ran to his aid, they noticed that his speech was slurred and his hands were shaking violently. Concerned for his well-being, the Good Samaritan had telephoned for an ambulance, and Hay was rushed to hospital. Doctors there soon diagnosed Hay as suffering from a brain tumour, which may have affected his memory. Further examination revealed that his condition was terminal. Errol Hay had between three and eighteen months to live. Asked if he still wished to give evidence in the case, Hay said that he did, because he wanted justice for Freddie Knights' family.

When Errol Hay entered the dock to give his evidence, he looked a shadow of his former self. Gaunt and unsteady on his feet, he did his best to avoid all eye contact in the courtroom. However, he soon showed that he was no shrinking violet and that the terrible disease that was slowly killing him hadn't yet affected his memory or his almost gloating attitude as he attempted to send his former friends to prison for the rest of their lives. To give himself kudos in the eyes of the jury, Hay informed the court that he wished to reveal for the first time who had taken part in an armed robbery with him several years earlier. Hay said, 'It was my father and my brother-in-law assisting me in the £7,000 Indian-shopkeeper job. My father's now aged 70, but he was helping me. I wouldn't tell the police before, but this is the first time I've come clean.'

Having earned a degree of credibility for such a breathtaking betrayal, Hay turned his attention to the Sayers brothers and Rowe. Hay claimed that he had attended the last three days of the Freddie Knights murder trial in Leeds, but Jonathan Goldberg QC, who was representing John Henry, pointed out that a covert operation by police to gather video evidence around the court had failed to capture him. Hay was adamant that he had attended the trial and said that John Henry had spoken to him through the glass of the dock, but a prison officer named Paul Richardson claimed that Sayers was flanked by guards and that there would not have been an opportunity for any such conversation to take place. Hay then claimed that after the trial he was driven to a phone box in Hetton-le-Hole, where he had put on an Irish accent to make the phone call to Robert Black. However, Black had made no mention of this to police, instead insisting that the caller had a strong Geordie accent. Finally, Hay, who was clearly becoming frustrated at being caught out, said that when he made the call he had offered Black £20,000, but the juror had told police that the figure was £10,000.

As Hay stood rooted to the floor of the dock in silence, Jonathan Goldberg QC stunned the court by saying, 'If you did make the call, you did it on behalf of a rival crime family in Newcastle called the Conroys. Paddy Conroy would go to any length to get John Henry Sayers in trouble. Conroy was at Leeds Crown Court because he hates John Henry Sayers and wanted to see him go down. I'm going to suggest to you that, if there is any truth that you made that call, you did it to wreck an acquittal, because Sayers had done so well in the trial. The rivalry between Sayers and Conroy is the stuff of legends in Newcastle. Paddy Conroy was there not as a supporter; he was there because he hates John Henry Sayers.'

Hay mumbled that he was not working for the Conroy family at the trial, and added, 'I was approached by Stephen Sayers to bring Mark Rowe along as backup. He was there for muscle. The Freddie Knights family had the Conroys with them on their side at the trial. Mark Rowe is a big man, and I was asked to bring him because he's a good friend of mine. I've come here to tell the truth and cleanse my soul. I want justice for the family of Freddie Knights.'

The morning after Hay finished giving his evidence, he underwent life-saving brain surgery. Some say it was successful; others, who wish Hay ill, claim that it went tragically wrong. Regardless of anybody's point of view, Errol Hay lived, but his illness remained terminal.

Jonathan Goldberg QC is considered to be 'Premier League' when it comes to barristers. He has defended Charlie Kray, the Brinks-MAT robbers, and Nicholas Jeffries, the civil engineer acquitted in 2006 of manslaughter and health-and-safety charges arising from the Hatfield rail disaster. Mr Goldberg also appeared in the House of Lords in the landmark 2005 human rights case of R vs Goldstein, which redefined the common-law offence of public nuisance. To put it mildly, he is a good man to have on your side when facing legal difficulties. There was little surprise, therefore, when he halted John Henry's trial by revealing a sinister flaw in the prosecution's case.

Hay had told the jury that, after making his initial call to the juror, he travelled to a second phone box, less than two miles away in Hetton-le-Hole, to ring a different number, in Leeds. But it emerged that the police had launched an investigation to analyse call records from the second box identified by Hay. The evidence gathered by the detectives showed the call could not have been made from any of the 14 phone boxes in Hetton-le-Hole. When a further forty-eight phone boxes were checked in a three-mile radius around the area, they too drew a blank for any calls made to Leeds. The police handed the evidence over to the prosecution, who realised that it did not support Errol Hay's story. As a result, it was not disclosed to the defence. Highly respected Crown Prosecution Service solicitor David Kingsley Hyland OBE, the head of Northumbria Police's complex casework unit, claimed that he had simply taken his eye off the ball, and insisted he had intended to pass the information on to the defence during the course of the trial. But the judge, Mr Justice Cooke, ridiculed the prosecution, claiming they had failed to be 'full and frank' in disclosing key evidence that would damage their case. He said, 'I have no doubt that Mr Hyland was looking to minimise the damage to Errol Hay's credibility and to the prosecution case by making as limited an admission as possible.' He added, 'The material was undoubtedly damaging to the prosecution and assisted the case of the defendants in what is essentially, from the prosecution's perspective, a one-witness case. The defendants knew that the police had been unable to trace a kiosk from which the second call was made but had not appreciated that the police inquiries revealed that the second call could not have been made from the box identified by Errol Hay nor that the billing information established that the call could not have come from any phone box in the area. In my judgement, Mr Hyland was always looking to avoid disclosure by giving an admission in as limited a form as the documents allowed.' He concluded, 'For all these reasons, therefore, the indictment is stayed on the grounds of abuse of process.'

John Henry, his brother Stephen and their co-defendant Mark Rowe sat impassively while their accusers squirmed in their seats. They knew they were going home to their families for Christmas.

Outside the court, Jonathan Goldberg QC told reporters from the *Newcastle Evening Chronicle* that the allegations against his client would never have reached trial if it had not been for the Sayers family's notoriety in Newcastle: 'This long, complex and ridiculously expensive police investigation seems somehow to have lost sight of the fact that their horse was lame from the off. It was always a surprising decision for the CPS to bring these serious charges on the wholly uncorroborated word of a man like Errol Hay. He was a career criminal and drug dealer who had fallen penniless in Thailand, where he was washed up and unemployed and living off the earnings of prostitution from his Thai wife. He had the idea of phoning an old contact in Northumbria Police and offering to sell his evidence against John Henry Sayers in exchange for a substantial reward. What is worse, the CPS lawyer Mr Hyland failed to dampen the police enthusiasm for the case, let alone his own. If Mr Sayers had been a plain and simple Mr Smith, we do not believe this case would ever have come to trial on such poor evidence.'

The honourable Mr Goldberg was undoubtedly correct about the Sayers name resulting in their facing such serious charges on such flimsy evidence. But, like all villains, Sayers, Conroy and others do little or nothing to talk down their names or their reputations when it suits them. To have a name is to be a Somebody, and to be a Somebody in this world is deemed an achievement. But once you have a name linked to criminal notoriety, like it or not, it is impossible to live down. Even if these two powerful families do ever decide to retire, it is unlikely they will ever be able to do so in peace. The cruel finger of suspicion will forever be levelled at them whenever anything happens in Newcastle, regardless of their innocence or guilt. Michael 'the Bull' Bullock and Paddy Conroy have effectively retired from crime but remain inseparable friends. John Henry Sayers is trying to rebuild his life following his release from prison. His brother Stephen is doing likewise.

No doubt they all consider themselves to be decent men who love their wives and children, but all men who carry the responsibility of fatherhood should look closely at themselves and ask if they would be happy for their children to follow in their footsteps. For most old-school villains who know about the misery a life of crime brings, the answer would be 'No,' and so the members of these notorious families should remove themselves and their loved ones from the environment they have been immersed in, make peace with themselves and one another and enjoy whatever time they have left on this earth, because ultimately nobody wins and we will all end up with 'names' in any event – albeit on a headstone in the graveyard.